D1058214

The 360° Corporation

THE 360° CORPORATION

From Stakeholder Trade-Offs to Transformation

SARAH KAPLAN

STANFORD BUSINESS BOOKS
An Imprint of Stanford University Press
Stanford, California

Stanford University Press
Stanford, California

© 2019 by Sarah Kaplan. All rights reserved.

Printed in the United States of America on acid-free, archival-quality paper

Library of Congress Cataloging-in-Publication Data

Names: Kaplan, Sarah, 1964– author.

Title: The 360° corporation : from stakeholder trade-offs to transformation / Sarah Kaplan.

Other titles: 360-degree corporation

Description: Stanford, California : Stanford Business Books, an imprint of Stanford University Press, 2019. | Includes bibliographical references and index.

Identifiers: LCCN 2019014666 (print) | LCCN 2019017661 (ebook) | ISBN 9781503610439 (ebook) | ISBN 9781503607972 (cloth : alk. paper)

Subjects: LCSH: Social responsibility of business. | Corporations—Social aspects. | Industrial management.

Classification: LCC HD60 (ebook) | LCC HD60 .K3647 2019 (print) | DDC 658.4/08—dc23

LC record available at https://lccn.loc.gov/2019014666

Cover design: Kevin Barrett Kane
Text design: Kevin Barrett Kane
Typeset by Motto Publishing Services in 9.2/15 Spectral

For Anita: to the moon and the stars and beyond

CONTENTS

ACKNOWLEDGMENTS

THE FIRST DEBT OF GRATITUDE goes to the MBA students in my Corporation 360° course at the University of Toronto's Rotman School of Management upon which this book is based. I have taught the class fifteen times to nearly six hundred students, and it has been their engagement, questions, and ideas that have pushed me to develop and refine the model I present in this book. I am equally grateful to my research assistants over the years—Stephanie Gibson, Matthew Literovich, and Rachel Megitt—who have helped me develop my syllabi and refine the insights. The Rotman School also deserves a big thank-you for just saying yes when I proposed to teach a course that no one had ever taught in a business school before. Charles Fishman, whose incredible book *The Walmart Effect* was an inspiration, generously came to Toronto multiple times in person and via Skype to engage with my students and me. I have had numerous guests visit my class who have all provided important and often contrasting perspectives and insights: Iwona Gwozdz, Oliver Horton, Rob McClinton, Kathleen McLaughlin, Lesley Smith, and Chris West (all from Walmart); Eric Grimes (Nike); Shelley Martin (Nestlé); Mauro Pambianchi (SmartCentres); Daniel Salmon (BMO Capital Markets); Marcelo Affonso and his team (Amazon); Brad Stone (*Bloomberg Businessweek*); Marina Strauss (*The Globe and Mail*); Professor Rick Locke (formerly of MIT, now at Brown University); Professor Harry Mahler (OCAD); and Professors Lisa Austin, Tiziana Casciaro, Wendy Dobson, Richard Florida, Rafael Gomez, Heather-Anne Irwin, Brian Languille, Geoff Leonardelli, Anita McGahan, Kerry Rittich, Maria Rotundo, Brian Silverman, Dilip Soman, Anil Verma, Joseph Wong, and Jia-Lin Xie (all of the University of Toronto). My Slump Management doctoral research group, with whom I still meet on a regular basis, always help in a pinch. I have had many other great academic interlocutors, too many to list here, whose work is incorporated and cited in the book. I am grateful for my team, chiefly Alyson Colón and Victoria Heath, at the Institute for Gender and the Economy for holding down the fort so that I could finish up the book, and for Rotman's amazing marketing team, especially Steve Arenburg, Karen Christensen, and Ken McGuffin, for their enthusiastic support. Kristina Moore and Hannah Townsend at the Wylie Agency have been exactly the kind of agents I needed—no muss, no fuss, and extremely effective. Steve Catalano, my editor at Stanford University Press, was an enthusiastic counterpart who helped hone the message of the book along with two helpful reviewers. Thanks to my parents and sisters—Hesh (who caught a lot of typos!), Meredith, Esther, Sharon, Rachel, and their partners and kids—for always being there for me, and especially to my sister Esther Kaplan, whose lifetime of social justice activism has kept us in a constant and evolving dialogue about the role of the corporation in society. Most importantly, it is my partner, Professor Anita McGahan, who inspired me to teach this course and write this book. Her commitment to addressing the world's most difficult challenges—especially global health—has shone a light for me, and it keeps our dinner-table conversations always lively. Plus, she believes in me, and that has given me the space I needed to live with and work on the ideas in this book.

The 360° Corporation

THE CORPORATION IN SOCIETY

WHEN I STARTED TEACHING at the Wharton School in the early 2000s, a prevailing mantra amongst the students was "learn, earn, return." That is, get your MBA (learn), go out and make a lot of money (earn), and then, later in life, give back to society through volunteering and charitable giving (return). This is a particular mind-set that separates what people do to earn a living from what they might do for society. It's a mind-set that's reinforced in many business schools, still today, by the fact that ethics is offered as a completely separate course from all of the other disciplines that business students study. And even more worrisome, that the ethics courses often reinforce Milton Friedman's dictum that firms have an ethical responsibility to the shareholder alone (as long as they play by "the rules of the game.")[1]

Thankfully, when I ask my students today about "learn, earn, return," they say they haven't heard of it. Maybe this is because I now teach at Canada's leading business school, and there's a different kind of ethos up here. More likely it is because there's a new generation of students who don't see these issues as separate. Given the social and environmental problems today, they are not interested in working in a world where profits matter at one point in time and social responsibility at another (later) time. They aren't seeing, and indeed won't tolerate, the disconnect.

This change in the winds has produced efforts like the B Corporation (B Corp) movement, which encourages for-profit firms to become certified as benefit corporations, which meet standards for social and environmental performance. About 2,500 companies around the world have been certified to date. The B Corp values state:

> That we must be the change we seek in the world,
> That all business ought to be conducted as if people and place mattered,
> That, through their products, practices, and profits, businesses should aspire to do no harm and benefit all,
> To do so requires that we act with the understanding that we are each dependent upon another and thus responsible for each other and future generations.[2]

In 2017, the founders of B Lab, the organization that carries out the B Corp certification, wrote an open letter to business leaders calling on them to reject the profit and ethics divide: "In the current environment of rising insecurity, fear, hate speech, and violence, and in the absence of trust in our economic system, all business leaders have an unprecedented responsibility and opportunity to build a more inclusive society."[3]

That these folks would write a statement like this is probably not so surprising. They are the B Lab people, after all. What's perhaps more surprising is that, at about the same time, Larry Fink, the CEO of BlackRock, an investment firm that manages more than $1 trillion in assets wrote in his own "Letter to CEOs":

> We . . . see many governments failing to prepare for the future, on issues ranging from retirement and infrastructure to automation and worker retraining. As a result, society increasingly is turning to the private sector and asking that companies respond to broader societal challenges. Indeed, the public expectations of your company have never been greater. Society is demanding that companies, both public and private, serve a social purpose. To prosper over time, every company must not only deliver financial performance, but also show how it makes a positive contribution to society. Com-

panies must benefit all of their stakeholders, including shareholders, employees, customers, and the communities in which they operate.[4]

The conclusion: companies cannot neglect the variety of stakeholders that surround them.[5] You might arrive at this conclusion for different reasons—that "clicktivists" might create social-media storms about company missteps; that consumers might get turned off by irresponsible firms; that the famous millennial workers might just walk away from companies that don't have a socially responsible value proposition; that investors are demanding adherence to environmental, social, and governance standards; that you have a personal responsibility to address your company's role in facing urgent social and environmental challenges, and so on.

However you get here, the next question is, How do you do it? The big problem: meeting these stakeholder demands often requires action that could compromise profits. It is not as simple as saying, "just do it." Improving worker conditions, investing in environmental advances, addressing the impacts of consumerism, creating talent pipelines for marginalized communities, or stopping polluting activities are all costly. Costly in terms of cash, costly in terms of time, and costly in terms of organizational disruption.

Yet just the fact that they are costly doesn't give organizations an excuse to "go slow." In fact, the urgency for action could not be greater than it is today. Rising seas are already flooding communities; pollution is choking cities; the artificial-intelligence revolution will create major dislocations as jobs are replaced with robots; progress toward gender and racial equality is stagnating. The question of "how" is nontrivial.

I created a course at the Rotman School to see if I could figure out the answer to that question. I called it Corporation 360° because I wanted us to look at the stakeholders that surround companies from all directions, all 360 degrees. It turns out that there aren't easy answers. There aren't step-by-step instruction manuals or simple tool kits. (Note to self: business books aren't supposed to admit that there aren't easy steps!) My students and I have spent the last nine years thinking hard about the role of the corporation in society, and about what companies might do to deal with the trade-offs created by stakeholder needs that conflict with the corporate bottom line. We went looking for ideas and inspiration from scholars, investigative journalists, corporate leaders, NGOs, and policy makers, and I'm grateful to all of the people and organizations whose work made this book possible.

I'm not any closer to a quick solution, but I have distilled some principles for action. I have also discovered pitfalls that anyone interested in making progress can try to avoid. This book reflects these ideas. I've done my best to make the guidelines as tractable as possible by suggesting four modes of action that range from identifying the trade-offs all the way to thriving when these trade-offs seem intractable. Mastering the four modes is what the 360° Corporation is all about.

Some will say that the argument in the following pages is too nuanced. I guess I'm not worried about that, because the problems are complex. If I gave you simple answers, I'd by misrepresenting the reality that leaders face every day as they try to work their way through the trade-offs they face. In fact, one of my messages is that successful companies will actually flourish in this complexity, using it to come up with exciting experiments and fruitful innovations into future ways of working. My aspiration: that the four modes of action outlined in this book provide the signposts you need to move forward. At the same time, I hope they give you enough space to construct your own new paths.

PART I

INTRODUCTION TO THE 360° CORPORATION

CHAPTER 1

CREATIVE DESTRUCTION REDUX

How Stakeholder Needs Create Performance Trade-Offs

EVEN BEFORE HURRICANE KATRINA hit the Gulf Coast in August 2005, Walmart's Emergency Operations Center sprang into action. Managers started with the usual stuff. Their sophisticated information systems had already told them that when hurricanes strike, people want flashlights, tarps, generators, bottled water, and strawberry Pop-Tarts. Yes, strawberry Pop-Tarts. Logistics teams quickly got these items to the stores in advance of the storm. But as Katrina hit land and its seriousness became apparent, the company shifted from priorities of supply and demand to loss prevention—dispatching armored trucks to get cash out of the stores and executing plans to prevent looting.

Amid this shift, an interesting thing happened.

In addition to stocking shelves with the right Pop-Tarts and safeguarding their stores against looters, managers at Walmart stores all over the affected areas were opening up their warehouses to supply food, water, and clothing to local residents and emergency workers. Orders came down from Walmart headquarters to deliver canned food, peanut butter, and other supplies directly into the disaster zone, and to distribute them—for free. In other words, Walmart was taking action that didn't directly benefit its bottom line. The company had thrown out the corporate disaster-relief playbook.

Walmart employees often arrived in distressed areas before FEMA did. After the storm, Philip Capitano, mayor of Kenner, Louisiana, home to the New Orleans airport, would look back on Walmart's role and acknowledge that during the worst of Katrina,

> the only lifeline in Kenner was the Walmart stores. We didn't have looting on a mass scale because Walmart showed up with food and water so our people could survive. . . . The Red Cross and FEMA need to take a master class in logistics and mobilization from Walmart.[1]

On top of this, Walmart then donated $17 million in cash, more than 100,000 meals, and a hundred truckloads of free merchandise to the areas that had been most severely affected by the storm, and, in an unprecedented move for the company, ensured jobs for all of its displaced workers. "I want us to respond in a way appropriate to our size and the impact we can have," CEO Lee Scott said. It worked. By mid-September 2005, only 13 of the 126 stores that had been shut down by Katrina remained closed, and the company had relocated 97 percent of the displaced employees.[2]

This was an instance in which Walmart's incredible scale and deep capabilities in logistics were truly able to shine. In the wake of Katrina, the company was able to mobilize its whole distribution network, on an extremely compressed timeline, to get supplies from all over the country to precisely where they were needed. Aaron Broussard, president of Jefferson Parish in Louisiana, put it this way on NBC's *Meet the Press*: "If the American government would have responded like Walmart has responded, we wouldn't be in this crisis."[3]

Walmart received a lot of positive attention for its response. Former presidents George H. W. Bush and Bill Clinton, who were heading up a hurricane-relief fundraising effort, praised Walmart for its quick action. Lee Scott appeared on CNN's *Larry King Live* to describe Walmart's work. A September 6 *Washington Post* article was titled "Walmart at Forefront of Hurricane Relief." These reactions are an indication of how rare it is for a company to act altruistically, as Walmart did. Walmart was only doing what many would agree was the right thing, but too often, if a course of action doesn't lead to a profit, a company will simply choose not to do it.

But was it all so altruistic? It is surely the case that the workers on the ground in '05 were motivated by the desire do the right thing, but from a corporate standpoint there are questions worth raising about Walmart's less explicit incentives. Hurricane Katrina came at a critical moment for Walmart, just as it was facing negative press about a slew of issues. Robert Greenwald's movie, an aggressive takedown of Walmart's practices titled *Wal-Mart: The High Cost of Low Price*, was about to be released. News stories revealed that Walmart's lowest-paid workers made so little that they qualified for Medicaid and food stamps. So perhaps it's no surprise that, as Walmart was beefing up its disaster-relief efforts, it was also firing up its public relations engines by hiring the top international PR firm, Edelman, to get the word out.

As an article published in *Advertising Age* a month after the flood put it: "Millions in corporate-image advertising in the past year failed to do much to help Wal-Mart's reputation. . . . But now, in the wake of Hurricane Katrina, Wal-Mart is getting the kind of advertising no marketer can buy."[4]

More critical observers argued that the aid efforts were the least that Walmart could do. After all, the company had received millions of dollars of government subsidies through infrastructure assistance and tax rebates for distribution centers it had built in the area. *Ad Age*'s conclusion: Walmart's efforts after Hurricane Katrina were "laudable but not heroic."[5]

Walmart announced subsequently that quarterly profits were hurt by a mere $.01 per share. But the stores also benefited in the longer term by creating shopping wish lists for victims of the storm. In short, critics argued that Walmart, rather than being altruistic, did the bare minimum, and that its efforts, while they may have seemed well intentioned, were simultaneously motivated by the company's bottom line.

So it's tricky. What is a corporation to do? Should companies do only what's in the shareholders' interest? Some view this as the corporate mandate: do only what is good for the owners of the company's stock. Should Walmart have taken only actions that increased profits and sales? That is, should it have sold as many Pop-Tarts as possible to the people who made it into its stores but left its displaced workers out to dry, without jobs for a foreseeable future? Was it appropriate for the retailer to help the workers and the communities simply because it was the right thing to do, even though many saw it as a transparent attempt to burnish its public image? In this case, perhaps we can deem Walmart's decision a no-brainer. But what would have happened if the interests of the shareholder and those of other stakeholders such as communities, workers, consumers, suppliers, and the environment had conflicted irreconcilably? This is the crucial debate for corporations in the twenty-first century—not just during crises but on a daily basis.

This book is designed to provide some answers to these questions, showing leaders how to engage with stakeholders in ways that are productive for everyone. Many recognize that a consideration of a broad range of stakeholders is important, but few know exactly how to do it. Indeed, few even appreciate the ways their business models make implicit, if not explicit, trade-offs across stakeholders. I'll argue that taking stakeholders seriously can lead to innovative business-model transformation. This is not just about how to make the business case for diversity or for sustainability—though that's of course a part of the story—it is about how companies can look through the lenses of different stakeholders and see new ways of doing business. This change might be effortful and filled with uncertainty, but when companies come out the other side, they'll be ready to participate in the twenty-first century.

For Walmart, the experience of the Katrina crisis was transformational—it provided a window into a new way of being. It began a series of explorations that have led it to make radical changes in how it does business, including commitments to zero waste, 100 percent renewable energy, women's economic empowerment, and many other initiatives. The complexities of that moment offered a path forward for the company.[6] This is the message I want readers to take away from The 360° Corporation: trade-offs, conflicts, and challenges can be the source of innovation and transformation.

TRADE-OFFS

Today, increasingly, corporations are being asked, pressured, forced, encouraged, regulated, and coaxed to consider a broader set of stakeholders in their calculations. There are many reasons for this. The 2008 financial crisis focused attention on how corporations can have broad-ranging effects on society. Climate change has attuned people to the potentially toxic effects of corporate policies. The global supply chain is more visible than ever before, and many consumers are more conscientious when it comes to their buying habits than they were in the past. In the current political environment, people are looking to corporations to pursue social-policy agendas. The net effect has been that, more and more often, companies need to consider stakeholders *other than* the shareholder in developing their strategies and managing their organizations.

It has been an extraordinarily rapid sea change. In 2011, only twenty of the S&P 500 companies produced sustainability or responsibility reports along with their annual reports to shareholders. In 2015, the figure was 81 percent.[7] Some countries—Denmark, the United Kingdom, South Africa, and soon the entire European Union—require all companies to report on environmental, social, and other related issues. The Global Reporting Initiative database included reports from 5,481 companies around the world in 2015.[8]

Some think that this turn toward a multiplicity of stakeholders is a good and much-needed development. They see corporations as deeply implicated in many social ills, from pollution to poverty, to discrimination, to global inequality—and also as potentially powerful actors in finding solutions to these social challenges. Others are genuinely opposed to the change, not because they don't want to fix these kinds of problems, but because they feel that tasking the corporation with managing them is likely to lead to suboptimal outcomes.[9] These opponents of corporate social responsibility (CSR) are concerned that taking away from the singular focus on creating economic value (as measured by total returns to shareholders) is either unethical or would open up the corporation to many inefficiencies. It would be hard, they claim, to monitor and control managers' performance when multiple objectives are at stake. It is also worrisome to turn over social agendas to corporate decision makers.

The challenge for those who want to consider these diverse stakeholders (and the worry for those who think it's a bad idea) is that each stakeholder comes to the party with different interests and views about what is of value. When these interests aren't aligned, corporate leaders are required to make *trade-offs*. For example, when the capital costs of installing pollution-control filters on a power plant or the operating costs of raising chickens in cage-free environments or the costs of improving conditions for workers in Bangladeshi clothing factories are high, those costs are likely to erode the financial returns of the companies implementing these changes or to prevent firms from undertaking the changes to begin with. Even more than just creating conflicts between stakeholder interests and financial returns, the needs of different stakeholders may be at odds with each other. When Walmart charges low prices, its decision benefits consumers—but those low prices have historically been based on low wages for workers. When consumers win, workers may lose.

These are either-or choices. The demands are irreconcilable. And if you're a corporation facing these choices, once you conclude that your decision is either-or, you're stuck. Governments might pass regulations requiring pollution controls or improvements in living conditions for animals on industrial farms, and thus make your decision for you, or you look to your firm's existing guidelines, which probably advise you to act in the way that will maximize the return to shareholders. Indeed, some economists and business leaders believe that in every case, a corporation ought to adhere to Milton Friedman's 1970 dictate: "There is one and only one social responsibility of business: to use its resources and engage in activities designed to increase its profits so long as it stays within the rules of the game, which is to say, engages in open and free competition without deception or fraud."[10] In short, one should not decide in favor of any stakeholder other than the shareholder.

How then can diverse stakeholders be accommodated? Government regulation is certainly one means. Regulations give social values a place at the table by requiring firms to conform to rules about pollution, worker safety, zoning, water use, and so on. These regulations create the "rules of the game" to which Friedman referred. Yet given the power that corporations have to influence government policy through lobbying, one might be concerned that regulations won't get us all the way to where we need to be. Granted, we are gradually seeing companies *voluntarily* taking on responsibilities in these domains, beyond what is regulated, but this voluntary action does not diminish the underlying trade-offs. If corporations are surrounded on all sides by stakeholders who are making trade-offs increasingly salient—suppliers, workers, consumers, the environment—then the solution is to become what I call the 360° Corporation.

The 360° Corporation is an organization that can productively and effectively address the tensions created by these trade-offs. This book offers signposts to leaders who want to spearhead the 360° revolution. In it, I argue that companies can develop explicit and coherent plans for addressing the tensions created by trade-offs. As I'll explain throughout the following pages, sometimes there's a win-win. Sometimes, creative thinking may lead to an innovative, mutually beneficial solution. There are still other times when a solution is not particularly appealing to any stakeholder, and yet it's still the best way to go (for now). In these cases, there are considerations and strategies that can help business leaders make the best possible decision. *The 360° Corporation* will address all of these modes of action and serve as a comprehensive playbook for managers, CEOs, and innovators who are burned out by constantly being tugged in many (360, to be exact) different directions.

A precursor to mastering trade-offs the way that only the 360° Corporation can is, of course, knowing what the trade-offs *are*. I call this Mode 1 because it is the starting point. There is no possibility for action without a clear understanding of who is gaining and who is losing. Trade-offs are implicit in every business, but most organizations haven't analyzed them enough to see them clearly. Indeed, in my conversations with leaders in many companies, they often have not even thought about how their way of doing business embeds a series of potentially unintended choices about which stakeholders to value and which to disregard. Getting clear on the trade-offs makes the tensions evident, and this lays the groundwork for three additional modes of action.

The predominant rhetoric today is to make a business case for action. This is what I call Mode 2 action, and it allows leaders to rethink the trade-offs. This is at the heart of the shared value concept that is so popular. There might be ways to reframe actions to be win-win, with benefits for both the shareholder and other stakeholders. If supporting a local school system in Bangladesh where your company manufactures garments improves the quality of workers over time and assures the support of the company by the community, then that's a pretty easy win. It's not just CSR; it's good for business. This is the origin of things like the business case for diversity—if you can show that increased diversity leads to more innovative output of project teams, then diversity is not just good practice, it's smart economics.

My argument here: shared value can take you only so far. There are plenty of situations where a business case is just not evident. Then companies can move into Mode 3, which takes them beyond shared value. When win-wins are not immediately evident, companies can seek out innovative solutions—new technologies, new processes, new ways of doing business—that allow them to innovate around the trade-offs. This is where the transformative possibilities of the 360° Corporation emerge. If your shoe-manufacturing process creates a lot of wasted materials, the answer may not be to just cut the materials more efficiently. It may instead be to come up with an entirely new manufacturing process that knits the upper of the shoe in one piece (think of Nike's Flyknit). If your just-in-time delivery system is leading to higher pollution and energy use, the answer might not be to find a way to stuff the trucks with more product. It might instead be to redesign trucks entirely (Walmart has done this in collaboration with Peterbilt in the Advance Vehicle Experience program) or to find new ways to deliver products (maybe one day, Amazon's drones). Mode 3 is transformative.

Mode 4 is the toughest. Sometimes there are just no solutions—even innovative ones—to be had. In Modes 2 and 3, there's still a way to make the business case—what makes social sense also makes economic sense, at least with enough creativity, investment, and work. Mode 4 is necessary when the trade-off is still somehow intractable, when acting for a stakeholder other than the shareholder might hurt the shareholder, and vice versa. In these cases, companies must find ways to function *with* the tension rather than do away with it. In the long run, these tensions can generate creative insights. In the present moment, companies must find ways to thrive within tension, often by initiating some experiments for future solutions. The key here is not to give up but instead to find ways to engage stakeholders in productive dialogues. These dialogues will not always be smooth. In fact, the most productive ones will likely be filled with conflict, but also filled with possibility.

Table 1.1 gives you a short guide to the modes of action in the 360° Corporation.

To be clear: companies can operate in multiple modes of action at the same time. For some issues, they may only be assessing the trade-offs (Mode 1); for others, they may be acting based on a business case (Mode 2); for still others, they may be innovating around the trade-offs (Mode 3); and for others, they may still be stuck, unsure how to resolve the trade-offs but working on it (Mode 4). Of course, some companies may not be doing any of this.

Becoming the 360° Corporation can be challenging, and the best way to learn the process is to observe it in action. To that end, this book focuses primarily on two large, well-known organizations, Walmart and Nike, and on the many different stakeholders that these companies must balance on a daily basis, revealing how frequently interests and agendas can conflict, and highlight-

TABLE 1.1. Four Modes of Action for the 360° Corporation

Mode 1. Know your trade-offs.	Most organizations have not analyzed their business model to understand the trade-offs implicit in their choices for how to do business. The precursor is to evaluate who is winning and losing in the status quo.
Mode 2. Rethink trade-offs.	It may be possible to construct a business case for a particular intervention that resolves the trade-offs in a win-win solution. This is the essence of shared value. The challenge is that most companies never move beyond Mode 2. They get stuck in the business case.
Mode 3. Innovate around trade-offs.	Companies can get out of the business-case trap through innovation. Rather than accepting the trade-offs, companies can innovate new ways to deliver value and break the trade-offs.
Mode 4. Thrive within trade-offs.	In some cases, the trade-offs are intractable. But that doesn't mean that companies shouldn't try to address them. Organizations may wish to hold the trade-offs in tension—thinking about what experiments in future solutions are possible or how long-term goals can be pursued without compromising short-term returns. Companies can engage in productive and pluralistic dialogue with stakeholders.

ing the trade-offs that arise most often in today's globalized economy. These are companies that—though far from perfect—have transformed substantial parts of their businesses through their engagement with the trade-offs created by the interests of different stakeholders. Each chapter examines a different stakeholder and Walmart's or Nike's response to that stakeholder's agenda. We'll also see examples of other companies along the way to demonstrate precisely how organizations can operate in the different modes of action. The goal is to provide you with very practical examples of how the companies uncovered the trade-offs (Mode 1), how they found business cases for action (Mode 2), or, more interestingly, how they sought out innovative solutions (Mode 3). We'll also see cases where the companies struggled for years with the tensions created by the trade-offs before they were able to find a solution (Mode 4).

In telling these stories, I am not trying to glorify Walmart or Nike, or any other company. Nor am I vilifying them. What you will see in these stories is the unvarnished reality of the struggle with trade-offs and of the work to find meaningful solutions. This struggle is what's interesting.

WHEN ONE "WIN" WINS

The conversation about coping with stakeholder trade-offs has been dominated for some time by the notion of shared value. Michael Porter and Mark Kramer—two of the most visible proponents of this point of view—suggest that CSR is not about balancing or blending different interests.[11] Instead, they insisted in their 2006 article "Strategy and Society" that "The essential test that should guide CSR is not whether a cause is worthy but whether it presents an opportunity to create shared value—that is, a meaningful benefit for society that is also valuable to the business."[12] There are lots of actions that can both benefit society and feed the bottom line, so many consider Porter and Kramer's definition successful, reasonable, and productive.

Yet others bristle at the implication that no social objective should be pursued if it doesn't meet the performance criteria of the shareholder. That is, Porter and Kramer's definition of *win-win* holds that you can achieve the first win only if you will also achieve the second. They go further to suggest that "generic" social issues that do not enhance a firm's competitiveness or operations should not be considered. Only those social issues that affect operations in the value chain or have an impact on the external competitive environment are worthy of attention, and they should be prioritized according to how much impact they would have on the firm. For example, if Nike wants to institute a recycling program for used shoes, it might make a case for the program by pointing out that the used shoes can be ground into new materials that reduce manufacturing costs. Likewise, if a Walmart store wants to donate money to the local Girl Scout troop, it might justify the donation by arguing that the goodwill accrued will decrease opposition to future store openings or expansions in the area.

In this approach, corporate priorities still dictate which social issues are worth addressing. The more we expect firms to take on these responsibilities, especially to the extent that company strategies become substitutes for government regulation, the more we relinquish social policy to the corporate bottom line. This means that some issues are addressed in extremely powerful ways. When Walmart, for example, shifted to concentrated liquid laundry detergent, it claimed that in just the first three years the switch would save 400 million gallons of water, 95 million pounds of plastic resin, and 125 million pounds of cardboard, as well as reduce pollution and fuel usage that comes from shipping.[13] This was a textbook example of Porter and Kramer's definition of a worthy cause. On the other hand, issues that don't fit the textbook may not get noticed.

What if the interests of different stakeholders are in conflict? We see this often in the case of environmental issues. Those who oppose greenhouse-gas emissions push to close down coal mining and coal-fired power plants, but this often affects workers in coal-mining regions for whom there are no reasonable alternative forms of employment. Or take Walmart's "Everyday Low Price" model. This approach is attractive to consumers, especially those of little means, because products are offered at affordable prices. But Walmart has historically achieved low costs through a low-wage employment model, which has meant that some of its store workers live below the poverty line. Or take Nike's positioning as the producer of high-performance sneakers. Athletes and regular consumers benefit by having shoes that meet exacting performance standards, but this has historically required the use of toxic glues that had the potential to harm workers and the environment during the manufacturing process. As most leaders today know, these situations, in which consumers win but the environment or employees or some other stakeholder loses, are much more common than situations that are win-win.

Finally, what if shareholders have mixed motives? Maybe they don't all want only financial returns? The growing industry of socially responsible investment funds highlights this possibility. In 1995, there were about 50 mutual funds that took into account some social issue. One of the first was Pax World Fund, which was started by two Methodist ministers in 1971 and restricted investment in alcohol, tobacco, gambling, defense, weapons, and animal testing. Today, the number of such funds is well over 500. As the field has grown, more specialized funds have emerged, including Barclay's Women in Leadership ETN, launched in 2014, or the First Trust ISE Global Wind Energy ETF, launched in 2008. It is estimated that today more than 15 percent—at least $21 trillion—of the world's investable assets are allocated to socially responsible investments.[14]

We also see sovereign wealth funds and major retirement funds making choices to divest from certain companies that don't meet some social standard, as when the Government Pension Fund of Norway divested from Walmart in 2006 due to, as they stated, "systematic violations of human rights and labor rights," and from mining company Freeport-McMoRan due to "serious environmental damage."[15] Recent campus protests have pushed many universities—including Oxford, Edinburgh, and the London School of Economics in the UK and the University of California and Yale University in the US—to divest from companies responsible for greenhouse-gas emissions and fossil-fuel extraction. The California Public Employees' Retirement System has for many years banned investing in tobacco companies even though the divestment has been financially costly to the retirement fund.[16] The Interfaith Center on Corporate Responsibility, a coalition of faith-based and values-driven organizations such as pension funds for nuns, explains on its website that its constituents "view the management of their investments as a powerful catalyst for social change."[17]

All of this signals that investors—whether individuals, foundations, endowments, or sovereign funds—are now including not only financial returns but also social criteria such as workers' rights or the environment in their calculus of what counts as total returns. In short, even if you are a staunch believer in the total returns to shareholders model, it is probably not offering the clear-cut guidance that this model once did. The best practices for assessing and navigating these situations will be at the heart of this book.

CAN THE SOLUTION REALLY BE WIN-WIN?

I admit it. I drank the total returns to shareholders[18] Kool-Aid like everyone else in the 1990s. Indeed, in my 2001 book *Creative Destruction*, written with a colleague of mine from McKinsey & Company, Richard Foster, we based our claim about the mythical nature of sustainable competitive advantage on the observed inability of firms to maintain abnormal total returns to shareholders over the long term.[19] We argued that if firms were going to perform for their shareholders, they would have to change (that is, create and destroy) at the pace and the scale of the market. We also pointed out that this was an extraordinary challenge, one that few firms would be able to achieve. We went in search of excellence, and excellence turned out to be hard to find.

But that notion of excellence was defined by whether or not firms could provide superior returns to their shareholders in the form of share price appreciation plus dividends. I spent more than two decades researching and consulting to companies about how to meet that aspiration. It was hard enough to do, and I soon realized that this definition wasn't even complete—in addition to the shareholder, interests of other stakeholders needed to be figured into the equation. The question remains: What is a corporation to do?

If you go looking for it, there is some indication that companies are adjusting to the inadequacy of the total returns to shareholders ethos—often adopting the shared value framework. Nestlé, for instance, says on its website, "Being a global leader brings not only a duty to operate responsibly, but also an opportunity to create long-term positive value for society. We call this *Creating Shared Value*, and we embed it firmly across all parts of our business."[20] Walmart's "2016 Global Responsibility Report" states, "We seek to create value for stakeholders across business and society, because *shared value* enhances the quality and viability of solutions. We believe that our social and environmental programs are of interest to long-term shareholders because they strengthen the systems we rely on as a retailer."[21]

The insight to be gleaned from these statements is that sustainability and other social objectives can be linked to business strategy (we are deep into Mode 2 here). Saving energy is not only about reducing pollution but about reducing internal costs to the firm. Improving worker safety is not only about doing good for employees but about reducing the costs of accidents. Improving the productivity of coffee farmers is not only about helping the rural poor in developing economies but also about increasing quality and reducing cost of inputs to manufacturing.

This isn't merely a theoretical argument. A whole swath of research has found that CSR writ large can contribute to the bottom line, at least under certain conditions. The benefits of different strategies include improved customer loyalty, lower capital costs, support from activists and communities (or at least lack of protest), superior access to or lower cost of key inputs, or improved employee productivity.[22] Thus, firms can reasonably pursue social goods, at least when those also improve the profits of the corporation. Such activities would not be in opposition to Friedman's dictate because they would be in service to the shareholder. Addressing stakeholder concerns could also improve firm performance. This is precisely what made the idea of shared value so motivating.

The concept provided a language for talking about the pressures companies were facing from stakeholders without disadvantaging the shareholder. On the other hand, this approach can be considered purely instrumental because, under this rubric, meeting stakeholder needs is possible only to the extent that shareholders benefit too.

TOWARD THE 360° CORPORATION

My view is that we need to expand beyond instrumental views of stakeholder management. While the idea that there might be win-win solutions lying all over the place is deeply appealing, it doesn't give us much guidance in situations where that magic combination is hard to find. Mode 2 simply isn't enough for a company in the twenty-first century.

Over the past nine years, I've explored these challenges while teaching a course at the University of Toronto's Rotman School of Management called Corporation 360°. When I arrived at Rotman in 2009, I wanted to do something different. Business schools tend to slice companies into little pieces. Strategy, marketing, organizational behavior, accounting, operations, and finance are all different topics in the core curriculum of most business schools. Perhaps more shamefully, most schools also teach ethics as a separate course, as if ethical considerations were somehow distinct from other business decisions. This is in part a necessity: faculty are trained experts in their disciplinary domains, and courses are designed to give students some frameworks to think about specific topics. But this silo-like structure neglects the fact that most business problems require multifaceted responses. I wanted my students to consider what happens when looking at companies from all of the different views—a 360° perspective—exploring the overlaps and contradictions when a variety of stakeholders are considered. Rather than teach a different case for each topic—as we tend to do in business schools—I ask the students to examine one company—sometimes Walmart, sometimes Nike—over and over again, seeing what it looks like from the standpoint of different stakeholders.

As I say in my syllabus,

> What new insights emerge when we examine one company from multiple perspectives? What can we learn through the intersections of the insights that come from each business discipline? Further, what insights develop when we compare the corporation as an engine for creating and capturing

private value (and thus providing returns to the shareholder) to that of the corporation as embedded in society and therefore affecting value creation (or destruction) at the *public* level? We will discuss the tensions that arise for the leader when attempting to manage across these different requirements. We will examine the corporation in society, studying the impact of its choices about labor management, globalization, location, sourcing, and other issues on social welfare. At the end of the course, we will take the perspective of the leaders of the corporation and seek to understand how they can make important strategic choices for their company in the face of the many challenges and obligations we uncover in the course.

You will see my students throughout this book. They have been extraordinary partners in pushing the conversation to the cutting edge and beyond. Across the last several years, we have worked collectively to come up with a methodology for thinking about the complexity of these issues. The goal of this methodology is to become the 360° Corporation, the corporation that works to address the tensions created by the differing interests of the stakeholders that surround it.

It's an approach for moving beyond shared value, an approach for business-model transformation, an approach that will enable leaders in any organization to be part of the 360° revolution. By addressing trade-offs through four modes of action—knowing trade-offs, rethinking trade-offs, innovating around trade-offs, and thriving with trade-offs—leaders can respond to the needs of the variety of stakeholders of their organization in ways that lead to exciting, transformative, and sustainable futures for all.

This book explores the pros, cons, possibilities, and opportunities of the four modes using two in-depth cases and many other examples. The Nike and Walmart cases offer rich examples of places where tensions arise and solutions—often extremely creative ones—are developed in response to the challenges posed by the conflicting interests of different stakeholders. Readers of this book will experience the approach that my own students experience, that of circling 360 degrees around a company to see it from every possible angle.

Mode 1. Know your trade-offs

Chapter 2—"know your trade-offs"—continues Part I's introduction to the 360° Corporation by examining **Mode 1**. The precursor on the path to the 360° Corporation—Mode 1—is to recognize that *every business model has at its core an ex-*

plicit, or more likely implicit, set of choices about trade-offs. In some ways, this is not news. Michael Porter himself made his reputation by telling managers that they must make choices, and that strategy is as much about what you decide not to do as what you decide to do.[23] We teach in our strategy classes that companies risk getting stuck in the middle if they try to be all things to all people. Many airlines, for example, have cut costs and services in order to compete with low-cost carriers such as Ryanair, but their costs will never be as low as that of the true low-cost leaders. Ultimately, they offer services that no longer appeal to high-end business customers but can't compete on price: they're stuck in the middle. There are trade-offs. If you choose a differentiation strategy, your customers will likely be more willing to pay, but your costs will also likely be higher than that of a company that has chosen a cost-leadership strategy (think of branded pharmaceuticals vs. generics). The discussion of trade-offs has long been a hallmark of business strategy.

What we are less likely to acknowledge is that business models also involve trade-offs that affect the interests of a wide range of stakeholders. In fact, most companies don't think about it this way at all. If they are pushed on CSR or sustainability, they think of it as an add-on to the core of doing business. They don't actually see how the existing business model carries the trade-offs in it and how real responses will require thorough examinations of the business models themselves. As an obvious example, when companies lay off workers to achieve greater operational efficiency, the stock market often rewards these actions, but obviously the workers suffer if they aren't placed in a new job with equal pay, equal benefits, and equal opportunities. Perhaps less obviously, a retailing model, such as Walmart's, based on just-in-time delivery of goods will create efficiencies in managing working capital but may also contribute to road congestion, fuel use, and pollution due to the many trucks on the road delivering goods at just the right moment. Worse, if the goods are delayed, companies might compensate with air freight, which just multiplies the fuel costs and pollution. Likewise, a manufacturing model such as Nike's that depends on goods made in low-cost labor markets might benefit the consumer but could put the manufacturer's factory workers in jeopardy if the low costs come with flimsy worker protections and frequent safety violations.

Often these trade-offs occur because the stakeholders do not have a place at the table. They are not part of the conversation. Who should be at the table? This is a tricky question, one that academics are still struggling to answer.

Some economists and legal scholars take a property-rights view to argue that those who are investing, one way or another, in the creation of value ought to be at the table where business decisions are made.[24] This criterion might include the workers in a manufacturing plant, but it would likely exclude the communities who might have to live with polluted waters created by that same manufacturing plant. Sociologists and political scientists take a different tack. They have pointed out that legitimacy is not something that can be defined abstractly or technically. The creation of legitimacy is a social and political process by which those who have power or find a means to shape the dialogue (for example, through social-movement activism) become the legitimate stakeholders in a particular conversation.[25]

Think of the people living in Bhopal, India. Before the Union Carbide methyl isocyanate gas leak resulted in a devastating explosion in December 1984, one might not have thought of these people as primary stakeholders. Many of them were living in shantytowns near the plant and had no power over Union Carbide's decisions. They were not consulted about the placement of the plant nor about any of the safety measures that were (or were not) installed. Indeed, the plant was likely built in that location precisely because these people didn't have power. But 8,000 of them died throughout the two weeks after the blast; 100,000 sustained permanent injuries; and at least another 500,000 were affected in some way by the incident.[26] These stakeholders were not considered because, prior to the explosion, members of the Bhopal community hadn't been given a place at the table. The next chapter (Chapter 2) shows what it looks like when companies do engage with stakeholders and how such engagement can lead to a deeper understanding of the business models with which they operate. It will demonstrate how to uncover those trade-offs—making the implicit explicit. This is the first step to becoming a 360° Corporation. The key insight: every business model has trade-offs embedded in it. You need to learn to uncover and understand your own trade-offs.

Mode 2: Rethink Trade-Offs

Part II of the book takes us to **Mode 2**: rethinking trade-offs. Once a company understands that a business model is in fact a set of decisions about whose interests are being valued and whose are not (Mode 1), it becomes evident that solutions will require a rethinking of that business model.

Chapter 3 lays out the business-case logic behind notions of shared value and win-win solutions. Most people who want to address worker, environmental, or other stakeholder concerns feel pressed to make the business case for . . . you name it: diversity, the environment, better treatment of workers, and so on. This is the essence of win-win—what I call Mode 2 action. This is about finding the intersection of particular interventions that benefit stakeholders with those that also benefit the business. At Walmart, installing LED lighting systems saves energy costs for the company while at the same time reducing energy use and pollution for society. As long as the costs of the LED lighting are not too high, the business case can be made for adopting it. Similarly, Walmart's support of food banks means that the retailer pays much less to send material to landfills, and it simultaneously supports the food needs of local communities. This not only reduces costs but also builds goodwill in the communities where Walmart operates, which can be helpful for a company whose entry into new communities has often been protested.

These are the kind of win-win solutions that are conceptualized through the idea of shared value. They support the profitability of internal business operations and reduce constraints in the external competitive context. What managers are discovering is that there are many *more* places where the business case can be made for actions that also take into account benefits to a broad range of stakeholders. It is the low-hanging fruit. The shift in mind-set represented by the shared value concept allows managers to creatively consider all sorts of actions that somehow did not seem possible in the past. They now have a language for talking about how acting for stakeholders other than the shareholder can also be good for the shareholder.

Yet what we observe in practice is that the corporate bottom line still dictates which initiatives get taken up to create mutual gains. In other words, some great ideas that would be a win for certain stakeholders get left by the side of the road because they don't meet the financial litmus test. Regardless of what lip service is paid, one win—the dollar—always wins.

Chapter 4 shows how the business case can lead to forward momentum but also how companies can get trapped in the business-case logic and miss seeing bigger opportunities for change. Overindexing on the business case takes a whole host of options that you might want to consider off the table. Most companies—even those that recognize trade-offs—never move beyond this point. This is particularly true when we consider the business case for diversity as an example. Most companies think that they will motivate action by arguing for the business case, claiming that diversity in teams has been shown to be associated with more innovation and higher performance. Yet it's pretty clear that making the case for diversity has so far failed to induce much progress in organizations, and even worse, having to prove the business case inadvertently implies that corporations shouldn't be more inclusive unless it can be shown that inclusion is better than the (what in North America is still a largely white, male, heterosexual) status quo. Thus, the business-case logic can become a trap that keeps people thinking only about incremental solutions. From this analysis, we can conclude that the shared-value or business-case approach can only get you so far, and may actually limit progress by narrowing your view to include only those possibilities anchored by the bottom line.

Mode 3: Innovating Around Trade-Offs

How does a company get out of the business-case trap? Part III offers insights in how to innovate around the trade-offs through **Mode 3** action. There are many situations in which the business case cannot be made. Let's reconsider LED lights. If the cost of LEDs is too high to justify a target return on investment, there is no business case for installing them. What happens then? Is that the end of the story? The shared value framework can't take us further, but organizations are discovering other means to address the trade-offs that come from considering other stakeholders.

Companies tend to treat CSR as an add-on to the day-to-day business. The reality is that they will have to transform their business models to meet their stakeholders' calls. If you can't make the business case according to the existing business model, an alternative is to innovate *in* the business model itself.[27] Take just-in-time manufacturing: we generally laud these systems as efficient and cost effective but rarely explore the hidden costs within them. From another standpoint (that is, another one of the 360 degrees), just-in-time means more trucks and fewer trains and boats (the less-polluting and more-efficient systems). Just-in-time means factory employees working mandatory overtime to meet deadlines and often cutting corners on safety. Just-in-time means that suppliers often spend more to stock items they will need to deliver at the drop of a hat. Chapter 5 shows how the most innovative companies have found ways to respond to these issues not just with regulatory compliance but with innova-

tion: new modes of transportation, new packaging, new design processes to reduce rush orders, new management processes for factories, new ways of engaging with local communities.

The good news: as I discuss in Chapter 6, the different needs and desires
of stakeholders can actually be a source of innovative ideas. Nike provides an
example of this. In 1997, after a sustained campaign by activists against labor
practices in the overseas factories where the company's sneakers were manufactured, Nike began what would end up being a very long (and ongoing) process to take the concerns and needs of these workers into account. The firm began with the establishment of new safety standards, but it became clear over
time that this wouldn't be enough because simple attempts to comply with standards didn't improve the lives of workers to the degree that everyone had hoped.
One eventual response was Flyknit, an entirely new manufacturing process for
sports shoes that weaves the shoe, rather than using cutting and gluing techniques. This approach produces much less material waste than the use of cut-
out patterns, saves money in materials, and reduces waste to landfills. But most
importantly, this innovative change in the company's own design processes
meant that Nike's demands on the factories did not inadvertently create pressures that led to worker-safety violations.

In Nike's case, the stakeholder interests—that is, workers' and environmental well-being—were brought to the surface through worker protest and
consumer pressure. But consideration of these interests triggered innovation,
which meant that Nike could shift into Mode 3. This happens when the win-
win business case is not immediately evident, but a corporation recognizes that
this is not a reason to give up on the objective. Innovation is central to addressing trade-offs.

On the other hand, innovation is not some magic wand that easily and un-
problematically solves problems or eliminates trade-offs. In fact, it's often challenging, costly, and disruptive. It may lead to the creative destruction that comes
with new ways of operating that outmode existing ways of doing business. As
with any kind of innovation, it may challenge the status quo in ways that are uncomfortable to people used to doing business in a certain way. You don't have
to wait for disruptors from the fringe. If you follow your stakeholders, the disruptors may never catch up to you. To really make progress on addressing stake-

holder pressures, companies will need to innovate in the ways they do business. Doing this in response to stakeholders' desires and needs can be a source of real competitive advantage.

The key insight derived from Mode 3 is that innovation often allows managers to find a win-win in situations where, at first, it seems like there isn't one.

Mode 4: Thrive Within Trade-Offs

But what about the cases where innovation isn't (yet) possible? Where new solutions to trade-offs cannot (yet) be imagined? Part IV looks at how companies can face down intractable trade-offs. Sometimes innovation can't take us as far as we need to go. What do we do, for example, with the tension created by wanting to sell more product (as any company must) and the costs associated with consumerism, waste, and environmental damage? In those cases, organizations are finding ways to *maintain* the tensions created by trade-offs in what I call **Mode 4** action. The solutions listed above conform to an underlying business-case logic, but even when that logic cannot be sustained, and when a business case can't be made, firms may still want to hold the trade-offs in tension in the organization. Indeed, researchers who study organizational paradoxes argue that organizations can live and even thrive with the tensions.[28]

In Chapter 7, I focus on the challenges posed by the tension between the desire to sell more products and the social costs of consumerism. I show what it means to get stuck between competing interests and what experiments are taking place to move beyond the impasses. Chapter 8 takes a look at sustainability initiatives specifically: how they got their start in Mode 2 business-case thinking, what innovations have been sparked through Mode 3 action, and finally how companies have managed in Mode 4 when they haven't found solutions.

I show how tensions between stakeholders can be the fodder for experiments of all kinds that would allow the organization, over time, to invent new, unprecedented, and sometimes radical solutions. Companies actually must rely on these tensions in order to push themselves forward. The conflict leads to action. If all resolutions to conflicts across stakeholders were easy win-wins, they would have been accomplished by now. When we can't innovate and we don't want to resort to leaning on the business-case logic, we might just be stuck with energy-efficient light bulbs and concentrated laundry detergent as the poster children of corporate sustainability initiatives. The biggest challenge for leaders today is addressing the conflicts where people cannot find the win-win and cannot (yet) innovate around the problem.

This is usually achieved by separating the activities aimed at pursuing one goal from those aimed at pursuing the other. Goals might be anything from sustainability to workforce diversity to labor standards in the supply chain, and organizations often create special initiatives to achieve them. Such initiatives are given permission to enact changes in policy even if the straightforward business case for them cannot be made. They may also pursue stakeholder needs in certain more receptive or more demanding markets but not in others where the environment is not favorable.

Alternatively, this separation can sometimes be accomplished across time. Organizations may position the needs of the stakeholders as long-term strategies in contrast to short-term operating-profit requirements. While many stakeholder needs are actually quite urgent, the tendency to position them as longer-term objectives is a means to hold the trade-offs at bay. Instead of stalling action when the business case is not yet evident, the organization can keep the issues alive by framing them as long-term projects or pilots.[29]

They are operating in Mode 4 to uncover potential future solutions by running experiments, entering into partnerships with NGOs, working with consortia of other companies facing the same challenges, making long-term research investments with uncertain payoffs, or involving stakeholders such as workers or communities in problem-solving.

Economists have argued that branching off initiatives or funneling stakeholder needs into long-term strategies will be counterproductive. The beauty of using total returns to shareholders as the primary metric, they assert, is that it is a focusing device, one that allows a single objective to specify how the trade-offs will be navigated and resolved.[30] Once you introduce multiple objectives, they argue, you might as well have no objectives at all because managers will be confused or will simply use the ambiguity to pursue their own interests. In some economists' opinion, holding shareholder and stakeholder requirements in tension is simply bad business. Psychologists and moral philosophers, however, would suggest that humans are more capable of accommodating multiple values at the same time than these critics imagine.[31] Indeed, given what we know about cognitive biases, there is no evidence that having one objective makes individuals any less susceptible to bias than having multiple objectives.

Therein lies the beauty of Mode 4. Companies may actually thrive precisely where the tensions are most evident. The more intractable the trade-offs, the more creativity can be thrown in their direction. Leaders will be required to run experiments in order to see what might work. Such experimentation is not simply about testing hypotheses but about identifying problems, generating provisional solutions, and iteratively revising them as new data emerge from the experiments. Experiments of these sorts allow organizations to move forward, if somewhat imperfectly, even as they invent the solutions.[32]

Further, Milton Friedman's argument that total returns to shareholders should predominate in corporate decision-making is tempered by the fact that, as research shows, some shareholders *want* companies to pay attention to other stakeholders and make their investment choices accordingly.[33] They want companies to operate in Mode 4 because they are looking for companies to create new futures.

The key message: even where there aren't innovative solutions, companies can learn to thrive within the tensions created by intractable trade-offs. These tensions, rather than being confusing or problematic, can actually be the source of organizational adaptability and resilience.

Part V concludes the book with two perspectives—what the 360° Corporation means for you as a leader and what it means for you as a citizen. In Chapter 9, I offer a CEO primer on spearheading the 360° revolution. There are nine principles that will underpin the actions in each of the modes. They start with asking questions, and they end with just getting moving. The epilogue turns the mirror onto the stakeholders themselves, reflecting on how they can most productively influence corporate action.

Because this book is published by an academic press, it had to undergo peer review. In that process, one of my reviewers made the following observation about how personal the four modes of action can be:

> There is a way that [the author's] thinking is likely to have even broader implications . . . [they can be seen as] four modes for managing trade-offs and conflicts in any decision-making setting. Consider a simple personal

example—not hypothetical, a decision I made today: Should I go to an academic meeting or spend time with my grandchildren? Mode 1 thinking helps
me understand that there can be a conflict between these two choices—
something that rarely occurred to me earlier in my career. Mode 2 suggests
that I might be able to reconcile these conflicts, say, by bringing a grandchild to the academic meeting as a special treat. Mode 3 suggests another
possibility—Skyping into the meeting or texting with my grandchildren during the meeting. Mode 4 suggests that sometimes there is no way to resolve
the conflict—as when a grandchild is performing in a play while the meeting is going on. In this setting, I have to do the right thing—which for me is
going to the play—and then explaining that decision to colleagues who expected me to be at the academic meeting.[34]

My hope is that you find your own ways for these ideas to change how you live
and work. There aren't easy answers. The only means to make progress is to begin the journey. These 360° explorations give you signposts along the way.

YOU'VE GOT TO WALK BEFORE YOU CAN RUN

Knowing Your Trade-Offs (Mode 1)

HOW DOES A FIRM MAKE MONEY? This is the first question I always ask myself when I'm introduced to a new company. It seems like a basic question, but it leads to an exploration of how the company actually ticks. Asking that question tells you what the business model is. It tells you what trade-offs the company is making. Most people consider corporate social responsibility and attending to stakeholders an add-on to doing business, but in reality, trade-offs between stakeholders are rooted in every single business model, whether it's the neighborhood corner store or Procter & Gamble. Companies often fail to recognize that business models always embed within them choices to favor some stakeholders and not others, but this is the first step in being a 360° Corporation. That's why I call this Mode 1. Knowing the trade-offs is the first step to effective management of trade-offs.

The basic idea behind the trade-offs we're talking about here is that an activity undertaken by an organization will benefit some stakeholders but create costs or disadvantages for others. To the extent that the organization does not bear this cost, it can be considered a negative externality. That is, the group that experiences the cost doesn't have control over the decision to incur it. It's called an externality because the stakeholder's costs are external to the firm and to profit-and-loss calculations. One of the conversations occurring in the sustainability space is that companies should internalize externalities in order to make decisions that account for the various stakeholders affected by choices. When we ask how a firm makes money, we are also implicitly asking a question about trade-offs and negative externalities.

In Rotman's first-year MBA strategy course, we often start asking this question with a case on Walmart.[1] We look at Walmart in 1994, when its growth in the US market was a staggering 26 percent per year, when it was just moving beyond its roots in the South and only beginning to gain footholds in the Mexican and Canadian markets. In a way, this was "peak Walmart" because the company still existed in its pure form as a chain of discount department stores. Here's what we discovered.

Walmart is famously known for what the company calls its Everyday Low Prices (EDLP), and concomitantly for its ability to negotiate good deals with its suppliers. Founder Sam Walton was a great innovator in the market of discount retailing because he decided to skip the distributor middlemen and go straight to the suppliers. As Claude Harris, Walmart's original buyer, told his staff, "You're not negotiating for Walmart, you're negotiating for the customer." Even big branded companies like Procter & Gamble have found their brands do not allow them to control the relationship with Walmart. According to Harris,

> Well, now we have a real good relationship with Procter & Gamble. It's a model that everybody talks about. . . . But let me tell you, one reason for that is that they learned to respect us. They learned that they couldn't bulldoze us like everybody else, and that when we said we were representing the customer, we were dead serious.[2]

It was true in 1994 that Walmart was much more profitable than its competitors—Kmart, Target, Caldor, Ames, Bradlees, and others. When you look at the income statement, though, the purchasing costs of Walmart's products (cost of goods sold) aren't any lower as a percentage of sales. Why might that be, given the company's extraordinary negotiating skills? It turns out that Walmart's purchasing costs were in part higher because its "Buy American" program that directed it to source from higher-cost local suppliers. Launched in 1985 (and relaunched in 2013), the program was aimed at supporting local economies. Whether it was part of Sam Walton's sense of corporate responsibility or, as some economists argued, simply enlightened self-interest (Walmart needs to support local economies so that people can afford to shop at Walmart), it meant that there were cases when Walmart paid more for goods that competitors sourced more cheaply from abroad. The company got a good deal from those suppliers, but it wasn't the same as sourcing from China or Mexico or elsewhere.

A BUSINESS MODEL BUILT ON LOW WAGES

If the retailer's higher profits did not come from savings in purchasing goods, where did they come from? Dissecting its income statement further allows us to surmise that the company actually made its greatest savings in labor costs. Why were these costs lower? Some of it comes from pure happenstance: Walmart started out and was still primarily located in rural and Southern locations where wages were lower than in cities or in other regions of the US. Another stroke of good luck: once the company instituted a stock-ownership plan for its workers, low wages could be compensated by a very rapidly growing stock price. Probably most importantly, Walmart had fought hard to keep its employees from unionizing.

When a shop is unionized, wages tend to be higher. Unions also provide a collective force for negotiating better working conditions or resolving worker issues. Walmart has always argued that unions are simply a costly third party that gets in the way of the company's direct relationship with its workers (whom the company calls associates). To protect this relationship, Walmart has gone to great lengths. When the butchers in the Jacksonville, Texas, store voted to unionize, Walmart announced that it would shift the company's meat purchases to prepackaged products, thus eliminating meat cutting in the stores altogether.[3] When workers in Jonquière, Quebec, voted to unionize, Walmart closed the store not long after, claiming that it was no longer a profitable location. Walmart created a document for all store managers called, "A Manager's Toolbox to Remaining Union Free."[4] It states: "Wal-Mart is strongly opposed to third-party representation. We are not anti-union; we are pro-associate." It then goes on to provide a "Union Hotline" phone number that managers were to call at the sign of any potentially union-related activity—all the way from suspicious conversations to passing out handbills to protests. Once managers call the hot-line, "Delta teams" made up of representatives from global security, labor relations, and media relations come from headquarters to run the store, and workers are offered "education" about unions.[5]

All this is to say that Walmart has always been serious about keeping labor costs down. Once you know that the company's business model is based not so much on the lowest cost of supplies but instead on the lowest cost of labor, you understand why.

This is the value of understanding the business model. It tells you how the company makes money, and it also reveals just which stakeholders are advantaged by the system and which are disadvantaged. In the Walmart model, consumers win. They get low prices on goods they want. Because many of Walmart's shoppers are low income, these prices really make a difference. This is what motivated Sam Walton and continues to motivate Walmart leaders since his time. Walmart provides access to goods that many people might not be able to afford otherwise. In the Walmart model, many suppliers also win. As long as they can stand up to Walmart's tough negotiations, they get access to sales in the largest retailer in the world. It doesn't work for all suppliers, but it's a gold mine for many.

On the other hand, workers might not win—or might not win anymore. Maybe in the 1980s and 1990s when employees got stock grants and those appreciated tremendously, the low wages made a little more sense. Today the story is different. As growth has slowed for Walmart, the company has been under increasing pressure to lower costs even further. As an example, the *New York Times* documented how the retailer contracted for cleaning services from providers who employed undocumented workers and violated overtime, workers' compensation, and Social Security laws. Although these workers were not directly employed by Walmart, according to the *Times*, "The use of illegal workers appeared to benefit Wal-Mart, its shareholders and managers by minimizing the company's costs, and it benefited consumers by helping hold down Wal-Mart's prices."[6] Although Walmart and the contractors ended up paying fines for their actions, these kinds of actions seem like a natural risk from a business model based on low-cost labor. These contractors provided the lowest-cost labor possible—only they had to do it by violating the law and workers' rights.

Comedian Jon Stewart covered the case in his Comedy Central *Daily Show*.

After showing a clip of a Walmart customer saying she was "stunned" that Walmart would employ undocumented workers, he retorted: "You're 'stunned' that Wal-Mart is using illegal immigrants? Lady, you just bought a sweatshirt for 29 cents!"[7] Of course, I'm not saying that acting illegally is an intended part of how any company might make money, but this example shows that some managers might be tempted to push the boundaries in the service of a particular business model.

WHEN THE BUSINESS MODEL BREAKS

Walmart's low-wage model has been under considerable pressure from unions, workers, and public opinion of late. OUR Walmart, a union-backed group of Walmart workers, has staged effective walkouts and protests around Black Friday shopping days and also conducted extensive media campaigns. Under then-new CEO Doug McMillon, the company announced in 2015 that it would increase the minimum wage to $10 for workers who were making less than that. They also increased the next level of department-manager pay to a minimum of $13 per hour (from the previous minimum of $10 per hour).[8]

How could this be possible? Wage hikes would surely undermine the low-wage business model. On the other hand, critics had asked why Walmart could not simply follow the path of Costco—a partially unionized shop that has paid its workers substantially higher wages than Walmart did, even at its comparable Sam's Club warehouse stores. Author Liza Featherstone found that in the mid-2000s,

> A Sam's Club employee starts at $10 and makes $12.50 after four and a half years. A new Costco employee, at $11 an hour, doesn't start out much better, but after four and a half years, she makes $19.50 an hour. In addition to this, she receives something called an "extra check"—a bonus of more than $2,000 every six months. A cashier at Costco, after five years, makes about $40,000 a year. Health benefits are among the best in the industry, with workers paying only about 12 percent of their premiums out-of-pocket while Wal-Mart workers pay more than 40 percent.[9]

One could pin this difference to the presence of unions. But that may not be the full story. In the end, Costco's business model is just fundamentally different from that of Walmart or even its Sam's Club division. As Featherstone points out, Costco's revenues per employee are five times as high as Walmart's. Some of this comes from the pure productivity of the workers: higher-paid workers are likely to be happier, and happier workers will tend to work harder. Some of it comes from the fact that Walmart and Costco just sell different stuff. Says Featherstone,

> While Wal-Mart sells a $199 swing set, at Costco we find a "summer fortress play system" for $1,499.99. A set of patio furniture at Wal-Mart was $199 in early summer; a patio *heater* at Costco is the same price. Costco's Web site promotes a $5,000 hot tub with a stereo. On Wal-Mart's site last week, the most prominent item was a $48 bike.[10]

Costco has about 4,000 SKUs (different products) while Walmart has 130,000. It's just a different business.

When you ask why Walmart can't just imitate Costco, it is because Walmart's business model would have to change radically. Walmart leaders couldn't just increase wages without changing how they think about how they make money.

This is just what Walmart is having to do. Along with the company's wage increase, it has also invested in worker training. The goal: higher sales and greater customer satisfaction. Note that the higher pay and benefits at Costco have resulted in much lower employee turnover. Lower turnover means that workers will be more experienced, and this could lead to more productivity. Lower turnover also means that employees end up costing even more because their wages rise as their seniority increases. Once the goal is to improve employee satisfaction in order to get better customer service, then the pressure is on to increase employee productivity. Not surprisingly, a headline ran shortly after McMillon's announcement: "Wal-Mart Cuts Some Workers' Hours After Pay Raise Boosts Costs."[11] As commentator Tim Worstall points out, we shouldn't be surprised:

> This isn't rocket science, isn't an unknown in the US retail scene. Costco pays very much higher wages than Walmart. It also employs about half the amount of labor per volume of sales. Costco is therefore simply in a different model along that same spectrum of trading off hourly productivity against

hourly wages. And note the obvious point here: Costco pays much better but also uses many fewer labor hours.[12]

This is not to say that Walmart should avoid increasing wages. Paying a living wage is only fair, and there may be benefits to the business. But increased wages will require Walmart to make money in a different way than the company has in the past. If its Everyday Low Prices were based on low labor costs—lower than its competitors'—then higher wages mean that the company will have to keep total wages lower some other way (through productivity and fewer employees) or find other places to reduce costs. This is where sustainability initiatives might come in—lower energy and waste costs might create more flexibility on the bottom line. Then we are talking about even more changes to the business model.

A clear-eyed analysis of the trade-offs embedded in the business model make the potential options for action more apparent.

A BUSINESS MODEL BUILT ON A PYRAMID

It is not so different for Nike. The company's story isn't about low wages for workers but instead about conditions in the supply chain. To understand the story, you need to ask the basic question: How does Nike make money?

Nike's founders, Phil Knight and Bill Bowerman, made their start selling performance shoes to competitive athletes. Athletes themselves, their orientation was always first and foremost to the top of what they called the market pyramid. They didn't do marketing in the early days; they just put their shoes on great track-and-field athletes such as Steve Prefontaine and Alberto Salazar. As Phil Knight said, "[We saw] our 'core consumers,' the athletes who were performing at the highest level of the sport [. . .] as being at the top of a pyramid, with weekend jocks in the middle of the pyramid, and everybody else who wore athletic shoes at the bottom."[13] While the top of the pyramid did not buy many shoes, the large volumes of consumers at the middle and bottom of the pyramid wouldn't buy shoes at all without the brand and reputation created by the top of the pyramid. Why else would Nike spend millions on sponsoring top athletes such as Serena Williams in tennis, Michael Jordan in basketball, Wayne Rooney in soccer, or Michelle Wie in golf? The Nike swoosh doesn't sell itself. Nike spends big on sponsorships, on advertising, and on innovation and design.

The company's mission, "Bring inspiration and innovation to every athlete* in the world," where the "*" comes with the note: "If you have a body, you are an athlete."[14] Staying ahead in the athletic-wear market means constant innovation in performance and design. The shoe must function for the top athlete, but its design must also appeal not just to "sneakerhead" collectors but also to the mainstream consumer at the bottom of the marketing pyramid.

It turns out that Nike operates in another pyramid. In the 1990s, critics called this the "pyramid of exploitation."[15] While consumers spent one hundred dollars or more for a sneaker, the workers who manufactured them were often working for a few pennies per shoe. Estimates suggest that only four cents of each dollar paid for a shoe covers the labor costs for making the shoe. Materials cost nearly twenty cents, and Nike's profits are about the same.[16] Because marketing expenses are so high, there is little left over to pay for the making of the products themselves.

With that low pay for factory workers came other problems such as poor or unsafe working conditions and involuntary overtime. When these conditions became public in the late 1990s, Nike at first resisted change. But when, as CEO Phil Knight admitted himself, "The Nike product has become synonymous with slave wages, forced overtime and arbitrary abuse,"[17] the company eventually had to do something.

The challenge, of course, was how to address the interests of the factory workers while not compromising Nike's ability to make money. Being at the cutting edge means having a constant stream of new products and designs tailored to the different global markets. But this "fast fashion" can put extraordinary pressures on factories that must turn products around quickly with little advance notice. Nike's solution, as I'll talk about much more in Chapter 6, was to rethink the business model. The company did not just demand that its supplier factories comply with labor and environmental standards. This would appear to be the simple solution, the one that would not require Nike to change much. Instead, Nike changed how it designed its products so that the factories would not have to operate on such tight deadlines; it changed its relationship to the factories from one of pure sourcing to partnership in applying new management techniques; and it developed new glues and manufacturing techniques that eliminated the need for toxic chemicals in the factories. This meant a whole host of transformations, not just in the factories but at headquarters in Beaverton, Oregon. R&D had to do research differently. Designers had to design differently. Planners had to plan differently.

CHANGING THE BUSINESS MODEL

One change leads to another, and making these changes is not simple. My own research, from *Creative Destruction* to today, has focused on this central question: How do you make organizational change? My studies—whether they were of large banks facing financial crises, communications firms facing the bursting of the tech bubble, or pharmaceutical firms responding to the rise of biotech—have all drawn the same conclusion: remaking the business model means remaking the organization. The way a company makes money is embedded into its daily routines. To change the model, you need to change the routines. To change the routines, you need to change how people think about what they should do and the incentives for what should be done.[18]

The fact that the change is hard might in part be the explanation for why it has been so difficult for firms to take into account the interests of stakeholders. Because for the most part, doing so will require change. Organizations are inherently inertial. Change requires at least some dislocation—and often major transformation.

This is where the other modes of action come into play. Once the trade-offs are known, or once they are surfaced by external pressure from the stakeholders themselves, the organization can begin to engage productively with them. The four modes of action—Mode 1, knowing your trade-offs; Mode 2, rethinking trade-offs; Mode 3, innovating around trade-offs; and Mode 4, thriving within trade-offs—are not exclusive choices. They often go hand in hand. The best companies do them all.

A CLEAR-EYED ANALYSIS OF THE TRADE-OFFS

Trade-offs are not always obvious. If identifying trade-offs across stakeholders hasn't been a conversation in the past, a company might not have systems, information, or processes for understanding them. The risk to a company, though, is that the stakeholders might find their own ways to get their voices heard, ways that might prove to be quite costly to the company—strikes, lawsuits, social media campaigns, and protests may be the only way that stakeholders feel they can get into the conversation. Companies may want to consider whether they might be better off taking these concerns into account from the get-go.

One problem with understanding trade-offs is that they have been discussed as occurring only in some cases or under some conditions. In business schools, we teach ethics as a separate course, which can imply that ethical considerations are a "sometimes" thing. We worry about stakeholders only if there is a toxic leak or a product defect or an illegal action. The insight I try to communicate to my students is that every business decision involves trade-offs between stakeholders—whether it is Everyday Low Prices or pyramid marketing or manufacturing overseas or opening new stores. All business models embody these trade-offs.

Another problem is that, although stakeholder theory has been around for four decades or more, it has not always dealt successfully with trade-offs between stakeholders with conflicting interests, despite the fact that these trade-offs are inevitable. It seems hard to imagine a scenario in which the interests of shareholders, debt holders, employees, suppliers, buyers, consumers, environmentalists, and others would be aligned. Yet the recommendations from stakeholder theory have often simply been to find a way to balance these interests.[19] A clear-eyed view into the trade-offs would make it obvious that this kind of balancing act may not often be possible.

What can companies do? I have found that there are two approaches that anyone can take: inside-out and outside-in analyses of the company and its context.

First, really understand how the business model works. In all my years consulting with companies, I was surprised to find how little the executives I worked with knew about the specific mechanics that produced their returns. A good start would be to create an ROIC (return on invested capital) tree. In a way, this is classic value-based management, and the first step I took in most of my projects when I was a management consultant.[20] You break down the components that contribute to your margin and to your invested capital. The goal is to break them down far enough that you understand what the business-unit-specific and operational drivers of value are.

Margin comes from revenues and costs. For revenues, it might be customer mix, salesforce productivity, percentage of accounts that are revolving, dollars per visit, or the like. For costs, it might be fixed-cost allocations, capacity utilization, operational yield, billable hours, cost per delivery, and so on. The same can be done for invested capital that comes from working capital (such as accounts payable, inventory turns, accounts receivable) and fixed capital investments. Each of these factors will have a number attached to it, but at the same time the number represents a set of activities and choices (for example, what the salesforce does or how often you pay your bills).

But the process extends beyond value-based management in then considering how each of those specific levers involves the various stakeholders. Salesforce productivity obviously involves the salesforce workers themselves, but it might also involve customers who might be pushed into buying something they don't understand or can't actually afford (think of subprime mortgages as an example). Capacity utilization might affect the environment if the push to use equipment keeps operators from conducting maintenance and repairs that could prevent leaks or explosions (think of the Bhopal disaster). This is the first conversation a company might have. Most companies have the tools to do this kind of analysis but haven't pushed it far enough to see what it looks like from the perspective of different stakeholders.

The broad movement toward producing sustainability or corporate responsibility reports—done well—can be a crucial component of Mode 1 action. Even if these reports start out mainly as a PR exercise, they can force companies to come up with measurements for what they are doing and how they are making progress. Measurements matter a lot, because as the old adage goes, what gets measured gets done. That's why I put in the caveat above about reports being done well. Figuring out what to measure and how to measure it isn't always obvious. As Nike points out in its "FY16/17 Sustainable Business Report,"[21] there isn't always guidance. There is a plethora of emerging accounting systems—social return on investment, social accounting, social auditing, sustainability reporting, and triple bottom line, to name a few—but any system of quantification depends on who the company counts as a stakeholder.[22] Determining who and what counts shapes the creation of the system; and consequently, once you have the accounting system in place, it reifies those choices.

Still, taking a stab at what would matter is important. Once you know the carbon footprint of every shoe you make, you can set a target for reducing the impact. Once you know how much water goes into making a cotton T-shirt, you can look for creative solutions to reducing water use such as closed-loop water recycling or using recycled cotton. Once you know how many safety violations exist in your factories, you can make upgrades or sever relationships with vendors.

Nike's and Walmart's reports are state of the art.[23] Nike's includes a table with its 2020 targets for everything from carbon footprint to use of sustainable materials to renewable energy to landfill diversion. Walmart lists its commitments across a broad series of categories from deforestation to emissions reduction to animal welfare to toxic chemicals. Both reports show exactly how the company has performed over the past years. This exercise has more than a reporting function. Of course, the numbers end up in a report, but the real benefit comes from the work that the company puts into understanding the issues, creating meaningful measurements, and setting targets.

This first step is an inside-out approach. A **second** step would be an outside-in approach. This would involve getting the stakeholders themselves to sit at the table to speak about what matters to them and why. In 2005, when Walmart's CEO at the time, Lee Scott, decided to make a push toward greater environmental sustainability, he invited leading critics to the table. The former head of the Sierra Club, Adam Werbach, became an advisor. Scott reached out to Steven Hamburg, a professor of environmental studies who had written a scathing report in 1994 on Walmart's environmental record, and asked him how to avoid just "greenwashing" their way forward. Rather than defend himself against the criticisms, Scott decided to listen. By listening and engaging, he was able to see a way forward, one that involved Walmart taking the lead on a Sustainability Index for suppliers and on moving toward zero waste and 100 percent renewable energy. Of course, Walmart isn't there yet, but the company is a lot further along than it would have been if it hadn't truly engaged with environmental critics.[24]

Similarly, we can take lessons from ACT UP, the AIDS advocacy group, and its spin-off, the Treatment Action Group, whose members fought in the late 1980s and early 1990s to have a seat at the table when pharmaceutical companies were deciding on research priorities and designing experimental protocols. The protesting got them to the table, but it was being at the table that allowed them to work together with researchers to get key drugs to market for those suffering around the world (more about this in the Epilogue). In Germany, of course, labor unions or other employee representatives have half the seats on the boards of directors (the *Aufsichtsrat*), so their voices are present at the highest levels of organizations right along with those of the shareholders. These are but a few of the mechanisms by which stakeholders can become part of the conversation.

Why is this important? Bryan Stevenson, anti-death-penalty advocate, legal scholar, and executive director of the Equal Justice Initiative, put it this way at *Fortune* magazine's CEO Initiative in 2018. Speaking to an audience full of CEOs, he said that, in the face of climate change, poverty, anti-immigrant sentiment, poor educational systems, and disease, our economic leaders and CEOs "have a critical role to play":

> When we isolate ourselves, when we allow ourselves to be shielded and disconnected from those who are vulnerable and disfavored, we sustain and contribute to these problems. I am persuaded that, in proximity, there is something we can learn about how we change the world, how we change the environment, how we create healthier communities. I am persuaded that there is power in proximity. Too often we wait until we think we have all of the answers before we get closer to those who have been marginalized. I am actually persuaded that we have to find ways to get closer to the disfavored, the marginalized, the excluded, the poor, the disabled, even if we don't have any answers about what we will do when we get there. The power is in the proximity. Many of us have been taught that if there's a bad part of town, you don't put your business there . . . I am persuaded we need to do the opposite. We need to find ways to engage and invest and position ourselves in the places where there is despair.[25]

In both cases—inside-out and outside-in—the challenge is to be honest about what the company's strategies and activities look like to other stakeholders. It requires a certain amount of vulnerability. Here, defensiveness is the enemy of insight. The input won't all be pleasant, and it won't all be easy to deal with. Still, it is the starting point for a journey to becoming the 360° Corporation that can lead to better outcomes for everyone.

• PART I SIGNPOSTS

- Corporations are increasingly expected to address the interests of multiple stakeholders. It is no longer entirely a "total returns to shareholders" game. This pressure comes from "clicktivists" creating social-media storms about company missteps, consumers getting turned off by irresponsible firms, millennial workers just walking away from companies that don't have a socially responsible value proposition, and investors demanding adherence to environmental, social, and governance standards.

- The urgency for moving beyond the bottom-line mind-set has never been greater. Rising seas are already flooding communities; pollution is choking cities; the artificial-intelligence revolution will come with major dislocations as jobs are replaced with robots; gender equality is stagnating.

- The shared value framework that dominates corporate discourse these days can inspire companies to think differently about stakeholders, but it doesn't deal with cases where there is no win-win. A fundamental question is how to move beyond the limitations of shared value thinking and deal with intractable trade-offs.

- The 360° Corporation offers a new model for addressing these challenges. The 360° Corporation is an organization that engages in four modes of action: knowing trade-offs, rethinking trade-offs, innovating around trade-offs, and thriving within trade-offs.

- Every business model has trade-offs embedded in it. Few companies recognize that each business choice involves a choice to favor some stakeholder needs and values over others. These trade-offs are often implicit. The starting point, or Mode 1, is that you need to make them explicit: learn to uncover and understand your own trade-offs.

PART II

THE BUSINESS CASE FOR SOCIAL RESPONSIBILITY

Rethinking Trade-Offs (Mode 2)

CHAPTER 3 •

IS THERE A WIN-WIN?

The Search for Shared Value

MORE AND MORE, supposedly social issues are appearing on corporate agendas. We are inundated with the business case for a high-trust culture, minimum-wage increases, sustainability, corporate social responsibility (CSR), a purpose-driven organization, and so on. These issues, which might not always have seemed like corporate priorities in the past, are being pitched as business imperatives today using business-case rhetoric: what's good for society is also good for business.

This is the essence of shared-value, win-win solutions, what I call **Mode 2** action. Companies are increasingly finding that social good does not have to be a trade-off with the bottom line. Higher minimum wages or high-trust cultures are pitched as improving productivity. Sustainability is pitched as lowering costs. CSR is pitched as increasing the value of a company's brand or reducing downside reputational risk.

WHEN SHARED VALUE WORKS

These pitches have worked. For many managers trained to think that profit takes precedent, the idea of shared value has given them a path forward to dealing with the trade-offs that their companies' business models create. Companies can

- Justify the substitution of more expensive LED lighting for incandescent lights because they use less energy which is *both* good for the environment and cheaper to operate over the long run.
- Reduce the amount of packaging on products because it *both* saves plastic and cardboard resources and decreases the cost of packaging and shipping.
- Invest in improved worker conditions in the supply chain because it *both* creates better circumstances for employees and reduces costly employee turnover.
- Promote organic products because they *both* reduce the introduction of toxic chemicals into the environment and increase consumers' willingness to pay more for organic.
- Focus on recruiting women because it *both* provides increased job opportunities for women and gives the company access to a neglected talent pipeline.

I could go on. You won't find many companies anymore that don't have a story like this to tell. That is the predominant narrative in the sustainability reports that have become almost de rigueur for firms these days.

Walmart's "2018 Global Responsibility Report" starts with a letter from Chief Sustainability Officer Kathleen McLaughlin, who states [with my emphasis on the last line],

> Business exists to serve society. For Walmart, this is true in many ways. We're providing customers with convenient access to safe, affordable food and other products, creating job opportunities for our associates; helping suppliers grow their businesses that, in turn, employ others; and generating tax dollars that help support community life. The most successful businesses do all these things but go one step further—they aim to strengthen the systems on which they rely, such as retail employment or food production. Why? Not only to build customer trust and maintain license to operate, but also to enhance supply security, manage evolution of cost structure,

generate new revenue streams and attract talent. Strengthening societal systems is *not only the responsible thing to do—it maximizes business value.*[1]

Nike CEO Mark Parker tells us in his company's sustainability report, "What keeps us going is this simple belief: when Nike creates meaningful change within our own company and within the communities that we serve, we make a positive difference in the world. We expand our purpose as a company." The report details how Nike diverted more than 12.5 million pounds of factory and postconsumer waste from landfills through the Nike Grind program, and it makes sense because the revenues from the sale of Nike Grind sports and play surfaces went back into the company coffers to fund sustainable innovations. The company has worked with suppliers of footwear finished goods to eliminate outdated steam boilers, which made sense because it generated average energy savings of 15 to 20 percent at each location.[2]

These stories are powerful. Companies motivated by purpose find ways to achieve social objectives while still attending to the bottom line. This is Mode 2 action: looking for win-win solutions.

What does it take to get to the win-win? It's not easy. Even the low-hanging fruit take real effort to pluck. Think of Walmart's famous decision to require suppliers of liquid laundry detergent to ship it only in concentrated formulas. That would seem pretty straightforward. The benefits to the environment are clear: less water, smaller plastic containers, fewer shipping boxes, lower transportation requirements, and therefore less pollution. The benefits to the company are also clear: reduced shipping and logistics costs and positive media coverage. But this kind of change didn't happen overnight.

The commitment was made public in September 2007 at the Clinton Global Initiative meetings, but it had started three years earlier with an experiment with Unilever. To get Unilever to develop a concentrated version of its All detergent, Walmart had to promise equal or greater shelf space for the product, to increase marketing and to educate consumers. Unilever created the thirty-two ounce "All small-and-mighty" laundry detergent, which was three-times concentrated and could wash the same amount of clothes as a one hundred-ounce bottle of unconcentrated detergent, and Walmart pushed it out to consumers. This trial was a success—even allowing Unilever to increase sales of the All product, so Walmart started to move it throughout its supplier network—to Procter & Gamble, Church & Dwight, Dial, and others. Walmart required each and every supplier to make a broad range of changes: new formulations, new packaging, new labeling, and new advertising. It happened because Walmart had the clout to make it happen. Simultaneously, Walmart had quite a bit of work to do itself. It adjusted its shelf allocations, shipping patterns, and warehousing; provided interactive displays to explain the new product to the consumer; educated Walmart associates about its benefits; and offered promotions to get consumers to buy the new formulations. By May 2008, Walmart announced it had hit the target that only concentrated versions of detergent were available in its stores.[3] The lesson is that even with the lowest-hanging fruit, the work to get to the win-win is nontrivial.

By the way, the fact that Walmart didn't just proceed with an across-the-board mandate to all suppliers but started with an experiment with one product from one supplier is part of Mode 4 action, which we'll get back to in Chapter 8. If you are unsure of the win-win or don't know whether implementation is possible, experiments like this are a great way to move forward. The experiment created two benefits. First, in the design of the experiment, both Walmart and Unilever learned what the concerns were on both sides and worked to accommodate them. Second, once the experiment was a success, it created great leverage for convincing other brands to participate.

The laundry detergent story is a great one, not only because it is a simple evocation of the win-win, but also because it shows how hard even clear-cut changes can be. You can see why the suppliers might resist: Would they be able to get a comparable price for the concentrated product? Would they lose shelf space if the size of the bottles were smaller? Would they be able to recoup their investment in the new formulations and other changes? You can also see why consumers would be resistant: How do we know our clothes will get clean if we use less detergent? Why do these much smaller bottles cost more than the older big bottles? Even internally to Walmart: someone in HR has to develop new training modules; marketers have to develop new interactive displays; store managers have to get the displays into the store and figure out how to reshelve the products. In short, like any change, it required many different players to make investments and change behaviors. Why did it get done? Because the business case showed that the investments would be worth it, not just for the environment but also for the bottom line, and because senior leaders were committed to making it happen.

HOW TO GET STARTED IN MODE 2:
MAKING THE BUSINESS CASE

What does it take to get started in Mode 2? As I've argued, most of the research and practice to date on CSR has focused here. There is no shortage of advice on how to make the business case for social responsibility. Most of the recommendations come down to the same set of ideas. I'm going to make my own argument that business-case thinking takes you only so far, but not far enough. Let me just summarize the categories of business-case justifications that most scholars, consultants, and practitioners highlight:[4]

- **Reducing costs and increasing operational efficiency.** Whether it is installing energy-efficient devices to reduce operating costs, improving working conditions to reduce employee turnover, or creating water-neutral manufacturing techniques to lower water costs, doing things that are good for stakeholders can end up being good for the bottom line.

- **Reducing risks and preserving the license to operate.** When people talk about the license to operate, they mean avoiding anything such as protests or regulation that might prevent the firm from being able to do its business. Firms might want to invest in local communities to make sure that residents support a company coming to town (think of Walmart giving to local charities when leaders want to open up stores in a new location). Other firms might want to create voluntary standards in order to avoid more restrictive or inflexible regulation.

- **Creating competitive advantage.** In some cases, consumers may be willing to pay more for or be more loyal to products that are seen as socially responsible, whether it is a hybrid electric car, or products sourced from female entrepreneurs, or fair-trade coffee. Similarly, the most talented employees who have their pick of jobs might be attracted to firms with good employment practices. In these cases, investment in socially responsible practices is a means for firms to differentiate themselves and their products.

The more interesting question is, How do you go about generating the insights about these potential benefits? I'm more compelled by the process. That's why the modes I identify in this book are *modes of action*. What actions can you take? I propose three steps:

1. Go back to Mode 1: know your trade-offs.
2. Use the analysis of trade-offs to set goals.
3. Develop solutions and understand whose interests will be affected by them.

First, as I outlined in the last chapter, Mode 1 action to know your trade-offs is a precursor to doing anything about them. Inside-out analyses of the business and its impacts as well as outside-in engagement with stakeholders can help you know more about what to do. Sometimes it is hard to even know what the low-hanging fruit is. Analysis comes first. But I also hesitate to recommend this because some companies can get bogged down in analysis paralysis. It is sometimes easier to say "more analysis, please!" than to start acting. At the same time, it is the detailed analysis of the stakeholders and the impacts on them that generate the insights about win-win solutions. It's a balance. You can't skip the analysis, but you can't use it as an excuse not to move forward either.

The more truths you tell and the fewer myths you make in the analysis, the more likely you'll generate insights. If you look at Nike's "16/17 Sustainable Business Report," there's something particularly poignant about how frank the company is about where it's gotten and where it has not. CEO Mark Parker describes the value of the analysis this way:

> Throughout the process of pulling this report together, I've been thinking a great deal about what it means to lead in a time of such dramatic change. It's moments like these that offer the opportunity to hit the pause button and ask the big questions. Is it possible to grow the Nike brand into new markets while leaving a smaller footprint? As we transform our business model to move faster and be more consumer-centric, how does that affect a sophisticated value chain that employs over a million workers and delivers over a billion units a year? And how can we challenge ourselves to cultivate a company culture that is more inclusive and empowering? What poli-

cies and practices will accelerate the pace of change within our own teams? This report covers many of these complex challenges. It reveals our flaws and shines a light on our victories. Most importantly, it tells us where we need to work harder.[5]

Nike is not perfect. Critics may suggest that the company hasn't made enough progress, but the analysis is motivating. The gaps identified create "moonshot" goals (in the company's words), and they also show where the firm can start building win-win solutions. This is the **second** step: setting goals and targets, the process of which can be illuminating in and of itself. Nike's report includes a chart that explains an overall increase in water impact because, despite water-efficiency initiatives, there was an increase in cotton-based fleece apparel in its product mix, cotton being a water-intensive crop. This same increase in the use of cotton fleece also offset most of the company's energy-efficiency initiatives in the supply chain because cotton weighs more than other materials. The analysis makes very clear how interlinked different choices are. Energy- and water-efficiency exercises won't matter, or won't matter nearly enough, if other choices outweigh them.

An obvious action: use less cotton. That would be the win-win. Can Nike make the business case for that? Are other materials as inexpensive to buy as cotton? Will consumers be willing to buy products without cotton in them? Can Nike's attention to the environmental impacts of cotton increase consumer loyalty or reduce the risk of negative press or social-media activism? This is the conversation one can imagine people at Nike having. This is the **third** step: the explicit conversation about how to address the trade-offs. Sometimes the answer seems easy: use less cotton or in Walmart's case, stock only concentrated laundry detergent. Then it's a matter of making the case for action.

A lot of narratives are possible if there is willingness on the part of management. While action can be justified in terms of reducing costs, enhancing reputation (or avoiding a threat to it), assuring the right to operate in a community, or reducing operating risks, some of these are relatively hard to quantify. This can often put a stop to projects right there. Then again, most companies are experienced in quantifying strategic moves with high levels of uncertainty such as acquisitions. In the case of an acquisition, you build a spreadsheet and do the best you can to think about the synergies that can be achieved by combining operations, the increased market access, the enhancement to the brand, or other issues that are typically contemplated in such a deal. You calculate sensitivities so you know how far off you have to be in your estimates to change your decision. This suggests that the same can be done for any initiative that works to accommodate the trade-offs with a stakeholder. That it is difficult to quantify is not an excuse not to try. How much more might a consumer be willing to pay for a more sustainable product? How much does employee turnover cost in the supply chain, and how much could turnover be reduced? How vulnerable is a product source to water shortages, and what would the impact of such shortages be? Depending on the issue, the answers to these questions can be estimated and stress-tested.

Just like in making the case for an acquisition that management already wants to accomplish, different aspects of the case can be emphasized. When the spreadsheet doesn't produce a positive financial outcome for a deal, management might still make the acquisition based on strategic or competitive reasons. Addressing stakeholder needs is not that different. Playing up the importance of reputation as a decision-making factor will be particularly important for some kinds of consumer companies. Playing up the license to operate might be more important for a mining company, or even for a company like Walmart, which has seen protests over the years when it wanted to locate stores in certain communities. Thus, as with any business case for any strategic choice, making the case is an art, not a science. The better analysis you have on the trade-offs, the more you'll be able to make smart choices in building the case, but it still comes down to judgment and to will.

WHAT'S THE PROBLEM WITH THE BUSINESS CASE?

If you have any doubt about how important the business case is, just browse the internet for "the business case for sustainability" (172,000 hits) or "the business case for diversity" (119,000 hits) or "the business case for CSR" (48,300 hits). Law firms, consulting firms, industry associations, academics, and management gurus are all in the business of telling you how to make the business case, and more importantly, that making the business case is the essential first step to achieving whichever objective they've laid out: sustainability, diversity, CSR, and so on.

This all sounds great. What could be wrong with these ambitious goals for shared value?

Well, it turns out that the very act of making a business case for social responsibility can undermine the objectives.[6] It sounds strange to say—given that 300,000 or more pages on the internet will tell you the opposite—but here's the argument, and it comes in several parts.[7]

First, in our Western business culture, we have been imbued with a belief in markets. We generally have faith (and are taught that way in business school) that the market system works pretty well in driving economic output, and certainly better than any other system. One of the tenets of that market system is the primacy of the shareholder.

Second, anyone imbued with those beliefs in the market is going to find the business case for social responsibility particularly appealing because it is based on the idea that action in favor of other stakeholders will also benefit the shareholders' bottom line.

Third, and here's the rub, recent research by European scholars Sebastian Hafenbrädl and Daniel Waeger shows that, unfortunately, when you make the business case to these kinds of folks, it doesn't make them more likely to act. The appeal of the business-case idea is that the facts provided in the case should lead executives to invest readily in socially responsible activities. Yet the evidence from research across a large number of firms shows that this doesn't happen. Why?

The answer is based on something called system-justification theory. The idea is that we as individuals tend to justify and perhaps even idealize our existing social arrangements: in this case, the market system and those corporate practices aimed to generate returns for the shareholder. We tend not to want to acknowledge that these systems might be unfair or arbitrary because that would be destabilizing. Thus, if we are believers in the free market, we also want to believe that company activities are not illegitimate but instead serve the system's purpose—which is to generate value for the shareholder. In other words, we justify the system we are in. That's why we want to make a business case for social responsibility: because it fits into the system we believe in. We believe in the market, so the only legitimate actions should be the ones that sustain the discipline of the corporate profit motive.

The problem is that our justification of the system makes it harder for us to feel moral outrage and limits our ability to even see problems in the system that might cause inequalities or damage to other stakeholders. We can't feel that something is outrageous because it would destabilize our belief in the system.

Social psychologists even say that it would cause anxiety. Yet moral outrage is what actually motivates action. Without it, it is hard to provoke change in organizational systems that are naturally inertial. Therefore, and ironically, if we are the kind of people who need a business case in order to justify action, we are also the kind of people who are less likely to act even if a business case is presented to us. Moral outrage is inconsistent with belief in the business case.

This is why, I argue, we haven't seen as much action on diversity despite a decade or more of making the business case for it. We claim that greater diversity and inclusion should lead to better financial performance or more innovation, but getting there would simply be too disruptive of the status quo.[8] When we don't see results, we call the business case into question (more about this in Chapter 4). It's perhaps also why the business case for sustainability has been great at the low-hanging fruit but gets stuck tackling the higher impact and trickier issues. There are often real trade-offs that simply can't be resolved through a win-win business case, and using a business-case framework keeps us from addressing those trade-offs. Other recent research shows that the business case provokes people to focus more on economic than justice-based metrics of success. These might be fine under certain circumstances, but the moment there is a downturn in organizational performance, people exposed to a business case are more likely to see social-impact efforts (such as those aimed at achieving diversity) as unsuccessful and to support reducing investments in them.[9]

Michael Porter and Mark Kramer's shared value framework was critiqued in the *California Management Review* in precisely this way by business ethics researchers Andrew Crane of Bath University and colleagues. They argued, "Porter and Kramer claim to 'move beyond' any such trade-offs, largely by (it would seem) ignoring them. While seeking win-win opportunities is clearly important, this does not provide guidance for the many situations where social and economic outcomes will not be aligned for all stakeholders."[10]

Porter and Kramer were given a chance to respond. They went back to justifying the system, saying:

> The reason that creating shared value has gained so much traction and led
> to real change is exactly because it aligns social progress with corporate
> self-interest in a concrete and highly tangible way, including with those "old

strategy models" that capture the reality of competition and prevailing corporate practice. It is precisely the wishful thinking of writers like Mr. Crane that has led to so many corporate responsibility and sustainability arguments falling on deaf corporate ears, by insisting that profit-seeking enterprises need to abandon their core purpose for the sake of the greater good.[11]

The problem is that, to the extent that we buy Porter and Kramer's logic, we may also be avoiding any moral sentiments that would guide effective action. Let me clarify. I'm not arguing against making the business case per se. In fact, I think the process of generating the business case (Mode 2 action) can lead to rich analyses about the trade-offs between stakeholders and shareholders, and it can provoke insights into ways to move forward. It's the *process* of making the business case that is more valuable than the privileging of the business case as a goal and justification for action. Dave Stangis, the vice president of corporate responsibility and chief sustainability officer at Campbell's, puts it this way: "If I'm spending my days and time and my efforts on trying to build a business case, convincing the company to be more sustainable or to think like me, I think I'm wasting my time." According to *MIT Sloan Management Review*, "Stangis sees a trend to go ahead even without a solid case—a 'just do it' zeitgeist, more akin to startup entrepreneurs than efficiency-focused managers. A business case may emerge from the process of exploring sustainable solutions, from learning what is possible by taking action."[12] Here, the business case is developed as companies act rather than as a precursor to action.

To sum it up: the latest research suggests that the more we say we need a business case to give permission for action, the less likely we are to achieve, in Nike's terms, our moonshots goals. Building the business case is more useful as a process of discovery than as a justification for action.

CHAPTER 4 ●

GETTING STUCK IN THE BUSINESS CASE

How the Business Case for Diversity Blocks Progress

TO EXPLAIN THE POWER of the business case (Mode 2) as well as its limits, I need to take you on a tour through the issues—looking at the impetus for the business case, where the business case gets bogged down, and what companies like Nike and Walmart have learned from the projects they have undertaken. To get deep enough into the issues, we'll look at the business case for diversity in detail, where we'll see how complex social issues do not readily lend themselves to easily made business cases for action.

Indeed, the business case for diversity is one of the most striking examples of the challenges of the business-case logic. Diversity is pitched as helping companies win the war for talent or increase innovativeness in teams. This is the subject of countless reports by banks, consulting firms, and NGOs. "The evidence is growing—there really is a business case for diversity," trumpets the *Financial Times*. McKinsey & Company has gotten a lot of PR off of reports that argue, "Awareness of the business case for inclusion and diversity is on the rise. While social justice typically is the initial impetus behind these efforts, companies have increasingly begun to regard inclusion and diversity as a source of competitive advantage, and specifically as a key enabler of growth."[1]

Sodexo CEO Michel Landel makes the typical argument:

> I am firmly convinced that gender balance is more than a moral imperative or a "women's issue." Gender balance is at the core of what we stand for at Sodexo, where each of our 420,000 employees must have access to the same opportunities and be able to develop his or her career. By tapping into the full potential of men *and* women, Sodexo is stronger, more innovative, and better at serving its 75 million consumers worldwide.[2]

This business-case logic is the essence of Mode 2 thinking. It should be fairly straightforward to make progress on issues that are seen as social if they are simultaneously good for business. And this logic has been quite useful in getting social issues on the agenda of corporate decision makers. It is no longer unusual to hear diversity, sustainability, or ethical treatment of workers in the supply chain discussed in board rooms and among executive leadership teams. An implication of this win-win mind-set is that companies should easily be able to make progress. The idea of shared value is that we can somehow move beyond trade-offs that have constrained action in the past by growing the pie rather than just dividing it up.

Yet despite the many claims that greater gender equality will be good for innovation, employee engagement, or rigorous decision-making, progress has stalled.[3] One could conclude that making the business case has so far failed to induce much progress in organizations.

Even worse, having to prove the business case may inadvertently imply that corporations shouldn't be more inclusive unless it can be proven that inclusion is better than the (still largely white, straight, and male) status quo. In the famous win-win calculation, one win—the dollar—always wins. This approach takes a whole host of options that you might want to consider off the table. Most companies—even those that recognize trade-offs—never move beyond this point. Said one (male) board director to me recently, "We added a woman to the board last year, and it didn't really make much of a difference. It's not going to make sense for us to push this."

Thus, the business-case logic can become a trap that keeps organizations from moving forward on diversity (or other social issues). The shared-value or business-case approach may get you only so far and may actually limit progress by narrowing your view to include only those possibilities anchored by the bottom line.

IMPETUS FOR A BUSINESS CASE FOR DIVERSITY

The Women's Economic Empowerment program at Walmart has entailed a tremendous amount of investment in building up the supply chain of female suppliers to hit the company's goal of sourcing $20 billion in products from woman-led businesses. Launched in 2011, it has been an extraordinarily successful effort to get more woman-led businesses into Walmart's ecosystem. Not only did the retailer hit its $20 billion sourcing target, but it trained more than one million women in small global suppliers and worked closely with its major suppliers to improve the diversity of people in those companies' key account teams. What spurred on this investment? What justified it at the corporate level? It's a long story, but let's start with two vignettes from the early 1990s that take us to the impetus for Walmart's business case for diversity:

> Claudia Renati started working at a Sam's Club in Roseville, California, in 1993 as a marketing membership team leader. When the regional sales manager left, she took on the responsibility of running the regional marketing programs, a job she performed without additional pay or recognition in her job title. When she asked the Director of Operations to promote her into the position, he refused on the grounds that she had not gone through the Management Training Program. He also suggested that the only way she could be promoted into management would be if she were willing to relocate to Alaska. Yet, he then filled the position with a male next-door neighbor who had not gone through management training and had no experience in marketing. This happened repeatedly. None of the more than 20 men hired into marketing management positions were required to relocate, and Ms. Renati was always tasked with training these less qualified and less experienced men who were hired to be her supervisors. Renati then "spoke with Director of Operations again about my desire to move into management and the fact that I had spent nine years working at Sam's Club with little advancement. All of my evaluations . . . were excellent . . . [The director of operations] then asked me if I could stack 50-pound bags of dog food. When I told him I could not repeatedly lift 50 pounds, he told me there was nothing he could

do for me because, before I could become a manager, I would have to be Floor Team Leader and that requires stacking 50-pound bags of dog food. I know of several males . . . who never had to become Floor Team Leader and stack 50-pound bags of dog food before going into management. I had also never seen any written job description with this lifting requirement nor do I believe that one exists. I believe that this was an excuse for keeping me from advancing."[4]

Ramona Scott worked for Walmart in Florida from 1990 to 1998. As a personnel manager who had access to payroll records, she observed that male employees were paid more than female employees of equivalent seniority. She asked her store manager about the pay differences, and his response was: "Men are here to make a career and women aren't. Retail is for housewives who just need to earn extra money." When she asked about a merit raise she thought was given inappropriately to a male employee, she was told by a manager, "He has a family to support." She pointed out that, as a single mother, she also had a family to support. The manager simply walked away, and she did not receive a raise. She twice asked her store manager about getting into the Assistant Manager Training program, but her requests were denied with no explanation. "Shortly after that, he told me that in order to get along with him, I needed to behave like his wife. From his description of his wife, I understood [the store manager] to mean that he wanted me to wait on him and fix him his coffee. In fact, when the District Manager visited, [the store manager] would tell me to go get them coffee. After this second instance of being rejected for admission into the Assistant Manager training program, I decided to give up on further promotion."[5]

These stories come from the declarations of women in support of the class-action lawsuit filed against Walmart claiming a broad pattern of discrimination against women. Named Dukes v. Wal-Mart Stores, Inc. after Betty Dukes, one of the complainants, it was first filed in 2001. The complaint claimed that Walmart had systematically denied female hourly and salaried employees around the US access to promotions and equal pay. The plaintiffs' attorneys, led by Joseph Sellers, filed 110 sworn statements of the kinds described above from women who were current or former employees of Walmart in 30 states. The complaint asked the court to award 1.6 million women employed at Walmart at any time since December 16, 1998, lost wages and punitive damages. It also asked that Walmart be ordered to make reforms to its employment policies and practices.

This lawsuit has followed a long and winding path all the way to the US Supreme Court. The crux of a class action is that a representative plaintiff—in this case, Betty Dukes—can bring a claim on behalf of all members of a class of people. The big roadblock for moving forward is certifying that the particular group of people has enough in common in order to be considered a class. Walmart contested such certification in this case. While the Federal District Court (in 2004) and the Ninth Circuit Court of Appeals (in 2007 and again in 2009) both ruled in favor of certifying the Walmart women as a class, this decision was overturned on appeal by the US Supreme Court in 2011, claiming that the women working at Walmart around the US did not constitute a class:

> Without some glue holding together the alleged reasons for [Walmart's employment] decisions, it will be impossible to say that examination of all the class members' claims will produce a common answer to the crucial discrimination question . . . The only corporate policy that the plaintiffs' evidence convincingly establishes is Wal-Mart's "policy" of giving local supervisors discretion over employment matters. While such a policy could be the basis of a Title VII disparate-impact claim, recognizing that a claim "can" exist does not mean that every employee in a company with that policy has a common claim. In a company of Wal-Mart's size and geographical scope, it is unlikely that all managers would exercise their discretion in a common way without some common direction.[6]

In essence, and ironically, the court ruled that the class should not be certified because Walmart was too large, because the patterns observed were too pervasive. There was no specific company-wide policy that could be identified, other than local managerial discretion, that would lead to the patterns. No matter where one stands on these claims, it is easy to see that, even aside from the legal costs, these lawsuits were costly for Walmart. The lawsuits generated a substantial amount of negative press coverage and attention for Walmart. These stories, for example, figured prominently in Robert Greenwald's documentary, *Walmart: The High Cost of Low Price*.[7]

SOURCES OF BIAS

Can discrimination be that widespread? Why might managers exercise their discretion in a common way, perhaps even without some common direction? What is the "glue" holding together discrimination? The short answer is that discrimination is not a Walmart problem, or not only a Walmart problem. One has only to look at the ranks of management in the US and around the world, or the persistent wage gap between men and women, to know that something is still going on. In the United States, women represent 47 percent of the labor force but only 15 percent of executive officers and 4.4 percent of CEOs of S&P 500 companies.[8] As the *New York Times* reported in 2018, there were still about as many men named John as women in total at the helm of the largest US corporations.[9] In Canada, 39 percent of companies listed on the Ontario Stock Exchange still have no women on their boards of directors (and only 11 percent have more than three female members). Women's pay gap has been stuck at about 88 cents to the dollar that men received for a couple of decades.[10] Women are more likely to live in poverty than are men.[11] These aggregate patterns are pretty hard to dismiss. The question is, Why do they persist, especially when no one likes to think that he or she is discriminating, and companies have been implementing diversity management programs for years?

In the *Mad Men* days, we could attribute much of these differentials to hostile sexism. After all, those were the days when classified ads had separate listings for "Help Wanted-Men" and "Help Wanted-Women."[12] In the era of #MeToo, we know that hostile sexism exists still, as evidenced by the plethora of news stories and sexual harassment claims (more than 12,000 charges were formally filed with the US Equal Employment Opportunity Commission in 2017).[13] But in a stream of research starting in the 1990s, scholars Peter Glick and Susan Fiske identified another form of more insidious sexism, which they termed "benevolent sexism." Benevolent sexism is tricky because it is imbued with positive and prosocial feelings but remains sexist because it involves viewing women stereotypically and in restricted roles. An example would be saying that the female manager in a meeting should take the notes or organize the team lunch because she's "so much better" at these tasks. The problem is that benevolent sexism, even if it is a "subjectively positive orientation of protection, idealization, and affection directed toward women . . . , like hostile sexism, [it] serves to justify women's subordinate status to men."[14]

US Senator Kirsten Gillibrand tells a story about her experience as a young lawyer. Asked why people feel free to comment on women's bodies, she said,

> I don't know the reason, but I know it makes women feel undermined. When I was a young lawyer, I worked for months on this case. I worked weekends, gave up vacation, worked until midnight. And at the celebratory dinner afterward, my boss says: "Let's thank Kirsten for her hard work. And don't we just love her haircut?" It was heart wrenching. I thought, "After all that work, you're commenting on my hair?"[15]

Or examine this (rewritten) obituary of Albert Einstein:

> He made sure he shopped for groceries every night on the way home from work, took the garbage out, and hand washed the antimacassars. But to his stepdaughters he was just Dad. "He was always there for us," said his stepdaughter and first cousin once removed Margo. Albert Einstein, who died on Tuesday, had another life at work, where he sometimes slipped away to peck at projects like showing that atoms really exist. His discovery of something called the photoelectric effect won him a coveted Nobel Prize.[16]

That sounds a bit odd. But then take a look at the first lines of the actual 2013 obituary of rocket scientist Yvonne Brill published in the *New York Times*:

> She made a mean beef stroganoff, followed her husband from job to job, and took eight years off from work to raise three children. "The world's best mom," her son Matthew said. But Yvonne Brill, who died on Wednesday at 88 in Princeton, N.J., was also a brilliant rocket scientist, who in the early 1970s invented a propulsion system to help keep communications satellites from slipping out of their orbits.

As commentator Melanie Tannenbaum emphasizes, there's nothing wrong with mentioning a person's family life in an obituary. "The *problem* here is really that if 'Yvonne' were 'Yvan,' the obit would have looked fundamentally different."[17] By the way, the controversy over the bio led the *Times* to rewrite the obituary, which now starts, "She was a brilliant rocket scientist . . ."[18] The point is that these "compliments" disguise a dynamic that leads to subordination and discriminatory outcomes. If people focus on a young lawyer's haircut, her skills as a lawyer are undermined, even if the comment was meant to be flattering. Now, imagine the boss who made the comment about Gillibrand's hair. Had he been confronted, he might have said, "Wait a minute! I was trying to be nice! Aren't you just overreacting?"

Benevolent sexism has at its roots the implicit or unconscious bias that most of us—men and women alike—hold. Few of us wake up in the morning thinking that we are going to act in a way that is sexist. In fact, by 2018, most of us think that we are doing quite the opposite, that we are beyond being sexist (or racist) in this day and age. Yet research has quite convincingly demonstrated that this is far from the case. A test of implicit bias administered by researchers at Harvard University has now been taken by more than 17 million people. It shows that overall, about 75 percent of people hold some unconscious bias associating men with work and career and women with home and family.[19] If this is the case, it becomes very hard to take women seriously in the workplace. As we saw at Walmart, managers could more easily think that women work there for a little extra income while men are there for careers that allow them to support their families.

Implicit bias plays out at all stages of people's careers. We now have evidence that the wording of job ads can deter women from applying for jobs and that the best-practice use of employee networks to identify job candidates just reinforces the gender status quo. Further, a now very numerous set of experiments shows that when identical resumes are evaluated, the one submitted by "Greg" will receive twice as many callbacks as the one submitted by "Emily." A woman needs to have several years more experience or education to be considered the equivalent of a male job candidate. She will likely be offered a lower salary for the same job as the male applicant. Once on the job, studies show that women with the exact same performance evaluations will often receive much lower salary increases and bonuses. Women are often not given the same developmental opportunities, such as profit-and-loss responsibility or access to high-profile deals because they are perceived as being less committed to the job. Studies also show that women can be seen as competent or nice but not both and that women are penalized for success in "male" tasks.[20]

Understanding individual bias helps us grasp why improving diversity and inclusion is seen as a trade-off by many people and organizations. If our biases cause us to devalue the contributions of women, we will also think that including women will compromise meritocratic principles. This is the crux of arguments such as those made in the now-famous memo from (former) Google employee James Damore. He argued that women somehow don't have the characteristics required for the coding jobs in the firm and therefore aren't suited to them.[21] That memo got him fired, but it also got the *New York Times* to feature him in an article about the backlash against the women-in-tech movement.[22] In reality, of course, including women (or people of color) wouldn't compromise meritocracy at all because the problem is in our biased perceptions of quality, not actual quality.

What makes the challenge of gender diversity so difficult to solve is that the discrimination we observe is not only or even mainly about individual bias. The bigger problem is that these stereotypes are embedded in and reinforced by our systems of recruiting, evaluation, promotion, and retention.

Why should companies care about this bias? For the past few decades, those who have attempted to promote gender equality have been pigeonholed into making the business case for action. Promoting "womenomics" has become its own big business, with companies such as Ernst & Young (in its 2010 *Ground-breakers* report), McKinsey & Company (in its Women Matter project) and Goldman Sachs (in its *Closing the Gender Gaps* report) arguing that "it's not about morality or fairness or doing the right thing; it's not even about hiring smart people. Instead, it is about honing a competitive weapon. Diversity is a strategy."[23] These arguments seem to make the case that social justice—the view that women have the right to the same opportunities as men and to be treated without discrimination—has not been enough to motivate action.

Here is the business case that people make: in the war for talent, companies cannot afford to ignore or underutilize half of the workforce. Diverse teams produce more innovative outputs and foster critical analysis, often taking more risk-aware decisions (because women are often put in riskier situations than men).[24] Women, as consumers, hold the purse strings in households, sharing responsibility for upward of 85 percent of purchases, and therefore companies need to understand and empathize with their needs.[25] Women own nearly 30 percent of businesses in the US, and this number is growing at 1.5 times the national average rate.[26] Women control more than half of personal wealth in the US today and are set to inherit 70 percent of 41 trillion dollars of the wealth being transferred over the next two decades; they will therefore shape the patterns of investment in the economy.[27]

More and more, as Walmart and others have discovered, companies with poor records on diversity are subject to reputational risks that can harm performance by turning buyers or investors away. In short, as even international agencies such as the United Nations and the International Monetary Fund argue, "Empowering women is smart economics."[28] The Calvert Foundation pitches this literally as win-win with its Women Investing in Women Initiative, called WIN-WIN for short, a program to raise capital through Community Investment Notes, which are investment tools that allow people to invest in a portfolio of organizations and projects that empower women. Citing the kinds of data I list above, Calvert says, "These, and dozens of other statistics, show that investing in women is smart economics."[29]

IF YOU LET ME PLAY

What have companies done with this business case? Nike's journey is illustrative—both of what can be done, and of the pitfalls along the way.

Despite the fact that the company is named after the Greek goddess of victory, Nike has struggled in the market for women's sports apparel—when it missed the aerobics trend in the 1980s and let Reebok surpass it in sales, or more recently with the meteoric rise of Lululemon. The women's athletic footwear and apparel market is larger than the men's in the US, but it counts for only 20 percent of Nike's business.[30] While Nike is yet again making a big push into the women's market, its path has been littered with false starts and false notes.

Nike missed the aerobics trend out of what some have called arrogance. In 1982, its leaders looked at the launch of Reebok's Freestyle shoe, with its soft garment leather, and laughed at it. The shoe was deemed to be poorly made and unlikely to hold up in use. Nike underestimated the fact that the shoe's comfort would appeal to female consumers. It wasn't the latest high-tech running shoe. Indeed, Nike executives didn't even think of aerobics as a sport, saying it "was nothing more than a bunch of fat ladies dancing to music."[31] Said CEO Phil Knight in retrospect,

> We made an aerobics shoe that was functionally superior to Reebok's, but we missed the styling. Reebok's shoe was sleek and attractive, while ours was sturdy and clunky. We also decided against using garment leather, as Reebok had done, because it wasn't durable. By the time we developed a leather that was both strong and soft, Reebok had established a brand, won a huge chunk of sales, and gained the momentum to go right by us.[32]

Two years before Reebok launched its shoe, Judy Delaney, then a Nike product designer, pushed to get Nike to create an aerobics shoe. Her presentations were often put off to a rushed mention at the end of lengthy product meetings centered on running shoes. Then her proposals were rejected.[33] When the Reebok threat could no longer be ignored, Nike's response was to get into the market of women's leisure shoes. It also launched a television advertising campaign to try to draw women in. It featured famous triathlete Joanne Ernst, but closed with the tag line, "It wouldn't hurt if you stopped eating like a pig, either." As an *Adweek* columnist pointed out, it wasn't hard to see why that ad didn't go over well.

> Ooch. Among the semi-neurotic, and even among the confident, lines like that were likely to conjure up the sorry feeling of being the last girl picked for field hockey. And because many women are already morbidly preoccupied— and even obsessed—with what they and other women eat, the ads didn't help anyone.[34]

How could a company miss the mark on such an important market? When you consider the culture of the place, at least at its origins, it is less of a surprise. As several sources have documented, the leadership team "drank plenty, talked sports constantly, and fancied themselves brash and iconoclastic." Their management off-sites were called "Buttface" meetings. There was a lot of yelling.

Said one Nike executive at the time, "It was like working in a fraternity."[35] Even later, when the company had found a more effective way to advertise to women, it made sure that most of the print ads were placed only in women's magazines because Phil Knight worried that the advertising agency was "pinkifying the brand."[36]

Said Phil Knight,

> We thought [the Joanne Ernst ads were] very funny but many women found [them] insulting. They were too hard edged. We got so many complaints that we spent three or four years trying to understand what motivates women to participate in sports and fitness. We did numerous focus groups and spent hundreds of hours on tennis courts, in gyms, and at aerobics studios listening to women.[37]

The company set out, with its long-time advertising agency Wieden Kennedy, to rethink its approach to women. The resulting award-winning 1995 television ad, "If You Let Me Play," famously made talk-show host Oprah Winfrey cry. Narrated by young girls and using images of them playing sports, the ad told viewers:

> If you let me play sports . . .
> I will like myself more.
> I will have more self-confidence.
> I will be 60 percent less likely to get breast cancer.
> I will suffer less depression.
> I will be more likely to leave a man who beats me.
> I will be less likely to get pregnant before I want to.
> I will learn what it means to be strong.[38]

The ad was critiqued by feminists for depicting girls as victims who could be saved by men's magnanimity in letting them play sports. On the other hand, for many women, it did resonate. More than twenty years after Title IX of the US Education Act was supposed to have eliminated barriers to girls' participation in sports, many still felt that cultural barriers kept girls out. Nike was overwhelmed with calls and letters from women of all ages who loved the ad. Said Janet Champ, the advertising lead at Wieden Kennedy, the Nike executives "were SHOCKED at what a nerve it touched."[39] Twenty years after it was first broadcast, the comments it receives on YouTube continue to express these ideas. Wrote one young woman,

> My mom told me to stop running because my legs are getting too muscular. I stopped. But you know what? This morning I decided to run anyways. No one said we couldn't play sports, they just shove their opinions down our throat. We don't have to take it. Female, male, handicapped, short, tall, ill, depressed, happy, rude, smart, dumb, whatever. It shouldn't matter. Just go out and do what you want to do, no matter what people say.[40]

Ironically, although the ad did help Nike make greater inroads into the women's market, it simultaneously fanned the flames of emerging critiques about Nike's manufacturing practices, where the vast majority of workers making Nike shoes and apparel were women. In fact, as political scientist Cynthia Enloe has argued, Nike is able to achieve low-cost manufacturing precisely because its largely female workforce in other countries is paid less than even the low wages that men receive in those same countries.[41] It seemed that Nike was interested in women as consumers but not as producers. Adbusters, an organization that critiques consumerism, ran a poster of a young Indonesian women running barefoot made to look like a Nike "Just Do It!" ad:

> You're running because you want that raise, to be all you can be. But it's not easy when you work sixty hours a week making sneakers in an Indonesian factory and your friends disappear when they ask for a raise. So think globally before you decide it's so cool to wear Nike.[42]

On this issue, Reebok was no different. Although Nike's competitor had been giving out an annual award to prodemocracy activists since 1988, it adopted its own human-rights production standards only in 1992. These standards suggested that Reebok would seek out subcontractors that adhered to workers' rights, but did not, in those days, have much bite in terms of monitoring or enforcement.[43]

THE GIRL EFFECT

Nike has, through the Nike Foundation, begun to address that connection between how the company engages women and girls as consumers and how it

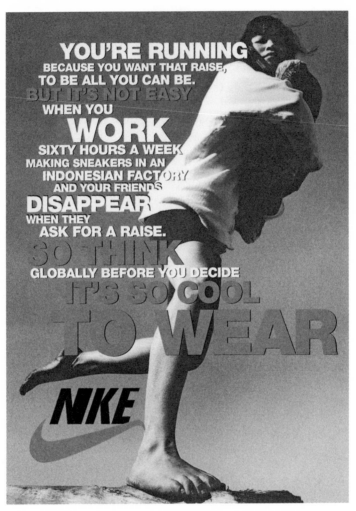

FIGURE 4.1. Adbusters' spoof ad of Nike. Source: "Unswooshing," Adbusters. Reprinted with permission.

tackles the challenges of the women and girls in the countries in which it makes its products. Nike launched the Girl Effect program in 2008—one that has subsequently spun out as an independent nonprofit—to focus on economic opportunities for girls in order to "break the cycle of intergenerational poverty."[44] The program's theory of change, articulated in a video ad that comes across very much like the "If You Let Me Play" ad, says the following in text animations:

The world is a mess. Poverty. AIDS. Hunger. War. So what else is new? What
if there was an unexpected solution that could turn this sinking ship around?
Would you even know it if you saw it? It's not the internet. It's not science.
It's not the government. It's not money. It's . . . a girl.

The ad goes on to suggest that a girl in poverty (illustrated with the word *flies*
buzzing around the word *girl*), will end up being stuck at a young age with a husband and a baby, hungry, in poverty, and perhaps HIV-infected. If only she got a
loan for a cow, which allowed her to become a small-business owner with a herd
of cows, she would then be admired for her "good sense" and invited by the men
of the community to the village council "where she convinces everyone that all
girls are valuable." Then the village thrives: peace, lower HIV rates, healthier
babies, education, commerce, sanitation, and stability. The whole country is
better off. "It's called the girl effect."[45] In other words, "Invest in a girl and she
will do the rest."

The problems Nike identifies are real. One quarter of the 600 million girls
living in developing economies are not in school, and nearly one-half are mothers before the age of 18. Problems with pregnancy and birth cause more deaths
among girls than any other cause. World Bank researchers estimate that addressing early school dropout, teenage pregnancy, and joblessness among girls
and young women ages fifteen to twenty-four could lead to dramatic increases
in GDP.[46] That Nike would be working to address these issues not only brings
resources but also attention to the challenges facing women and girls in economies around the world. The projects the company pursues through the Nike
Foundation and the Girl Effect, are real and have positive impacts on the lives
they touch.

On the other hand, consider the fact that much of this work is done in partnership with and funding from, for example, the UK's Department for International Development and the US Agency for International Development. This
raises the concern that development goals might be subsumed under corporate
objectives. Said feminist critic Maria Hengeveld, this program "thus helps Nike
to brand itself as the women's champion that it isn't and that it has never been."
These criticisms point out that the Girl Effect promotes market participation by
individual girls and women while eliding the effect of multinational corporations that may not offer adequate working conditions or a living wage.

"If You Let Me Play" has simply turned into "If You Let Me Trade." Girls are still conceived as resources, instruments, and victims, waiting to be saved by consumption and business. Women's supposed intrinsic desire to take care of their families and communities is still treated as an economic asset, rather than a problem of gender norms.[47]

We might also worry that corporate social responsibility projects like the Girl Effect might redirect or crowd out government or NGO-led initiatives that do not give corporations such as Nike the right kind of return on investment.

Walmart too has undertaken numerous initiatives to increase women's empowerment. Starting in 2011, the retailer set goals to increase sourcing from women-owned businesses, launch a women-owned online product marketplace, and increase the representation of women in Walmart-facing supplier teams.[48] These goals are integrated into the business and are supported by $134 million in grants from the Walmart Foundation.[49] Why do they do it? It's the business case again. According to Sarah Thorn, senior director of federal government relations at Walmart Stores:

> For Walmart, empowering women isn't just the right thing to do; it's also smart business. The majority of our 248 million customers are women, and women control well over $20 trillion of annual consumer spending globally. We also know that when we work with women, we have greater impact. Women business owners are more likely to hire and promote women inside their organizations. And women in emerging markets invest 90 percent of their income back into their families and communities. In the end, empowering women economically will make Walmart a more successful retailer, helping us better understand and serve our customers. We'll also be helping to build stronger communities in the countries [in which] we operate around the world.[50]

Walmart has also turned its attention to its own workers. In the US, unlike in most other developed economies around the world, paid parental leave is not a guarantee. As of January 2018, Walmart now offers ten weeks of leave at full pay for all birth mothers at any level of the organization and six weeks at full pay for other new parents. From a Canadian perspective, where paid leave is covered for many by unemployment insurance for twelve to eighteen months, this doesn't sound like a lot. But in the US, it is pretty revolutionary. Why did Walmart do it? Activism by OUR Walmart (a labor-union supported group that opposes Walmart's labor practices) pushed the idea along, and Walmart also came to see how this would benefit a company where 55 percent of the workforce is female.[51]

THE BUSINESS CASE ENABLES AND CONSTRAINS ACTION

While applauded by many as a game-changer or groundbreaking, Walmart's 2011 announcement of its Women's Economic Empowerment program came just a few months after the US Supreme Court decision denying certification of a class in the Wal-Mart Stores, Inc. v. Dukes case. The union-supported Making Change at Walmart campaign complained, "Wal-Mart's latest PR gambit is trying to cover up decades of unjust treatment of women. Wal-Mart causes systematic economic harm to women in the US and around the world, and that is precisely why Wal-Mart is trying to sell us on a new image."[52]

It's tricky. Taking action in the corporate context is thought to require a business case, but when the business-case logic is applied, it can undermine the impact or impressions the actions take. By claiming that empowering women, "will make Walmart a more successful retailer, helping us better understand and serve our customers," Walmart risks two things. First, the efforts might be seen as "pinkwashing," when in fact they are having real impact. Second, it implies that if these benefits—of better serving customers—are not realized, then the effort will be seen as a failure. The business case can constrain as much as it enables. If you pursue only Mode 2 actions about trade-offs, you are bound to get stuck along the way.

Indeed, Georgetown University legal scholar Jamillah Bowman Williams demonstrates in a series of experiments that making the business case for diversity may even generate negative beliefs about inclusion and increase bias in decision-making, while more legalistic and justice-based arguments are more likely to inhibit bias and increase equitable behavior (in particular because they trigger moral reactions).[53] Even worse, Oriane Georgeac and Aneeta Rattan at London Business School show that people who are the supposed beneficiaries of the business case for diversity (for example, women or those in the LGBTQ community) may actually be made to feel less like they belong.[54]

By Walmart's own reporting, the proportion of women in managerial roles at the company has improved, if slowly, over five years, with the percentage of first- and midlevel managers up from 40.4 to 43.5 and executives and senior-level managers up from 26.7 to 31.2 percent. That's ahead of other retailers, and Walmart is also one of a small cohort of Fortune 500 companies with three women on its board of directors. But as the company shifts away from general merchandise and toward grocery, the percentage of women in its workforce is declining overall.[55]

In 2017, Walmart announced that it had achieved its goal of sourcing $20 billion of products and services from women-owned businesses. More interestingly, according to Kathleen McLaughlin, chief sustainability officer at Walmart and president of the Walmart Foundation, "We've found that products from women-led companies have better sell-through rates and better margins." It has been a hard slog to make progress, with lots of lessons learned along the way. The company still hasn't succeeded in hitting its sourcing targets outside of the US:

> In China, for example, it's taken us years just to identify the women-led businesses [because there was no private or government data to help with the research]. In Japan, women haven't traditionally been encouraged to start businesses, so we had to begin with pitch contests there to inspire women to participate.[56]

The Walmart Foundation ended up having to give out $134 million in grants to train 500,000 women in the agricultural value chain, 60,000 women in 150 factories, 200,000 women in the US, and 200,000 women in emerging markets for workforce readiness. Then the company learned that it had to train the men too, so that they could create more-supportive work contexts for the women. Progress didn't come in the ways that Walmart expected and cost a lot more than its leadership might have anticipated, even to get as far as the retailer has gotten. To its credit, Walmart has treated this program as a learning opportunity, and many other retailers (and other companies looking to increase their sourcing to women-owned businesses) have looked to Walmart's experience as a case study for what it takes. Yet if all of these costs had been factored initially into the business case for action, would the payoff have been apparent?

Meanwhile, a 2016 investigative report by the Nation Institute's Investigative Fund (now known as Type Investigations) found that women working in Nike factories in Vietnam still experience poor working conditions—not only low wages but evidence of harassment and abuse. Nike admits that progress on improving conditions is mixed, but it is not for lack of trying. Critics such as Tim Connor, a lecturer on corporate and employment law at Australia's University of Newcastle argue that

> Investing in the Girl Effect costs Nike a lot less than it would cost to ensure that the hundreds of thousands of young women and girls employed in Nike's supply chain are paid a living wage. But ensuring [that] a living wage is paid to those young women would be a much more effective way of empowering a much larger number of women.[57]

Nike was in the press again in 2018 regarding poor treatment of women at its headquarters in Beaverton, Oregon. The situation had gotten bad enough internally that a group of female employees put together a survey about sexual harassment and discrimination and presented it to CEO Mark Parker in March of that year. To Parker's credit, this sparked a wide-ranging investigation at the firm that led to the departures of at least eleven senior executives. Said the *New York Times*, "While the #MeToo movement has led to the downfall of individual men, the kind of sweeping overhaul that is occurring at Nike is rare in the corporate world, and illustrates how internal pressure from employees is forcing even huge companies to quickly address workplace problems."[58] That overhaul led Nike to increase the wages of more than 7,000 employees (nearly 10 percent of the workforce) who had apparently been unfairly paid.[59] The overhaul didn't stop former employees from filing a class-action lawsuit claiming that they were "devalued and demeaned" by Nike, including receiving lower pay and promotion opportunities than their male colleagues and being ignored when they made complaints about it.[60]

Perhaps not surprisingly, Nike still struggles in its main markets to find a way to engage with female consumers. It launched the NikeGoddess initiative in the mid 2000s, which was meant to change how Nike would design for, sell to, and communicate with women. The company started an online magazine of the same name, developed the www.nikegoddess.com website, and created stores for women only. Pitched as a reboot of the women's effort, one in which Nike had to "wake up to the women's business and do it differently" (according to Nike's then–global footwear director for women, Darcy Winslow), it was meant to move beyond "If You Let Me Play."[61] Yet very little is left of these programs today. The magazine is gone. The website is gone. Nike has tried yet again to create new concepts for women, such as the 2014 launch of a women's-only store with fitness studio in Newport Beach, California.[62]

What all of this says about the business case is that it is often more complex to address trade-offs and grow the pie for shared value than organizational leaders would like to believe. Or even if they believe it, it may be hard to muster the commitment, resources, and willingness to create change to make the pie bigger. It is not enough to sprinkle diverse people on top of the existing organization or decide to serve female customers or engage with women in the supply chain. The stories from Nike and Walmart show that organizations will have to change how they work, how they develop products, how they manage the supply chain and all sorts of other activities if they want to be successful. Those changes are sometimes hard to make and potentially costly. It is true that the pie will likely be bigger afterward, but progress is not automatic.

What does this say about the possibilities for gender equality? From these stories, it is pretty clear that we have a long way still to go. With Soraya Chemaly's *Rage Becomes Her* and Anne-Marie Slaughter's *Unfinished Business* making the bestseller lists, Katniss Everdeen the hero of the *Hunger Games* trilogy, Wonder Woman taking the box office by storm, Hillary Clinton having run for president, and the #MeToo movement taking flight, perhaps we have reached a watershed moment?

That's the claim journalists made when tire manufacturer Pirelli announced its coveted high-gloss annual calendar—normally offering up arty photos of naked models—would feature in 2016 mostly fully clad women chosen for their accomplishments rather than their measurements: financier Melody Hobson, athlete Serena Williams, rocker Patti Smith, performance artist Yoko Ono, playwright and performer Ava DuVernay. "Along with Playboy's decision in October to end nudity in its pages," the *New York Times* said, "the Pirelli pivot seems to give real substance to the theory that we are at a flexion point in the public objectification of female sexuality."[63] And why? According to Antonio Achille of the Boston Consulting Group, it is because—wait for it—women as consumers represent "an enormous untapped opportunity... Women are superb brand ambassadors. Women share a positive car experience with more than 20 people on average, while men share experiences with only two."[64]

STEPS TO MAKE THE BUSINESS CASE
(WITHOUT GETTING STUCK IN IT)

Gender inequality is an illustration of both how the business case gets mobilized and how the trade-offs across stakeholders make action difficult. We could tell this same story about sustainability or consumerism or the supply chain (as I will in the next chapters), but this deep dive into gender helps us see how complex the trade-offs can be and how embedded the current set of trade-offs are in our culture, our systems, our processes, and even in our mind-sets. What's key to understand is that the status quo contains trade-offs already. When people advocate for gender equality, they are advocating for a rebalancing. The current balance gives tailwinds to some (straight, white men) and headwinds to the rest. Making the business case for diversity is seen as a path forward in creating the new balance. As we've seen, it can also trap companies into taking only the actions that meet the business-case criteria.

The business-case rhetoric risks centering the people and organizations that are already in positions of privilege. The pressure to make the case to those in power implies that their needs and interests must be met in order for action to be taken, a sort of "Prove to me that there's something in it for me." The concept of win-win should imply that all of the various stakeholders should benefit, but if the financial bottom line is the win that predominates over others, then companies are at risk of being seen as pinkwashing on gender equality, or greenwashing on sustainability. While economic profits are necessary for the survival of corporations, it is often hard to determine exactly what the potential benefits of progress might be. Overindexing on the business case might in and of itself create limits to what progress could be made.

What is a company to do? I identified three sets of actions in Chapter 3, but it is worth restating them through the lens of Nike's and Walmart's struggles and successes in achieving gender equality. What emerges from these stories is that making the business case is most usefully seen as a process of discovery rather than only as a justification for action.

First, start in Mode 1. The analysis is elucidating. Indeed, no matter if you are trying to operate in Mode 2, 3 or 4, knowing the trade-offs is a good start.

It's going to be difficult to make a smart business case if you don't first understand what the conflicting demands are. As we've seen in the discussion of gender diversity, the issues are complex, and these kinds of tough trade-offs aren't easily amenable to quick or simple solutions in organizations. Indeed, without careful analysis, we often get the root causes wrong. If we think that the problem is that women lack self-confidence, then we propose one set of solutions focused on training women to lean in or negotiate better.[65] If we realize (as research suggests) that the problem is actually that organizations do a pretty good job of making women feel unwelcome or not included, and this leads to what appears to be lack of sure-footedness, then we intervene on the organizational practices and culture.[66] The analysis of trade-offs and the causes behind them is really crucial to identifying the right interventions.[67]

Second, create targets and measure progress. Walmart's moonshot of sourcing $20 billion of products from women-owned businesses led the company through an exploration of what it would take to train and support these entrepreneurs. Setting the target is only the beginning. It starts the journey and keeps everyone pushing forward even as they encounter roadblocks along the way. This is what sustained Walmart's efforts and led the retailer to create new solutions and partnerships.

Third, recognize that making the business case is only a starting point for a conversation. Just asserting the business case doesn't guarantee action. In fact, the actions to make good on the promise of the business case, as the Nike and Walmart cases show, are often difficult, costly, and complex. That isn't to say that companies shouldn't start down the path. If the costs mount or progress is slower than anticipated, it might be easy to say that the business case didn't pan out. This is precisely the moment when companies should persist, because it is at those tough moments that insights into forward action materialize.

That's where Mode 3 actions come in: addressing trade-offs will ultimately require innovation and creativity.

PART II SIGNPOSTS

- Most research and practical advice on corporate social responsibility has been focused on making the business case (Mode 2 action). The argument is that doing something that addresses a stakeholder need can also be good for the bottom line by reducing costs and increasing operating efficiency, reducing risks and preserving the "license to operate," or creating competitive advantage by increasing customer willingness to pay. This is the essence of shared value.

- The advantage of the business-case logic is that it can inspire managers to think differently. For many managers trained to think that profit takes precedent, the idea of shared value has provided a path forward to dealing with the trade-offs that their companies' business models create.

- The latest research suggests that business-case thinking can also be a constraint on action. To the extent that the business case reinforces the logic of the existing system, it mitigates against people experiencing moral outrage at the social costs their businesses extract. Without moral outrage, it is hard to provoke change. Known as system-justification theory, this insight suggests that making the business case may actually block real progress.

- Making the business case may be more effective for plucking low-hanging fruit but gets stuck tackling the higher-impact or trickier issues where real trade-offs cannot be resolved through win-win solutions. The more we say we need a business case to justify action, the less likely we are to achieve our moonshot goals.

- Therefore, building the business case is more useful as a process of discovery than as a justification for action. The process starts with a Mode 1 analysis of stakeholder needs and trade-offs. Organizations should then set targets that will allow them to measure progress. Finally, they can use the analysis and targets to start a conversation about how to achieve the win-win. Having an explicit conversation about how to address trade-offs will help engage the organization in finding solutions.

- What all of this says about the business case is that it is often more complex to address trade-offs and grow the pie for shared value than leaders of organizations would like to believe. Or even if they believe it, it may be hard to muster the commitment, resources, and willingness to create change to make the pie bigger.

PART III

BEYOND THE BUSINESS-CASE TRAP

Innovating Around Trade-Offs (Mode 3)

CHAPTER 5

CSR IS NOT AN ADD-ON

Innovating in the Supply Chain

WHAT'S BEYOND THE BUSINESS CASE? When there are trade-offs between the goals of shareholders and various stakeholders and it doesn't seem like there's a way to make everyone happy, what can a company do? The last two decades of experience with the global supply chain give us a window into what might be possible. The ability to produce products in the global supply chain is what allows companies to sell products at reasonable prices to their consumers. For example, Walmart needs to offer Everyday Low Prices, and to get those low prices, the brands that sell to the retailer are increasingly turning to factories outside the US. The global supply chain from the likes of China, Vietnam, Honduras, and Bangladesh to the American, or Canadian or European shopping cart means that most brands are just that, brands that are attached to products made by other companies located far away from the brand's headquarters and transported to the consumers who want them.

As Charles Fishman, journalist and longtime student of Walmart, points out, Levi Strauss, which in 1980 had sixty clothing plants in the US, closed its last two US factories in 2004, a year after setting up a partnership with Walmart. The last 2,500 American production workers at the company lost their jobs.[1]

Why is it that Levi's or Walmart or Nike has moved its production overseas? Cost, of course. The firms are exploiting the comparative advantage that Mexico or China or Bangladesh has in labor and other manufacturing costs.

That sounds innocent enough. Workers in these countries do not have many economic alternatives, so factory work can be appealing. Low wages go a much longer way in these countries than they do in the US or other developed economies. It turns out it is not so innocuous.

The trade-off here is particularly intense. Consumers demand low prices. Retailers' margins are razor thin. The result is extreme pressure on vendors to keep costs low. Low costs mean poor working conditions—from unsafe buildings to long hours to low pay.

As a result, global retailers and global brands have been stuck for a long time in a compliance model—adhering to standards but not much else. Said differently, they have been sticking to Friedman's principle of following the "rules of the game" (regulations) but, beyond that, paying attention to the bottom line.[2] Getting unstuck has been hard—as it always is when trade-offs are the most acute. From Walmart and Nike and others, we are discovering that the gold standard for tackling the costs to workers and the environment from just-in-time delivery of products around the world has come from Mode 3 innovation around the trade-offs.

WHO IS TO BLAME?

On November 24, 2012, fire broke out at the Tazreen Fashions garment factory in Dhaka, Bangladesh. The fire burned for hours before firefighters could get it under control. When the alarms first rang, managers told the workers to stay in their seats. It was a false alarm, they said, go back to work. The managers padlocked the exits.[3] By the time smoke came pouring into the work areas, it was too late. The few open exits were too narrow for escape, and stampedes ensued. A dozen workers jumped to their deaths from upper windows. Many died of smoke inhalation near their workstations. At least 117 workers perished, and more than 200 were injured, though definitive counts have been impossible to establish because some bodies were never found.

Sumi Abedin, one of the workers, jumped out a window and managed to survive with some broken bones. "I didn't jump to save my life. I jumped to save my body, because if I stayed inside the factory I would burn to ash, and my fam-

FIGURE 5.1. Tazreen Fashions factory fire, Dhaka, Bangladesh, 2012. Source: Abdullah, Abir, European Pressphoto Agency, 2012. Reprinted with permission.

ily wouldn't be able to identify my body." In the aftermath of the fire, many stories like this one emerged, such as the son who called his mother to say he was dying for sure and couldn't get out, but he would tie his shirt to his waist so that his mother could find him among the bodies he was seeing on the factory floor.[4]

In the piles of debris examined after the fire were jeans, T-shirts, and shorts destined for North American retailer Sears, C&A (the European discount retailer), Sean ("Diddy") Combs's line of clothing, Hong Kong–based Li & Fung, and Walmart's private label Faded Glory.[5] According to the police, the factory had been in violation of several fire and safety codes prior to the disaster. How could that be? Major brands such as Walmart already had been touting their factory-inspection standards for years.

Who is to blame? There were some obvious targets. First, there were the garment-factory managers who kept the workers from escaping. The police arrested them shortly after the fire. Eventually they also indicted the factory owner, Delwar Hossain; his wife, Mahmuda Akhter; and several managers in charge of security and production on charges of culpable homicide by negligence. Many around the world, outraged by the presence of so many global brands, began to direct their attention to Walmart and its peers. People wanted to know why these brands were manufacturing their products in factories with such dangerous conditions.

But, Walmart argued, it was not to blame. The retailer had not contracted directly with the Tazreen factory, which had received two orange (higher-risk) ratings in previous Walmart-sponsored audits. In a statement after the fire, a spokesperson stated, "The Tazreen factory was no longer authorized to produce merchandise for Walmart. Without any notice to Walmart, a supplier subcontracted work to this factory without authorization and in direct violation of our policies. We have since terminated the relationship with that supplier."[6] Walmart contracted with Simco, an approved supplier. But Simco was unable to fulfill the order. It then transferred the order (and the fabric) to Tuba Garments without telling Walmart sourcing executives, which was in violation of Walmart's supplier guidelines. Simco leaders claimed they thought this transfer was legitimate because Tuba Garments had made products for Walmart in the past. Then Tuba Garments sent the order to another Tuba Group factory, Tazreen Fashions Ltd., without seeking permission from Simco or Walmart. Walmart is right to say that Simco violated policies in outsourcing its own outsourced work.

But questions remained. Investigative reports pointed to documents found in the wreckage after the fire showing that at least two different suppliers had subcontracted to the factory and at least five of the fourteen lines in the factory were dedicated to Walmart production. Said Scott Nova, executive director of the Worker Rights Consortium,

> If Walmart's claim that they were the victim of one rogue supplier had any shred of credibility, it's gone now . . . Walmart is limited to one of two options—to say, yes, we know these suppliers were using the factory or, two, we have no control over the supply chain that we've been building in Bangladesh for more than 20 years.[7]

Neither option is good for Walmart.

Was this just a problem of one or two rogue suppliers? It seems not. As Walmart's own "2014 Global Responsibility Report" shows, only 7 percent of audited factories were rated low risk (green); 29 percent were medium risk (yellow); 57 percent were higher risk (orange or red); and 2 percent were disapproved or unauthorized.[8] There are a few things to take away from these numbers. First, very few factories get clean bills of health. Second, most factories in use are problematic enough to require corrective actions and reauditing within six to twelve months. Third, in one year, 2 percent of factories were deauthorized. Two percent sounds small, but considering that these assessments occurred in more than 15,000 factories, that means at least 300 factories (per year!) are so much in violation of health, labor, and safety standards that they can no longer be used.

The numbers are getting worse. After the 2012 Tazreen fire, Walmart conducted more audits and held factories to more-rigorous standards. As a result, from 2012 to 2013, the percentage of factories rated as yellow and orange (medium and higher risk) reversed. While previously, more than 50 percent of factories were only at the yellow risk stage, in 2013, that number went down to 29 percent; the percentage of orange (riskier) factories went up from 24 to 57 percent. As Walmart increases monitoring, it gets better data on the full range of factories producing its products, which is increasing transparency. That the numbers are getting worse does not necessarily mean that the situation is getting worse; it's just that we know more about what is really going on.

Of course, it is a good thing that Walmart (along with many other companies) is seeking greater visibility into the complex global supply chain in which it operates. If the numbers get worse, the net effect will likely be greater attention paid to efforts to improve factory conditions, both because the company has more information internally and because there will be more pressure from other stakeholders externally. Indeed, the audits are a crucial part of Mode 1 analysis: they bring in the voice of the worker and give global brands a window into worker conditions.

These data tell us that the conditions at Tazreen were not unique. That fire got more press coverage than most, but in the six years prior to the Tazreen catastrophe, more than 500 Bangladeshi garment workers died in factory fires.[9] According to the Bangladesh Center for Worker Solidarity, more than 50 percent of Bangladeshi factories do not meet local legal fire-safety requirements. We have only to look to the Rana Plaza disaster, where the April 24, 2013, collapse of the factory building led to 1,137 deaths and more than 2,500 injuries. Walmart and a number of similar retailers, including Canadian retailer Loblaw (makers of the Joe Fresh brand), US-based J.C. Penney, French hypermarket chain Carrefour, Italian clothing chain Benetton, and the British chain Matalan all had products produced by the factory at the time of the collapse or in the recent past.[10]

Walmart emphasized that there was no production in that factory "at the time of the collapse," but according to the *New York Times*,

> One document, dated May 12, 2012, that was found in the rubble detailed a purchase order by a Canadian company, Fame Jeans, for "dark blue wash," "skinny fit" jeans to be delivered to Wal-Mart in the fall of 2012. Another document, dated April 27, 2012, discussed pricing for five styles of jeans, with the prices ranging from $3.41 to $4.50 a pair . . . After the *Times* questioned Wal-Mart about the documents on Tuesday, Allen Brandman, chief executive of Fame Jeans, said in an interview, "It's very clear that Wal-Mart did not authorize me in any capacity to work within this factory." He blamed a "rogue employee" for the order, who had decided to use the factory without Mr. Brandman's knowledge.[11]

Here, the rogue supplier blamed a rogue employee for the actions. Is that where we should leave it? Is it just a few bad apples creating the problems?

A CANADIAN CLOTHING DESIGNER TAKES THE BLAME

Shortly after the Tazreen fire, Sujeet Sennik wrote an op-ed in Canada's *Globe and Mail* newspaper titled, "I Designed That Cheap Garment. I Lit That Factory Fire in Bangladesh." He wrote:

> I would like to confess to lighting the recent fire that lead to the many deaths at the Tazreen Fashions Ltd. factory in Bangladesh. I am neither Bangladeshi nor a factory worker, and I have never set foot in the building that was set ablaze in late November. Nonetheless, I have ashen thoughts and blood on my hands . . . In Bangladesh, stories circulate that the Tazreen fire was arson. My point is, this fire was lit by me. I am the one who asked our factories to make a $9 blouse, and, by default, Bangladesh is one of two countries in which clothing can be imported duty free. My employers are happy that we will have this item on the floor en masse for next season's sales. Our customers have forced us to hack down the prices to be competitive in this market of cheap clothing and off-price bargaining that we call the Canadian

clothing sector . . . Perhaps one of the perished women was sewing the back neck of a garment to its collar. This operation in Bangladesh costs a fraction of a cent compared with what it would cost in Canada. I wonder whether she was holding on to the collar that I had asked her to sew to meet my cost target when she died. I know that our shipments are sometimes rushed at the last minute to make the vessel. Maybe that's why the managers asked some of the workers to stay seated when the fire started . . . The point is clear. I confess to the murder. The reason is clear. The collar that the Bangladeshi woman was holding as the smoke pushed through her lungs was destined for a killer-priced shirt next season.[12]

It is worth noting the irony of the Tazreen fire happening on American Thanksgiving, the day before Black Friday, historically the biggest US shopping day of the year. What Sujeet Sennik is saying is that he is guilty along with all of the rest of us in a system that expects ever-cheaper goods on demand. He designed cheap products because that was what his employer wanted. His employer wanted cheap products because that is what the consumer demanded.

Workers' rights critics blame the brands. Said Workers Rights Consortium Executive Director, Scott Nova:

The only way factories in Bangladesh can survive, given the prices that the western brands are willing to pay, is to operate unsafely. And that's why you get fires. And for all of their rhetoric about corporate social responsibility and all of these monitoring programs and audits, brands and retailers will not pay one penny more for factories.[13]

The government regulators in Bangladesh blame the brands. According to Mikail Shiper, a senior official in Bangladesh's Ministry of Labor and Employment, "The buyers write to us to improve working conditions. We asked them to raise prices by 25 cents per clothing unit that would go to workers' welfare. They refused, citing the financial downturn in their countries."[14]

The suppliers themselves blame the brands. Abdus Salam Murshedy is the managing director of Envoy Group, a major supplier of garments in Bangladesh. He is also the former captain of the national soccer team. Though he is a powerful man with many resources, even he says, "The buyers, they are our god . . . We cannot do all these things they ask, fire safety, when the prices are so low!" He traced the problem back to the prices retailers charged: "One thing I would like to know is why they have to do 'buy one, get one free.' This is money they're taking from here. Why do they do 'buy one, get one free'?"[15]

The brands blame the consumers. Consumers want low prices. Low prices translate into tight cost controls throughout the system. Who pays for improved conditions? This question had been under consideration well before the Tazreen fire. A number of retailers met with worker advocates in Dhaka in April 2011. In the meeting, there was a proposal for a memorandum—that would be contractually enforceable—requiring all manufacturers to pay higher prices so that factories could pay for safety upgrades. The costs are often perceived as prohibitive. Sridevi Kalavakolanu, Walmart's director of ethical sourcing, along with an executive from the Gap wrote a memo for that meeting, stating, "Specifically to the issue of any corrections on electrical and fire safety, we are talking about 4,500 factories, and in most cases, very extensive and costly modifications would need to be undertaken to some factories. It is not financially feasible for the brands to make such investments."[16]

This blame game is part of a system. A consumer gets two T-shirts for the price of one but does not see the effects of that price on the workers who make the shirts. The designer designs the T-shirts but also does not see all the way back to the people who will manufacture them. We can try to blame and even indict people and brands for specific actions (and we should), but focusing attention on the individual obscures a system that produces these outcomes. This system is broken.

Part of the reason the blame game exists is because it is hard to make the business case for change. As we can see, the global brands actually have engaged closely with the factories and labor representatives (Mode 1) but haven't always been able to justify the expense for those actions the labor representatives recommend. The trade-offs between profits and other objects are just too salient for many of the companies, companies that often operate on razor-thin margins. Mode 2 action may not be enough to make progress. The fallback ends up being a compliance approach.

A FIRST STEP: AUDIT AND COMPLIANCE

When issues of poor labor conditions in factories first came to light in the 1990s, an initial response by global brands was to insist that the factories they used were in compliance with local regulations as they were enforced by the governments in those countries. This ended up being problematic because it is unclear that governments can or will do much in the circumstances, then or even now. In Bangladesh, for example, the Bangladesh Garment Manufacturers and Exporters Association has become a major political power. Garment-factory owners have become members of Parliament and owners of news media and television stations. The government, recognizing the importance of garment exports, which represent 80 percent of foreign exchange, wants to keep the factories running at full speed. There are reports that factory owners have made payments to government officials to assure that regulations remain light and enforcement of them weak (unsurprising given that the country ranks 144 out of 176 on Transparency International's corruption index).[17] The country has created a special police force to monitor industrial zones and put down any labor unrest. Domestic-intelligence agencies track and intimidate labor activists.[18] Such regulatory capture means that the government, which should be acting in the public interest, leans instead toward the special interests of the factory owners.

After the Tazreen and Rana Plaza disasters, activists pushed global brands to take up the responsibilities for workers' conditions that were not being or could not be taken up by local governments. A coalition of trade unions proposed the multi-stakeholder Accord on Fire and Building Safety in Bangladesh in 2013, the signatories of which would commit to a legally binding inspection regime, including revealing the names and locations of all supplier factories and assuring rapid inspection and remediation. There were seventy-five original retail and brand signatories (and nearly 200 by the end of 2018), including Loblaw Companies, Carrefour, Adidas, Inditex (parent of Zara), Marks and Spencer, and H&M.[19] In addition, the Accord was signed by eight unions (such as the Bangladesh Textile and Garment Workers League) and four witness signatories—the Worker Rights Consortium, the International Labor Rights Forum, the Clean Clothes Campaign, and the Maquila Solidarity Network. The Accord requires independent inspection and a corrective action plan for any remedial actions required of each factory. Importantly, brands and retailers are bound to negotiate commercial terms with the factories that make it financially possible for them to comply with the action plans and maintain safe workplaces.[20]

Notably missing from the signatories were Walmart and other major North American retailers. Chafing at the legally binding nature of the Accord, these companies instead announced a separate, voluntary plan, the Alliance for Bangladesh Worker Safety. Walmart, the Gap, Costco, Canadian Tire Corporation, Hudson's Bay Company, Target, Macy's, and Sears, among other US and Canadian retailers became members of the group, whose goals were more modest. The purpose of the Alliance was to create standards and assessment approaches that could be implemented by qualified assessment firms. The Alliance was immediately criticized for being company-developed and company-controlled with no worker representative signatories to hold the retailers to account. The Alliance does not require the global brands to pay for repairs if the assessments reveal deficiencies other than through a voluntary loan program that was not a condition for membership in the Alliance.[21]

Certainly, many managers at Walmart and its counterparts are seriously and meaningfully concerned about the plight of Bangladeshi workers. The question is whether they can reliably remedy the problems when they are not ultimately contractually constrained by other stakeholders. Many companies are proponents of these forms of self-regulation as a substitute for regulation by the government or supervision by concerned stakeholders. The advantage for the firms that participate is that it levels the playing field for everyone. Every firm has to incur the extra costs, so it is a way of reducing harmful impacts without raising costs of any one firm relative to its competitors. No firm is at a competitive disadvantage. Yet the net effect is that it leaves the control of regulation in private hands without NGO or government oversight.

IS COMPLIANCE ENOUGH?

In both cases, whether legally binding or voluntary, the primary focus started with compliance. But as both scholars and practitioners have come to recognize, simply aiming to comply with standards, no matter how strict, is an impoverished way to cope with the complexity of the global supply chain. Signatories to the Accord and members of the Alliance have recognized this to a certain extent by including components for worker training, though most of those are focused on training workers to adhere to standards such as basic fire safety.

Independent of these compacts, some members have their own programs that move beyond compliance. Walmart, for example, has a partnership with several NGOs and government agencies (including CARE, World Vision, Swasti, USAID, and the Gates Foundation) to develop a training program for women in factories in Bangladesh, India, El Salvador, Honduras, and China. This is the potential wellspring for Mode 3 innovations. As part of its Women's Economic Empowerment Initiative (see Chapter 4), Walmart is working to improve the lives of supply-chain workers by giving them training in both work and life skills, including financial planning, health and wellness, time management, career development, and leadership. Walmart has now trained nearly one million women. According to Kathleen McLaughlin, chief sustainability officer at Walmart, when I interviewed her for a public event at Rotman, achieving these goals would not have been possible without the innovative partnerships the company developed with partner organizations that shaped the development and delivery of programming tailored to each country and location.

> In addition to training these women, we now have a model for doing this that anybody can use to do the same—and we want to share it; that's part of our theory of change. If we were just off on our own doing these things, we would probably produce some benefit—but we wouldn't really be shifting the system.[22]

She went on to talk about how important collaboration was for generating shared value, and especially how important innovative action is when the trade-offs seem hard to resolve.

> Where it gets tougher is on the other end: Are there business practices that are not creating immediate social value? A good example is animal welfare. If you look at issues like gestation crates in the pork industry, or cage-free eggs, these are production systems that have evolved over time, and that are not unique to Walmart. They're part of the food industry's efforts to satisfy rising consumer demand—but many people are not comfortable with them anymore. Changing those systems is going to require problem solving to create better systems, and that will require capital and operating expense, and so on. How that will evolve—in a way that doesn't increase the cost of the end product—is a real challenge that we need to work through. We can't do any of this by ourselves; for instance, we actually don't own any chickens—we buy eggs from other people, so, clearly, addressing this requires collaboration. The way we come at it is, 'Let's use the same problem-solving

ability that we would apply to any business problem,' because these are business problems, too. They require innovation in production approaches and collaboration with suppliers and other retailers.[23]

What companies are discovering is that sticking to the "rules of the game"—compliance with regulations—may not be satisfactory. **First**, for anyone committed to the social goals associated with stakeholder needs, compliance may seem unambitious. **Second**, the compliance mind-set may make it hard to come up with the required actions even to achieve the regulated objectives. What worked for Walmart, and as I'll show in the next chapter, what worked for Nike, were the Mode 3 efforts to transform the trade-offs into innovation challenges. The deeper the insight into the trade-offs and what causes them, the more innovative the solutions can be.

CHAPTER 6

STAKEHOLDERS AS A SOURCE OF INNOVATION

Transforming Operations

YOU WILL NOTICE THAT Nike's name wasn't mentioned in the stories of the Tazreen fire or the Rana Plaza collapse. In fact, Nike has only a few manufacturing facilities in Bangladesh. Nike's story began much earlier in the 1990s when journalists began to report on what its factories' working conditions looked like. A 1992 *Harper's* magazine article by activist Jeff Ballinger highlighted the plight of workers in Nike subcontractor factories in Indonesia. He displayed the pay stub of Sadisah, one of the workers in South Korean company Sung Hwa's factory in Tangerang (just outside of Jakarta). He showed that Sadisah made about fourteen cents per hour, worked sixty-three hours of overtime in the month for an extra two cents per hour and made about fourteen pairs of shoes every day. At that rate, the labor cost for making a pair of $80 Nike shoes was twelve cents. Ballinger contrasted this with the $20 million endorsement fee paid to Michael Jordan during that time.[1] The same year, demonstrators appeared at the 1992 Summer Olympics in Barcelona to call attention to the sweatshop conditions at Nike's factories.

A November 8, 1997, *New York Times* story really caused the issue to take off, when journalist Steven Greenhouse unveiled evidence from Nike's internal factory inspection reports conducted by Ernst & Young. He wrote,

> Workers at the factory near Ho Chi Minh City were exposed to carcinogens that exceeded local legal standards by 177 times in parts of the plant and . . . 77 percent of the employees suffered from respiratory problems. The report also said that employees at the site, which is owned and operated by a Korean subcontractor, were forced to work 65 hours a week, far more than Vietnamese law allows, for $10 a week.[2]

Two days later, Dara O'Rourke, a consultant to the United Nations Industrial Development Organization, published a report based on research in more than fifty Nike vendor factories in Vietnam. He concluded that Ernst & Young's report was deficient, and despite having identified many ways in which manufacturers did not live up to Nike's manufacturing standards (which the company called its Code of Conduct[3]), these auditors neglected a wide range of violations. O'Rourke went on to detail violations of Vietnamese labor laws on pay and maximum overtime hours, forced overtime, strike breaking, and physical and verbal abuse of workers. This was a crisis moment for Nike, and, over time, it led to a transformation in the manufacturer's practices.

Nike had been an innovative pioneer in outsourced manufacturing, having started out by marketing sports shoes made in Japan. In the 1980s, following the general trend of most footwear manufacturing in the US, Nike closed its last US manufacturing plant for footwear, located in Saco, Maine. At the time, Nike outsourced manufacturing to South Korea, but the South Korean companies were mainly subcontracting the work to plants in Vietnam, Indonesia, and elsewhere.

Nike's initial response to criticisms of working conditions had been to deny responsibility, claiming that these factories were owned by third-party contractors and were therefore outside of Nike's control. As pressure increased, Nike changed its strategy, hiring Ernst & Young and Price Waterhouse to perform internal audits. It also hired former UN Ambassador Andrew Young's company, GoodWorks International, to review contractor compliance with Nike's Code of Conduct. Young's June 1997 report was viewed by many labor activists as a whitewash because the research was conducted entirely with Nike officials in tow; it concluded, "We found Nike to be in the forefront of a global economy. Factories we visited that produce Nike goods were clean, organized, adequately ventilated and well lit."[4]

Despite these actions, the bad press continued. Headlines such as "Nike Invited to Answer Charges of Third World Exploitation," "Women's Groups Pressure Nike on Labor Practices," "The Just War Against Nike," and "Nike Supports Women in Its Ads but Not Its Factories" filled the press. College students around the country began to protest against Nike. With demand for its products weakening (profits dropped by half from 1997 to 1998), CEO Phil Knight made a now-famous speech at the National Press Club. Characteristically, he came out swinging, denouncing the press that described him as a "corporate crook, the perfect corporate villain for these times." At the same time, he somewhat incredulously acknowledged, "Nike products have become synonymous with slave wages, forced overtime, and arbitrary abuse." He provided a long history of the development of Nike's manufacturing approach over the years and pointed out that Nike shoes would cost at least twice as much to the consumer if they were manufactured in the US.[5] (That's the crux of the trade-off, right there!)

Despite his defensiveness, Knight announced six new actions that were the beginning of an extraordinary transformation of Nike from pariah to gold standard in offshore manufacturing approaches. The first was to improve the health conditions in factories to meet US Occupational Safety and Health Administration standards, in particular by innovating in new kinds of water-based glue that would not contain the toxic chemical toluene. Along with that, Nike raised the minimum age of workers in all footwear factories to eighteen, and sixteen in apparel and equipment factories (again, he emphasized, the same as in the US). The company also committed, at least in principle, to having monitoring done by independent NGOs and not just hired accounting firms. It expanded education programs and microenterprise loan programs in the regions where Nike operates. Finally, Knight also announced that Nike would fund university research "to explore issues related to global manufacturing and responsible business practices such as independent monitoring and health issues."

Knight concluded the talk by saying that these practices would represent standards for the industry, and, "they reflect who we are as a company. I don't necessarily expect you to believe that, but I will tell you this: It makes us feel better about ourselves." Of course, as opponents pointed out, the goal should not have been for Nike executives to feel better about themselves but to create better conditions for the workers who make expensive Nike gear.

As Knight predicted, opponents argued that Nike had not gone far enough. In a 2001 assessment, the Global Exchange labor activist group contended that the six initiatives had not been implemented aggressively enough—for example, factories were still being given advance notice of inspections so that they could clean up before visits.[6] The assessment pointed to a number of additional policy changes the labor group wished Knight had promised in his 1998 speech, including protecting workers who speak honestly about factory conditions; regular, transparent, independent, and confidential procedures for monitoring factories and worker complaints; decent wages; better working hours; improved health and safety procedures; and freedom to organize into unions. The group cited many continuing violations along these lines.

Fortunately, Nike didn't stop there. But to move forward, it had to transform its approach from one in which the supply-chain workers were adversaries to one in which they were partners.

LISTENING TO THE STAKEHOLDERS

Despite its deficiencies, the plan that Knight announced in 1998 was the beginning of an innovative—Mode 3—journey that has made Nike the gold standard in managing factories upstream in the global supply chain. It was at that point that Nike began developing an important in-house capability for understanding the details of the supply chain and assuring standards can be applied even to factories that are several degrees removed from direct relationships with the company. By 2004, Maria Eitel, Nike's vice president for corporate responsibility, said, "You haven't heard about us recently because we've had our head down doing it the hard way. Now, we have a system to deal with the labor issue, not a crisis mentality." Even a skeptical press noted, "You have to give Nike some credit for trying. It has performed about 600 factory audits since it built up its in-house monitoring staff two years ago, including repeat visits to those with the most problems."[7]

By the time of the Tazreen fire, Nike had already hired a head of sustainable business, Hannah Jones, who had oversight on these issues. She had been concerned for years about the dangers of outsourcing to Bangladeshi factories. She wanted Nike to step away. As in any company, Nike production managers were under pressure to keep costs down and felt that Bangladesh—one of the least expensive places to manufacture garments in the world—should be an important part of the sourcing strategy. Said Nike Chief Operating Officer Eric Sprunk, "Our competitors were moving fast into Bangladesh and the pressure was getting bigger and bigger."[8] Looking at how competitors had undercut Nike by $10 on a fleece jacket, the only difference they could find was the competitor's Made in Bangladesh label.

They faced a decision: How would they manage the trade-off between attaining lower costs to remain competitive and the risk of working with unsafe or abusive suppliers? This could have ended up being a showdown between two C-suite executives, Hannah Jones on the side of corporate responsibility and Eric Sprunk on the side of costs. Instead, as reported in the *Wall Street Journal*, Jones said to Sprunk: "Can we talk about this decision?" Through the conversation, they decided to have the two teams travel to Bangladesh together and see the situation for themselves. What they found were numerous safety violations within an existing supplier, from locked windows to fabric strewn over the production floor. Once everyone had witnessed the facts, no one had to take Jones's word that the supplier was in violation. Nike agreed to cut off relations with that supplier and reduce its presence to only four (more modern) factories across the country. Said Jones, "Did we pass up on margin because of that? Absolutely." Not an easy choice when Nike's gross margins had fallen by almost 3 percent in the prior year.[9]

Nike seemed to be saying that the problems in Bangladesh are too hard to fix. Better get out than get it wrong. While some have lauded this decision as a form of boycott that might put pressure on factory owners to enforce higher standards, Nike has also been criticized for not signing on to the compact that other brands that have stayed in Bangladesh have signed.

Perhaps Nike has the luxury of making this choice. As Hannah Jones pointed out, "Bangladesh represents a fork in the road for the industry," with one option leading to lower costs and the other to safer factories.[10] Nike, unlike Walmart or H&M or the Gap, is not playing the cost game. Perhaps it can absorb the higher costs of manufacturing in other more-expensive countries. Perhaps the cost to its brand image is higher if Nike is perceived to be participating in the abuse of workers. As corroboration, another reputation-conscious brand, Walt Disney, ended all manufacturing in Bangladesh after the Rana Plaza collapse.

INNOVATING WITH THE STAKEHOLDERS

On the other hand, Nike has not simply accepted the higher costs of choosing not to manufacture in unsafe environments. It has transformed a compliance challenge into an innovation challenge. This is the approach advocated by management guru C. K. Prahalad and colleagues with regard to sustainability initiatives, but it applies in this context as well: pursuing social good can be a source of innovation that leads to new sources of competitive advantage. Rather than simply comply, innovate. A company can get to the win-win but not with the current ways of doing business. Instead, the win-win is achieved through the path of innovation.[11] This idea takes us beyond shared value (Mode 2) to propose innovation as a means of resolving trade-offs across stakeholders (Mode 3). We'll look at Prahalad's argument more deeply in Chapter 8, but for now, let's see how Nike has used Mode 3 to innovate in its supply chain.

Nike has used the trade-offs surfaced by its outsourced-manufacturing business model as an opportunity to look at how the upstream processes of design, commercialization, and sourcing may be undermining efforts to improve practices downstream. Not only does price pressure translate into pressure on suppliers, but so do the demands of fashion and consumer taste. It takes a lot to get the right product on the right shelf in the right store. Just-in-time delivery and lean manufacturing mean that suppliers need to comply not only with price demands but also with changes in orders or rush jobs (to match consumers' changing buying patterns). The result might be forced overtime or other harsh demands on workers. Thus, even if a company like Nike invests in programs to improve workers' conditions in the factories, it might simultaneously be undermining those efforts with its own upstream practices.

Nike admitted as much in its "FY07–09 Corporate Responsibility Report."[12] Nike leaders began to focus on understanding the root causes of such problems as excessive overtime, work without breaks, and toxic chemicals in the workplace. They found that increased numbers of athletic-wear styles and requirements to switch between them, capacity miscalculations, long approval processes in merchandising (leading to rushed orders), and last-minute changes in colors and fabrics were all directly correlated with overtime. Similarly, Nike's choices about materials and glues led plants to produce more toxic environmental waste and to subject workers to potential physical harm. While recognizing that poor management at plants also caused these problems, Nike found that its actions at Nike headquarters, far away from the factories, contributed heavily to factory conditions.

Said CEO Mark Parker, "Ignorance is not bliss. You have to understand the systemic issues and work with factory partners to solve them."[13] Indeed, starting with the crisis in 1997, Phil Knight promised to engage with researchers on questions of the global supply chain, and Nike leadership did. One such scholar was Rick Locke, then at MIT's Sloan School of Management (and now provost at Brown University). Locke and a number of colleagues, students, and research assistants were given data from the three types of audits conducted in Nike's factories: the SHAPE audit of basic environmental health and safety (launched in 1997); the M-Audit of management and work conditions (launched in 2002); and the independent audits conducted on a 5 percent sample of Nike's factories by the Fair Labor Association, which is a multi-stakeholder initiative comprising brands, NGOs, and universities. These last audits are the only ones that are fully independent and based on unannounced visits by inspectors. The researchers also spent a tremendous amount of time in the field, visiting factories and interviewing the various stakeholders.

The work of Locke and colleagues is summarized in the 2013 book, *The Promise and Limits of Private Power: Promoting Labor Standards in the Global Economy.*[14] It doesn't paint a picture of Nike as perfect—indeed, no factory got a score higher than ninety on the hundred-point M-audit scale, and more than one-fourth scored below fifty—but it does give us a glimmer of what is possible with the right systems and approaches in place. Where have these insights led the company? The insights have led it to work closely with the factories to build capacity in lean manufacturing. Rather than creating flexibility and responsiveness to production demands on the backs of the workers, the goal is to help plants run just-in-time systems effectively as part of what Nike calls a "manufacturing revolution." Perhaps even more importantly, the insights have led Nike to rethink its planning processes to enable more lead times in ordering and create as many global products (rather than multiple products tailored to local markets) as possible in order to reduce the number of styles. Further, Nike's whole product-design process is implicated. The many choices made in Beaverton, Oregon—in design, materials, assortments, and demand forecasting—have been reshaped by a commitment to improving conditions in the supply chain.[15] Tough conversations and expansive innovation are signatures of the approach that Nike has developed over the years.

The disappointing news is that over the first half of the 2000s, according to Nike's own auditing measures, most factories did not improve in their compliance. However, Locke identified some conditions under which compliance was the highest. In particular, the more engaged the brand is with the factory, the more the factory is compliant. That means not just frequent visits from compliance officers, but visits from sourcing directors and production teams, which helps develop better practices. This suggests that it is not just (or not only) policing and auditing that make the difference. Instead, face-to-face contact may generate more initiatives to improve production processes such as lean manufacturing or total quality improvement. It may also lead to greater trust that moves the working relationship from being adversarial to being collaborative.

Because of the limitations of the traditional compliance-focused model, more and more companies, Nike included, are refocusing on capability-building efforts. As in health care, prevention is much more effective than treatment. Capability building aims to help managers organize more effectively so that they can avoid putting their workers in unsafe or abusive conditions. This new model—adopted by Nike as Generation 3 compliance and by the Fair Labor Association as the sustainable compliance program FLA 3.0—engages with factories to help them develop technical knowledge and management systems to run high-performance organizations.

What's so challenging is that it is not even enough to address operations within headquarters and the factories. Nike acknowledges that to achieve its compliance objectives for the workers who make its products, it needs to reach into the community to assure such things as access to basic services and financial management training (the same kind of thing Walmart found for women's empowerment). The system that needs fixing is not just throughout Nike's (or any global brand's) supply chain but into the communities that connect to it.

A key observation is that the innovation came from working *with*, not just *for*, the stakeholders. The guidance from C. K. Prahalad and others is right: stakeholder trade-offs can sometimes be solved through innovation. Beyond this recommendation, it is clear from the Nike and Walmart cases that the innovation comes from deep engagement with the stakeholders. This approach, when it is most effective, goes beyond "inclusive innovation"—innovation that is aimed at enhancing the well-being of disenfranchised populations—to become "embedded innovation." This concept was developed in the field of global health by Anita McGahan and collaborators, but it can usefully be extended to this conversation.[16] They argue that embedded innovation starts with a commitment to solidarity with stakeholders, treating them as the focal point of innovative problem-solving. This kind of innovation is based on a deep understanding of the contexts in which the stakeholders exist and involves them in the innovative process. At the same time, the innovative process brings in state-of-the-art thinking from around the world to find solutions.

Nike's journey is illustrative. The company engaged with top scholars (Rick Locke and colleagues from MIT) along with the factory workers and communities on the ground. What they came up with was a very different set of interventions than they might have anticipated going into the process, and that looked very different from a pure compliance model of action.

As Brian Stevenson of the Equal Justice Initiative said, the power is in the proximity. Getting close to your stakeholders—truly engaging with them—is what will generate solutions.[17]

INNOVATING TO FIND THE WIN-WIN

There are indicators that the global movement to improve labor standards has had an effect. First, because factories are rarely dedicated to producing for only one brand, they are now likely to be facing audits from multiple different companies with their own standards. Locke finds that the higher the proportion of reputation-conscious companies sourcing from a factory, the more likely the factory will be compliant with health, safety, and labor standards. The different brands in one factory often work together to ensure that standards are met. A further sign of hope is that newer factories tend to get higher ratings than the older ones with which Nike has had a longer-term relationship. This might imply that as the labor-standards movement has gained momentum, factory owners around the world may be more likely to establish factories that meet higher standards.

The experience at Levi's is similar. An early mover on factory-compliance initiatives in the 1990s, Levi's still struggled with worker turnover and absenteeism, a sure sign that work conditions were not desirable. It launched an initiative called, straightforwardly, Improving Worker Well-Being. Discovering that there was no one-size-fits-all for the seventy-two factories and 140,000 participating workers around the world, Levi's leaders tasked vendors to come up with plans. These vendors discovered they couldn't do that until they asked their workers what was going on in their lives. In Mexico, vendor Apparel International organized peer-led sessions with an NGO, Yo Quiero, Yo Puedo (I Want, I Can) to learn about worker experiences and train supervisors. The vendor made seemingly small changes at work, like providing better fans and water fountains, shaded parking for motorcycles, and microwaves in the break room. Importantly, it got the supervisors to communicate better with employees—more coaching and less shouting. The result: lower absenteeism, lower turnover, and changes in how the staff interact. "It's a win-win situation, believe me," said Oscar González Franch, the president of Apparel International.[18]

Here's how *Fortune* magazine described it:

> Levi's efforts, *and the business case for them*, all become clearer when you zoom in on one of the vendors that are on board . . . The goal is to build a network of more productive, better-run factories—with happier, healthier employees and lower rates of costly absenteeism and turnover. That would be good for suppliers, but also for Levi's, which will get more reliable, cost-efficient sourcing partners—while generating positive vibes that resonate with young talent and with consumers who want their values reflected in everything they buy.

Levi's and its vendor also invested in the town itself, for example, by improving the health clinic and creating a playground. It innovated in the financial model to support the well-being program by creating a foundation that sells products made by local workers from Levi's scraps. Says Levi's CEO Chip Bergh, "This goes way beyond making a profit. We are demonstrating there is an opportunity for companies to redefine their role in society, and that's good for business." Despite these efforts, wages are still low, and even with all of these initiatives, they are not rising. The one thing Levi's might not be able to do (because it wouldn't be good for business, one presumes) is increase wages. These innovative solutions have improved worker well-being, but the profit constraint is still there.

Let's be clear: factory conditions are still poor in many locations. Daily we see in the news reports of factories that employ children, use toxic chemicals in unsafe conditions, pollute the waterways, force overtime work, or house workers in terrible dormitories. The list goes on. What we can learn, then, from an analysis of Nike's (and Levi's and Walmart's) efforts is that there are ways to make things better, and the solutions involve collaborative innovation among all of the stakeholders, many of whom have competing interests: the brands, the suppliers, the suppliers to the suppliers, NGOs concerned with labor practices and environmental impact, consulting and accounting firms that conduct audits, and, of course, governments.

STEPS TO INNOVATING AROUND TRADE-OFFS

The trade-offs here are intense: performance-driven companies with tight margins unintentionally create conditions that might be detrimental to the environment, public safety, and workers throughout the supply chain. In the case of worker conditions in the supply chain, even when good Mode 1 analysis of the trade-offs is done, action may be stymied if companies stay in Mode 2—business case—action. Where we have seen success is when companies moved toward innovative solutions to break the trade-offs. Walmart ends up creating whole new partnership models to train workers. Nike ends up transforming its whole design and manufacturing process.

For leaders interested in moving toward Mode 3, here are a few key steps.

First, I know I'm starting to sound like a broken record, but start in Mode 1. That is, innovation is not possible without deep insights into what the experiences of the stakeholders actually are, not (only) through reports but through on-the-ground fieldwork to get behind the numbers. Sometimes it is unpleasant or stressful to engage with stakeholder representatives who might be enraged about existing conditions. Phil Knight's 1998 speech reflected that discomfort—he seemed befuddled at being chastised for something he felt was out of his control. It's worth keeping in mind, though, that outrage has as its base a compassionate caring for those stakeholders who are affected by the actions of corporations. The outrage is most productively heard as an invitation to listen and learn. The outrage can serve as an effective call to action, something that keeps you going even if the going gets tough.

Second, don't get trapped in Mode 2. What is clear from these examples is that there is not always an immediate win-win. Building a business case for better worker conditions flies directly in the face of delivering products to consumers at reasonable prices. The demands created by those prices are often used as an excuse by global brands and local vendors not to take action, or not to be as aggressive in making change as stakeholders would like. If the stakeholder concerns get immediately incorporated into a conversation about the business case for action, it may be hard to find solutions that work for everyone. In the case of factory conditions in the global supply chain, the fixes are sometimes expensive—so expensive as to make it potentially difficult to justify action. The conversation needs to hold the business-case logic in a bubble while the innovation process is allowed to unfold. Of course, the conversation must come back to how the solutions might be funded, but instead of being the starting point, the question of funding should rather, and eventually, be part of the innovation itself.

Third, cocreate with the stakeholders. In the end, no company can innovate *for* stakeholders and get it right. The company must innovate *with* stakeholders. It's impossible even to know what the pain points are for different stakeholders, such as factory workers, without consulting them and engaging them. Creating platforms to work with stakeholders is useful for both identifying the problems and generating the solutions. The state of the art is embedded innovation: an innovation process in which the stakeholders are at the center of the inquiry. Nike's big step forward in addressing factory conditions was when it started working with the factory owners and workers to come up with solutions. Those efforts pointed to opportunities to change work processes within the factories, but they also pointed to the ways that Nike headquarters was creating the conditions for time crunches and stresses at the factory.

Fourth, take an expansive view. You'll likely need to look more broadly than you think you need to. If Nike had tried to solve the problem of worker conditions in factories by just focusing on the factories, it would have never gotten there. The more it examined the root causes of the pressures on factories in places like Ho Chi Minh City, Vietnam, the more Nike leaders realized that those pressures stemmed from what was happening at headquarters in Beaverton, Oregon. The result was a rethinking of design processes, of order processes, and of global product mixes. Nike had to let go of its existing business model. It also meant that headquarters had to shift its mind-set from compliance to innovation. Every tension created by a compliance demand needed to be transformed into an innovation question. A key insight: innovative solutions are unlikely to be narrow but will rather address the complex systems that create the trade-offs.

CODA: WHAT HAPPENS WHEN STANDARDS IMPROVE?

I asked my students about Sujeet Sennik's op-ed.[19] Did they think that Western consumers, brands, and retailers were responsible for the poor factory conditions in countries like Bangladesh? Some said yes for all of the reasons outlined above: we as consumers and managers are part of a system that creates and tolerates such factory conditions. Others, however, disagreed. Many of my Canadian students felt that it was the local governments' responsibility to set and enforce regulations. Global brands, they argued, should not have to be enforcers of good standards but should simply follow the rules and regulations of local countries. Government—which should represent the citizens and not the interests of corporate profit—should or could be a central instrument for ensuring fair working conditions. Being from Canada, a country with a great deal of regulations that are mainly extremely well enforced, these students perhaps have more faith in the role that regulation can play in developing economies where governments may not always have the will or the skill to enforce laws.

Other students in the debate, particularly those from Pakistan, Bangladesh, and Thailand, argued from a different perspective: we should think about the alternatives for these workers. Most come from the countryside where they would have engaged in subsistence farming. The factory jobs, however difficult, provided more opportunities to feed and potentially educate their children than they would have otherwise. These workers were already working long, uncomfortable, often-dangerous hours before they came to the factories. So global brands should not pull out of these countries just because work standards are poor.

Even as global brands try to do the right thing by cutting off relationships with noncompliant suppliers, my students' concerns have been realized. When Walmart ended its relationship with Simco, its action put 20,000 workers out of jobs at least temporarily. Or in Nike's case, when it pulled out of a vendor called Lyric Industries, the supplier had to find another buyer, this time a Japanese retailer with much tighter profit margins than Nike's. To manage the demands of this new customer, Lyric's factory doubled its overtime hours, according to the general manager, Sakr Rahman. "They want their clothes on time no matter what . . . We had to tell the workers that the new buyer has a new mind-set, and that means different rules."[20] If global brands leave Bangladesh as Walt Disney and others have done, where do they go? They are likely to seek out low-cost manufacturing in other countries (Vietnam, Cambodia, Pakistan) where the situation is much the same but the problems are less in the limelight.

That's how Bangladesh became a major center for garment manufacturing to begin with. For years, China was (and is) the world's manufacturing hub for clothing, computers, and many other products that Western consumers buy. Following a well-known pattern of development, as standards of living rose, workers in China began to demand higher wages and better working conditions. Workers began protesting and using social media (to the extent the efforts were not suppressed) to raise visibility on the issues. Ensuing labor shortages, accompanied by government efforts to increase the minimum wage, led manufacturers to pay higher wages and therefore increase their costs. They could certainly shift some manufacturing to lower-cost areas such as Western China or Vietnam, but they could not feasibly abandon the expensive infrastructure they had built. The solution was to go upscale, manufacturing their own brands or incorporating more value-added goods. This led global brands to search elsewhere for lower-cost suppliers.

Of course, this story is part of a long history. The pictures of the Tazreen Fashions factory fire are hardly distinguishable from pictures from the 1911 Triangle Shirtwaist Factory fire in lower Manhattan.[21] The same smoke coming from the windows. The same locked doors and inadequate fire escapes. The same bodies of teenage women who leapt to their deaths to escape the flames. That early twentieth-century tragedy mobilized public opinion against such working conditions. An estimated 400,000 New Yorkers came out to pay their respects to those who died and to protest those conditions. The New York State legislature created the Factory Investigating Commission, and within three years, in what became a model for the whole US, New York passed dozens of new laws regulating fire safety, work hours, toilet facilities, eating facilities, and other worker conditions. These reforms had previously been blocked by opposition from manufacturers fearful of the increased costs, but they ultimately became models for the rest of the US and part of the movement to achieve the occupational health and safety standards we have in most advanced economies today.

FIGURE 6.1. Aftermath of Triangle Shirtwaist Factory fire, 1911. Source: GRANGER / GRANGER—All rights reserved. Reprinted with permission.

Worker protests are thus central to the story. Whether in 1900s New York City or 2015 Dhaka, when labor organizes itself, it creates possibilities for change. Prior to the Tazreen and Rana Plaza tragedies, massive protests in 2010 in Bangladesh had already led the government to raise the minimum wage for garment workers from $20 per month to $37 per month. Although unions have mainly been banned in Bangladesh, workers at individual factories have begun to organize (still, fewer than 5 percent of garment workers are represented by unions). At the Rosita Knitwear factory in 2011, workers elected an association. That same year, the company passed a factory audit with top marks. It received a grade of "good" for working hours, compensation, health and safety, and indeed for each of the twelve categories inspected. Yet just a few short months later, when a female employee brought a complaint that she was being pressured to have sex with a Chinese manager, it became a trigger for workers to protest for rectification of this complaint as well as other problems with pay and earned leave. But here, as elsewhere in the country, the factory owners along with the support of the police, pushed back. When the six weeks of confrontation damaged the Rosita factory, management fired 300 workers for vandalism and posted their names on blacklist notices for the entire economic zone. The president of the association was fired and jailed. Around the country, worker protest has been of keen interest to the police, who have been witnessed beating protesters, firing rubber bullets at them, and intimidating individual workers. Aminul Islam, one of the most outspoken labor activists in the country, was abducted by the national security forces and killed.[22] Such incidents, however, bring bad press, and in their own sad way may eventually generate more pressure for change.

With the higher standards that followed from the Triangle Shirtwaist Factory fire came higher costs. In pursuit of lower costs to meet the demands of consumers, manufacturing moved to Japan, then Korea, then China. And now Bangladesh. In essence, Western brands and Western consumers have exported the problem of labor standards abroad. Or in a twist, back to places like Los Angeles, which has been investigated by the US and California governments as one of the sweatshop capitals of the world. Where work is done without regulation, in the informal economy, workers are often undocumented immigrants from Thailand, Honduras, and all of the same places where global brands set up their manufacturing plants. The workers suffer many of the same problems that they face in plants abroad: unpaid overtime, low wages, piece-rate work, no breaks, and on and on.[23] We want high labor standards. We want cheap goods. To get both, we take advantage of low labor standards elsewhere or away from sight in the informal economy at home. This may not be visible to us in the shiny stores and internet portals where we shop, but embedded in each of the products we buy is a complex global supply chain where goods and people cross many borders on the way to producing finished goods.

The tide may be turning. As pressure from local labor and international forces grows, it may become unsustainable to operate factories in such poor conditions. If factories do not improve conditions, they may lose business to suppliers from countries that are better at enforcement. The conversation with my students points to a complex moral calculus. Is it better for brands to stay in a situation where factories might risk not being in compliance or to go? Perhaps, however, this question is based on a false dichotomy. The answer may be to stay but also to engage. This is not simply about assuring compliance with standards but about innovating throughout the supply chain. Global brands will certainly have to absorb some of these costs.[24] Will consumers also be willing to pay?

• PART III SIGNPOSTS

- When you start with the Mode 2 business case or win-win mind-set, it can often lead to roadblocks or incremental solutions. Most trade-offs don't have easy solutions, and innovation (Mode 3) will likely be necessary. The conversation needs to hold the business-case logic in a bubble while the innovation process is allowed to unfold. Innovative solutions may eventually lead to a business case, but they don't often start with one.

- The starting point is always Mode 1, but the more intractable the trade-off, the more likely that this will require not just reports and quantitative analyses but in-depth work with stakeholders to understand their issues and identify root causes. This may not always be comfortable, especially when stakeholders are outraged at one corporate practice or another. Companies should see outrage as an invitation to listen and engage.

- Sticking to the rules of the game—compliance with regulations—may not be a satisfactory means of dealing with trade-offs. First, for anyone committed to the social goals associated with stakeholder needs, compliance may seem unambitious. Second, the compliance mind-set may make it hard to come up with the required actions to achieve even the regulated objectives. Companies must transform the trade-offs into innovation challenges (Mode 3 action). The deeper the insight into the trade-offs and what causes them, the more innovative the solutions can be.

- No company can innovate *for* stakeholders and get it right. The firm must innovate *with* stakeholders in an embedded innovation process. Creating platforms to work with stakeholders is useful for both identifying the problems and generating the solutions.

- Companies will need to look more broadly than managers think they need to. Tough trade-offs should be transformed into innovation questions. A key insight: innovative solutions are unlikely to be narrow but will rather address the more complex systems that create trade-offs.

PART IV

THRIVING WITHIN INTRACTABLE TRADE-OFFS (MODE 4)

CHAPTER 7

DEALING WITH PARADOXES

Selling Sustainably

THIS QUESTION ABOUT whether the consumer will pay is a crucial one. It is often the most intractable of the trade-offs. What do we do with the tension created by wanting to sell more products (as any company must) and the costs associated with consumerism, waste, labor standards, and environmental damage? What about the cases where innovation isn't (yet) possible?

I'm going to argue that in those cases, organizations are finding ways to *maintain and thrive* within the tensions created by trade-offs in what I call Mode 4 action. Indeed, companies actually must rely on these tensions in order to push themselves forward. The conflict leads to action. If all resolutions to conflicts across stakeholders were easy win-wins, they would have been accomplished by now. When we can't innovate and we don't want to resort to leaning on the business-case logic, we might be left with only a few overly publicized cases of success. Concentrated laundry detergent, anyone?

The biggest challenge for leaders today is addressing the conflicts in which people cannot find the win-win and cannot yet innovate around the problem. Some companies are using sustainability initiatives as holding places for these tensions. Sustainability is an attempt to address a nearly intractable trade-off:

companies need to sell products to survive, but every product they sell feeds consumption and has an impact on the environment. The question becomes, How can a company make consumption less damaging or even neutral? It feels impossible. Yet companies are beginning to operate in Mode 4 to uncover potential future solutions by running experiments, entering into partnerships with NGOs, working with consortia of other companies facing the same challenges, making long-term research investments with uncertain payoffs, or involving stakeholders such as workers or communities in problem-solving.

The takeaway for Mode 4: even where there aren't innovative solutions, companies can learn to thrive within the tensions created by intractable trade-offs. These tensions, rather than being confusing or problematic, can actually be the source of organizational adaptability and resilience.

In this chapter, let's start by looking at how these tensions become intractable. The lens I'll use for this exploration will be consumerism and sustainability. We'll turn to solutions in Chapter 8.

CAMPING OUT OVERNIGHT FOR NEW NIKE SHOES

Basketball star Michael Jordan retired from the sport for a final time in 2003. But that doesn't mean that his Jordan-branded Nike shoes don't still attract attention. Coveted today by people who can barely remember the Chicago Bulls' six championships in the 1990s, Air Jordans remain a core of Nike's strategy to excite consumers. Consumers still go to great lengths to get their hands on the shoes. Anticipating the release of the Air Jordan Bred 11 shoes in December 2012 (retail price $185), people lined up overnight at the Madison Square Mall in Huntsville, Alabama, to get one of thirty-six wristbands that would allow them to purchase the shoes at a later date. An altercation broke out, and the police responded. When police used pepper spray, the Nike fans refused medical attention because they did not want to lose their places in line. In Houston on December 13, 2014, nearly fifty police officers arrived at the Willowbrook Mall late at night when the crowd waiting in line for tickets to buy the Air Jordan 11 Retro Legend Blue sneakers got rowdy. Said Katrice Stapleton, one of the people waiting there,

> I came out to get the 11's for my kids and so far it has been chaos. Complete chaos. They were throwing rocks trying to break the glass and get into the

store. That happened about three times and they tried to bum-rush the court to get into the mall.

That same month, a young man set up camp outside the Houston Galleria on a Wednesday in order to be first in line for the Retro Legend Blues that would go on sale on Saturday. He was hoping to get his younger brother the thing he most desired as a way to provide solace after their father had passed away.[1]

Starting in 1989, the Wieden Kennedy advertising campaign starring Jordan and actor-director Spike Lee as his character Mars Blackmon convinced consumers that "It's gotta be the shoes."[2] That was the beginning of $100-, $200- and higher-priced shoes. That was the beginning of the nearly cult status attained by certain shoes, and "sneakerhead" collectors and sneaker conventions where fans bought and sold collector-item shoes. Those Air Jordans that retailed for $185 might be found the next day on eBay for $700. Special items can easily trade in the thousands of dollars. These elite buyers of Nike products have a high willingness to pay for the right product. Many other consumers, wanting to "be like Mike" or to show off their taste, are willing to pay too.[3]

Playing to this elite is central to Nike's marketing strategy. As outlined in Chapter 2, the company thinks of it as a pyramid, with the sneakerheads and top athletes at the top and the mass consumer buying lower-priced Nike-branded shoes at the bottom. The manufacturer makes limited-edition shoes with extraordinary creativity—the Ronaldinho-signature Touch of Gold numbered-edition soccer boot, the Wu Tang Clan Dunk High in the Black/Goldenrod Friends and Family edition, the LeBron Zoom Soldier 8 FLYEASE made for people with disabilities who cannot tie shoes, the Nike Tennis Classic x colette—designed with French boutique Colette—for consumers at the top of the pyramid. Nike makes less expensive versions for those at the bottom. Although the base of the pyramid supports the company because that is the source of most of the revenue, the top of the pyramid supports the company by making the brand desirable. According to one Nike executive, "We've got to have the best shoe at the top of the line, even though it will, almost by definition, never make money. But without it, the market for the lower-priced shoes will go away."[4]

Then there are those who cannot afford the $200 and try to get the shoes another way. In May 1990, *Sports Illustrated* ran a cover story called "Your Sneakers or Your Life." The image was of a man with a pair of Air Jordan Vs hanging over his shoulder and a gun pointed directly into his back. Journalist Rick Telander documented in a way that no one had before the many crimes committed all across the US, mainly by teenagers and mainly in poor, segregated neighborhoods. Telander also raised the question of responsibility: "Should we demand that the sports shoe industry be held to a higher standard, than, say, the junk food industry? . . . Obviously, we are talking about something bigger than shoes here." Telander reflected 25 years later:

> I wanted it to be as devastating as possible. I wanted people to not be able to ignore this. It's kind of the point of any writer. You want to write things that people notice and help change things for the better. And if you can't change for the better, at least you get the facts out there and get rid of hypocrisy.[5]

Michael Jordan began to see the problematic implications of being a sports hero, and even more, engaging in extensive marketing efforts to build the Jordan brand.

Fifteen-year-old Michael Eugene Thomas loved Michael Jordan and the Nike shoes that carried Jordan's name. He displayed the box and the $115.50 receipt ("the price of a product touched by a deity") from their purchase. He cleaned the shoes every night. "We told him not to wear the shoes to school," said Michael's grandmother, Birdie Thomas. "We said somebody might like them, and he said, 'Granny, before I let anyone take those shoes, they'll have to kill me.'" Two weeks after he had finally gotten the shoes, this 15-year old was killed by another teenager, a basketball buddy, who just had to have the shoes. Said Michael Jordan upon hearing the news:

> I thought I'd be helping out others and everything would be positive. I thought people would try to emulate the good things I do, they'd try to achieve, to be better. Nothing bad. I never thought because of my endorsement of a shoe, or any product, that people would harm each other. Everyone likes to be admired, but when it comes to kids actually killing each other, then you have to re-evaluate things.[6]

The question is whether hero worship can motivate kids to overcome their circumstances or instead just entrench them in a cycle of unattainable desires.[7]

Fred Danzig, the editor of *Advertising Age*, wrote Telander a personal letter after the issue came out. He said he felt the issue was not just a shoe industry problem, "but one that involves every company, every ad agency and marketing executive." He referenced an *Advertising Age* editorial against gun violence decrying the power of the National Rifle Association that made this point, while acknowledging, "We know that one editorial doesn't solve anything and we will be pressing the issue at every opportunity in the hope that we can influence change for the better."[8]

Phil Knight of Nike had a different response:

> We can't make rules that keep drug dealers from wearing our stuff, and we can't solve the problems of the inner city, but we sponsor a lot of sports clinics for youth. And we're underwriting a series called Ghostwriting that the Children's Television Workshop is developing to teach kids how to read and write. We're doing it because we think it's the right thing to do, but we also want the visibility.[9]

Even here, Nike was engaging in the sell.

I BOUGHT THINGS I DIDN'T EVEN KNOW I NEEDED!

Walmart drives sales a different way. Far from creating an elite, aspirational brand, it uses its Everyday Low Price model to draw customers into its stores and get them to buy. Following Sam Walton's "stack 'em high and let 'em fly" philosophy, the company focuses on offering what it hopes will be surprisingly low prices to customers. The stores are filled with signs such as "Everyday Low Price," "Unbeatable," "Save even more," and "Rollback." The message is hard to ignore. Walmart's stated objective is to get people the best prices for what they need. The effect is to draw shoppers into buying more.[10]

Every time I teach the Walmart case for my course, I have my students conduct an ethnographic observation at a Walmart store. I want them to experience the ideas we cover in class. One student used the assignment as an opportunity to do his shopping for Canadian Thanksgiving dinner with a total budget of $140. He raved about the fact that the yams were right at the front entrance, the flour was on sale, and that the cinnamon and brown sugar were at eye level just next to the flour. "I felt like Wal-Mart was expecting me, that the employees had set that display just for me because in fewer than two minutes I had already found two items of my shopping list," he wrote in his report.[11]

> At this point, I was extremely excited to find cheap prices and see how well I was doing on my budget, so I started to give myself little treats such as an 8-pack Gillette Mach 3 Turbo razor cartridges that was selling for $24.75, when normally I buy this pack at Shoppers [Drug Mart] for $28.95.

By the time he checked out, he had gotten everything on his list and more, and also broke his budget by spending $156.

Here's how he wrote about it in the assignment:

> The core of Wal-Mart's strategy revolves around ensuring high volumes through low priced products. However, I wanted to know what exactly does Walmart do to ensure such volumes besides offering low prices. In other words, once the customer is in the store, which tactics are implemented to promote buying more? I went to a Supercenter to begin the experiment: I needed to buy certain products but I ended up leaving with more items than originally needed. Why? This is exactly what surprises me because I am a moderate person when it comes to shopping. I normally stick to my budget, do not buy more than I need, and once I am in a store I go directly to get what I want. However, this did not happen in this situation and I believe this can be attributed to the following strategies:
>
> • Making discounts highly visible: Throughout the entire store you can see these small signs announcing rollouts. Moreover, it is impossible not to see them as they pop out in every aisle even when you are looking straight ahead. I found myself just checking every item on every aisle that had a red sign on it. Not only did my time at the Supercenter increase but I also bought products that I did not need in the first place. I recall buying a family size pack of Special K just because it was selling at an unbelievable price: $5.34 (the normal size at Sobeys [grocery] costs around $8). I would not have bought it if the discount sign had not been visible. Even more, I would not have stopped to check the price. I would have passed it by without realizing I was in the cereal aisle. In addition, almost every product on sale was placed at eye level so it was not difficult just to turn my head and see what was being discounted.

- The right product in the right place at the right time: The feeling I had when entering the store that day is that they have been preparing for me. Just seeing the two top items of my shopping list right away at the entrance made me feel that they already knew what was on my list. In addition, 73 percent of the items that I bought that day were discounted. Everyone who has prepared a Thanksgiving dessert knows that the top four ingredients are pumpkin, vanilla, cinnamon, and all-purpose flour. "Conveniently" the last three items were next to each other. The same with the Coke and the chips, with the cheese and the crackers, and the list goes on.

- Volume discounts: I felt almost forced to buy bigger quantities. For example, I needed two 2-liter bottles of coke (which were selling at $1.87 each), but the six-pack of 2-liter bottles was only selling for $4.97, meaning that each bottle in the pack cost 82 cents (less than half of the unit price). This situation happened with a lot of items, such as lemons (unit price was 8 cents, but you could buy a bag of 16 lemons for 99 cents), onions (price per pound was $1.29, but you could buy a 10-pound bag for $6.99), and chips (unit price for Big Value chips was $1.44, but you could buy a pack of three different types of chips for $2.35). This made me feel pressured to buy the better deal even when I knew my guests were not going to eat that much.

- Layout: Thankfully, the food section was close to the checkout stands. And I say thankfully, because who knows what else I would have bought if I had walked through the men's clothing section or the home appliances floor. In this state of shopping frenzy, I walked through the personal care products area and left with a bunch of items that were not in my initial list. Nevertheless, Walmart is very smart when designing the layout of its stores. Whether you are buying groceries or medicine, Walmart makes sure you walk almost the entire store to find the products you need while at the same time entices you to check discounts for other products that were not part of your initial plan.

- One stop shop: This strategy is self-explanatory. Walmart has become the place where you can buy almost anything imaginable. Groceries, clothing, jewelry, medicines, personal care products, home appliances, insurance, eye exams, dry cleaning, tires, and so on. These strategies are not unique to Wal-Mart, because I have seen them in action at other retailers, but what I have not seen until now is all of them being executed together and with such precision.

He concluded, "I came to the Supercenter to run an experiment without realizing the subject of the experiment was going to be me."

It may be that Walmart's customers are not able or willing to pay much for any individual product, but Walmart relies on the fact that customers will buy many products, often including items they did not think they wanted or needed until they saw them on the shelves. Charles Fishman documented many cases of this in his book *The Wal-mart Effect*: a gallon of Vlasic pickles for $2.97, a garden-hose nozzle for $1.74, a DVD player for $39, a power lawnmower for $99.96. The lawnmowers are so cheap that you don't repair them when they break; you just replace them. No one actually finishes a gallon of pickles, but you can't resist buying them when they are so cheap! (Then again, this strategy ended up bankrupting Vlasic.)[12]

Nike and Walmart, in their own ways, have figured out how to get customers to pay enough for and buy enough of their products. In fact, both of these companies have been considered geniuses in their approaches to driving demand—whether through famously innovative advertising campaigns or famously prolific use of "Everyday Low Price" signs.

However, you only have to look at the overflowing trash dumps and the burgeoning storage-locker business to begin to question whether we have too much stuff. When our lawnmower breaks, we throw it away. When our house fills up with things we have acquired, we put them in storage so we can buy more stuff. As a result, the US self-storage industry added one billion square feet in just eight years (1998 to 2005) and today covers 2.5 billion square feet—that's seventy-eight square miles or three times the size of Manhattan.[13] These are the trade-offs: selling products vs. encouraging consumerism; selling products vs. taking care of the environment; selling products vs. ensuring good working conditions in the supply chain. It's a fundamental paradox. How do you do both at the same time?

ISN'T THIS JUST CONSUMER CHOICE?

Should we be concerned about how corporate sales efforts fuel these trade-offs? Do we think that Nike should worry that it is creating expensive products and marketing them to people (poor youth, for example) that cannot afford them? What about when one of those kids kills another one to get his shoes? Do we think Walmart should be held responsible for the fact that lawnmowers and DVD players are now nearly disposable? What about when crowds are whipped up into such a frenzy by Black Friday deals that they stampede into stores, beating each other up and ripping products out of each other's arms?

It is certainly tempting, especially if you are a student who has read too much Milton Friedman or a company spokesperson who is charged with defending your company's business model, to say that companies are not to blame. Consumers are making choices. Companies do what they do, and consumers will do what they do. They will buy what they need or want and won't buy what they don't need or want. This doesn't tell the whole story, however.

As sociologist Juliet Schor points out in her book *The Overspent American*, this answer is based on a conventional set of assumptions about the rationality of consumer choice that simply do not hold in practice.[14] It assumes that consumers have all of the information they need to make choices. This ignores the fact that much of the information directed toward them comes in the form of advertising. It assumes that preferences do not change over time. That is, that if someone eats a bacon and egg sandwich today because he wants it, he won't later regret that diet when he gets hypertension. It assumes that one individual's preferences are independent of another's preferences. Yet there is considerable evidence from research in marketing, psychology, and behavioral economics that people are influenced by others, and the way decisions are framed will change how they make their choices.[15] We buy more of a product if it is placed at eye level on the store shelves. We buy more products if we have a shopping cart to place them in. We buy more products when we have credit cards, or amazingly even when we simply see the Visa sign in the window of the store.

Drawing on Thorstein Veblen's early critique of conspicuous consumption, Schor offers an alternative to the rational model of consumer choice.[16] Being sociologically minded, she points out that our sense of social standing is connected to what we consume. This idea is the source of the expression, "keeping up with the Joneses." In an early twentieth-century comic strip by cartoonist Arthur Momand, the Joneses were the better-off next-door neighbors of the cartoon's main characters. Keeping up with them meant doing what they did, buying what they bought.[17] You engaged in this "upscale emulation" so that you would not appear lesser than those neighbors whom you could see and compare yourselves to day in and day out. In this view, consumption is not about fulfilling specific material needs but about attaining specific social goals. Others have suggested that such behavior might even be considered "defensive consumption."

We buy the SUV not because we want one but because we are afraid not to. If a fuel-efficient compact car gets into an accident with a larger, heavier SUV, the car and its passengers will likely suffer more damage and injury. If you have small children, what choice would you make?[18] Suddenly, the roads are clogged with SUVs.

Now in the twenty-first century, with the ubiquity of television and the internet, we no longer keep up with the Joneses but instead with the Kardashians. In the US, 35 percent of the population wants to be in the top 6 percent. Another 49 percent aspires to be in the next 12 percent. That nearly three-quarters of people want to be in the top 20 percent of wealth speaks to how far aspirations exceed what might be practical. It explains why people go into massive credit-card debt to get products they think they need, and maybe why people kill others for their sneakers. Said Telander in the *Sports Illustrated* article,

> Of course, these assailants aren't simply taking clothes from their victims. They're taking status. Something is very wrong with a society that has created an underclass that is slipping into economic and moral oblivion, an underclass in which pieces of rubber and plastic held together by shoelaces are sometimes worth more than a human life. The shoe companies have played a direct role in this. With their million-dollar advertising campaigns, superstar spokesmen and over-designed, high-priced products aimed at impressionable young people, they are creating status from thin air to feed those who are starving for self-esteem.[19]

Critics of consumerism, such as Naomi Klein in her bestselling (no pun intended) book *No Logo*, argue that corporate branding and marketing activities are central to this story. Indeed, she argues, "successful corporations must primarily produce brands, not products . . . [where companies foster] powerful identities by making their brand concept into a virus and sending it out into the culture via a variety of channels: cultural sponsorship, political controversy, the consumer experience and brand extensions."[20] Companies work to generate the (perhaps unattainable) aspirations that lead to what many have described as overconsumption. Brands originally emerged in the industrial revolution when products were no longer connected to local craftspeople but were mass-produced in factories. Instead of buying clothing from the local seamstress, people began to buy ready-made apparel. Manufacturers developed brand names to distinguish products that were no longer distinguishable by the craftsperson who made them. At some point, brands began to transcend the products they were meant to represent.

As I have traced out in the last few chapters, as companies outsource their manufacturing and logistics to others, the brand is what remains with the company. The brands can become the object of consumers' aspirations. The brand is what gives individuals the distinctiveness they seek. Klein even claimed that the Nike swoosh had become one of the most demanded tattoos in tattoo parlors around the US. A study of those sporting corporate-logo tattoos—Nike, Apple, and Harley Davidson top the list, but IBM is there too—found that people do so because they identify with the brand philosophy or lifestyle that it represents.[21] Consumption is what enables people to attain the lifestyle.

We know that branding and advertising work; otherwise the billions of dollars of expenses and the huge industry of agencies would not exist. A powerful example of their effect is when the Canadian province of Québec banned advertising to children of products such as fast food, arguing that children do not have the ability to make informed decisions about what products they desire. Researchers found that subsequently the Quebecers bought less junk food than they had previously and the children weighed less on average than other children in North America.[22]

Juliet Schor offers this critique of consumerism: when there is an aspiration gap, consumption crowds out alternative uses of income—savings, public goods, or even free time.[23] We can't save because we must spend our earnings on current consumption. We can't afford to pay more taxes that could support public transportation systems, research funding, or education because we can't spare the cash. The appeal of the recurrent election rhetoric about small government and tax reductions is a direct result of this calculation (though the result is that cuts in spending mean reduced investment in infrastructure, education, health care, and other things that help assure longer-term prosperity). We can't afford to take vacation or take the weekend off, or we feel we must take the second job because we must buy those extra goods. Consider that consumption not only affects inequality but also the environment. You only have to look at the overflowing trash dumps and the burgeoning storage-locker business to begin to question if we have too much stuff.

THE FAUSTIAN BARGAIN

The power of brands has a flip side to it. In response to the critique of branding in Klein's *No Logo* book, the *Economist* announced in the magazine and later in a debate with Klein herself that it was "pro logo." Brands are good for the consumer, the magazine argued, because they offer a guarantee of quality and reliability. They serve as a form of warranty because if the products or the actions of the company do not live up to the brand promise, that will compromise the value of the brand. A brand makes a company vulnerable because the company must become more accountable in order to live up to the promises implied by the brand. Said the *Economist* article, "The more companies promote the value of their brands, the more they will need to seem ethically robust and environmentally pure. Hence, brands are levers for lifting standards."[24] Nike's troubles in the 1990s with the conditions in its factories or when individuals committed crimes to get their shoes are prime examples. Nike responded by investing heavily to improve factory standards. In 2015, in response to a series of horrific mass shootings in the US, Walmart stopped selling Confederate flags (in whose name crimes were committed) and some assault weapons. After the 2018 school shooting in Parkland, Florida, the retailer announced it would raise the age required to buy any type of firearm or ammunition to twenty-one years (from the previous eighteen).[25]

When celebrity endorsers are involved, the calculus becomes even more complex. Michael Jordan discovered this when the labor conditions in the Nike factories first came to light in the 1990s. The media creates fame for Jordan, and Nike fosters this fame and benefits from it. In 1998, *Fortune* magazine calculated the value of Michael Jordan as a brand for the economy at more than $10 billion.[26] The media also connected Jordan to the problems of labor conditions. He largely kept silent at the time, but many charged that he was more concerned about his own brand than about the factory workers who made his products. "I don't know the complete situation. Why should I? I'm trying to do my job. Hopefully, Nike will do the right thing, whatever that might be."[27] Ironically, this may have hurt his personal brand.

Similarly, in 1996 when activists discovered that television morning-show host Kathie Lee Gifford's line of clothing for Walmart was manufactured in Honduran sweatshops, she tearfully announced a stance against poor worker conditions and handed out checks to the workers who had been unfairly treated.[28] She was tempted simply to discontinue her line of products at Walmart, but she was urged by none other than notoriously prolabor US Labor Secretary Robert Reich to use her celebrity to fight against sweatshops. "My first reaction was I don't need this, but they told me that I had a unique opportunity to make a difference by using what happened to me to stop the horrible practices of some of these manufacturers." She testified before Congress that manufacturers are now "morally compelled" to address child labor and other poor working standards. Labor leaders agreed: "Kathie Lee Gifford is a celebrity, a very influential and powerful person," and therefore was responsible for standing up for the workers, said Charles Kernaghan, head of the National Labor Committee.

In 1999, labor leaders again brought workers from a Walmart factory in Santa Ana, El Salvador, that manufactured Kathie Lee's products to speak at a press conference to denounce their long hours, low pay, and substandard work sites. Upset with the negative press that his wife was receiving, Kathie Lee's ex-football star husband, Frank Gifford, said in a press conference, "I resent what you have done to my wife. You have assassinated her character." However, it was this very pressure on Kathie Lee that led to her campaign to end sweatshop conditions. Interestingly, Kathie Lee attempted to encourage other celebrities to participate in a Washington, DC, rally against illegal labor practices but did not find many takers. "They're saying, 'It says in my contract that this can't happen to me.' Well, it says the same thing in my contract, too, and that didn't protect me." This is the Faustian bargain that companies and celebrities strike with each other. They feed off each other's marketing and fame, but they also can hurt each other if their practices don't line up with consumer expectations.

The arrow goes in both directions. Companies can hurt stars' brands, but stars can also inflict pain on companies. Pittsburgh Steelers quarterback Ben Roethlisberger has had an endorsement contract with Nike likely worth more than a million dollars per year. Michael Vick, another star NFL quarterback signed a deal with Nike in 2001, his rookie year. Golfer Tiger Woods has been in the Nike embrace since turning pro in 1996. His first five-year contract was worth a total of $40 million. As the contract was renewed in subsequent years, the numbers climbed to more like $20 million per year.[29] Nike signed these athletes for all the same reasons they developed their relationship with

Michael Jordan. Superstar athletes—because of their extraordinary sporting accomplishments—build the brand and increase demand.

But what happens when those athletes tarnish their reputations, often in fairly dastardly ways? Roethlisberger was accused in 2008 of rape at a Lake Tahoe hotel during a celebrity golf tournament. Although no criminal proceedings ensued, he did pay a settlement to the accuser. Then, in March 2010, he was again accused of rape. Again, the police chose not to press charges, but after a leak of the police report, it became clear that the police were more interested in getting autographs with the football star than in investigating the crime. Outraged, NFL commissioner Roger Goodell suspended Roethlisberger for six games and ordered him to undergo a behavioral evaluation. Michael Vick ended up going to jail after being convicted of animal abuse in a dog-fighting ring. After a domestic dispute that became public when Tiger Woods crashed his vehicle into a tree, it was revealed that he had conducted numerous extramarital affairs and sexual encounters.

Companies protect themselves with morals clauses in their contracts that give them fairly expansive rights to fine athletes and celebrities and terminate their agreements under such circumstances. But they don't always use them. Nike stuck with Roethlisberger despite those multiple accusations of rape (though no convictions). It dropped Vick but signed him again four years later after he got out of jail and returned to NFL play. It even doubled-down with Tiger Woods, using the crisis to create an advertisement repurposing a recording of his deceased father's voice to ask him, "what your thinking was . . . and did you learn anything."[30] Nike stuck with these athletes even when other companies did not. Ben's Beef Jerky dropped Roethlisberger from their advertising. AT&T, Accenture, and Gatorade dropped Woods.

Some analysts implied that this was purely an economic calculation. A study of Nike golf products comparing the thirteen weeks before and after the Tiger Woods scandal broke showed that sales did not change.[31] So why should Nike discontinue its relationship with Woods if he's still helping the company sell products? Consumers kept shopping. No collective boycott ensued. Similarly, Roethlisberger's brand of Marauder football cleats continued to sell. Can this be purely an economic calculation? Isn't there a moral choice embedded in the economic choice? In a scathing editorial in the *New York Times* after the second Roethlisberger incident, commentator Timothy Egan put it this way,

> Is there anything creepier than a big, beer-breathed celebrity athlete expos-
> ing himself in a nightclub and hitting on underage girls, all the while pro-
> tected by an entourage of off-duty cops? Well, yes. It's the big, corporate
> sponsor—Nike, in this case—that continues trying to sell product with the
> creep as their role model.[32]

One might draw the line at arrest and conviction. Vick actually went to jail, but Roethlisberger was never charged. Because of police misconduct, the line might not be so clear. Maybe the "bad boy" image is part of Nike's brand, though these incidents do make the "Just do it" slogan slightly problematic. On the other hand, because Nike is such a big brand, do they have a special responsibility to change culture around things like violence against women?

INTRACTABLE TRADE-OFFS

Whether we are talking about advertising expensive products to people who cannot afford them, selling wastefully large sizes of products in order to encour-age consumers to buy more, supporting antiheroes who represent misogynistic values, the question is: What responsibility does a global brand have in relation-ship to culture and consumerism? This is what I mean by a trade-off being in-tractable. The sales goals are in direct contradiction with social goals. For most companies, the sales goals outcompete the social goals, but what I want to fo-cus on is how companies could make productive use of these tensions. I dwell on these paradoxes at length in this chapter because I want to make clear ex-actly how hard it is to address them. No amount of win-win language will help.

Of course, governments can play a role in changing the rules of the game. Juliet Schor suggests a tax on luxury goods and status consumption, which could subsidize environmental initiatives to reduce the impact of consumption. Schor's argument would also support US Senator Elizabeth Warren's crusade to develop more meaningful regulation of consumer credit, so that consumers are not duped into going too far into debt in order to keep up with the Joneses.[33]

Consumers themselves have also started to act out, not only in periodic boycotts of products that are connected to poor labor standards or environ-mental violations, but also in critiques of consumer culture itself. The culture-jamming movement—taking its inspiration from wartime jamming of radio frequencies—has attempted to point out the hypocrisies in some brand claims.

The Adbusters organization often repurposes ads, such as taking images of Tiger Woods and morphing his smile into a Nike swoosh. Or altering the image of a Nike Air Jordan shoe with "Nike: $250. Sweatshop: 83¢." Or superimposing pictures of the swoosh on large numbers of sheep, exhorting viewers to "Break free from the corporate herd."[34]

Ironically, even these efforts can get re-repurposed, as when Nike invited consumer advocate Ralph Nader to be in a television advertisement with athletes and celebrities. The script called for Nader to hold an Air 120 shoe and say, "Another shameless attempt by Nike to sell shoes." Nader declined to participate, but Nike can't say it didn't try.[35] Then again, Adbusters also sells a magazine and has what it calls a "culture shop" where you can buy, you guessed it, some products!—Vegan shoes, Adbusters T-shirts, books, and flags. If branding and advertising are attempts to create distinctiveness, then counterculture has also become part of the sell.

What is apparent from these stories is that we can quickly exhaust the win-win calculation when it comes to some sets of trade-offs. **First**, if you operate only in Mode 2 (making the business case), lots of tough conversations are off the table. These trade-offs are so thorny that it is unclear if any Mode 3 actions to innovate around them are possible. This is where existing theories mainly leave off. We can't find shared value (à la Porter and Kramer). We can't find any innovations that solve the problem (à la Prahalad and colleagues). The answer, I argue, will be to hold the trade-offs in tension and use them productively to promote organizational resilience. This is what I call Mode 4 action: thriving within the trade-offs.

Second, as I signaled in Chapter 1, an emerging literature has begun to explore these intractable moments.[36] It suggests that instead of being afraid of paradoxes, organizations can (and should) embrace them. This can be accomplished by keeping the two sides of the trade-off separate: make profits short term and sustainability projects long term; address trade-offs in some product lines but not others; create sustainability teams that are authorized to pursue environmental objectives in certain projects separate from the rest of the business; run experiments with uncertain outcomes to find resolutions to the trade-offs. All of these require organizations to live with the tensions rather than ignoring them or sidelining one set of interests in favor of others.

CHAPTER 8

EXPERIMENTATION

Going Green, Not Greenwashing

THE COUNTERPOINT TO CONSUMERISM has been the sustainability movement. Companies have sought to inoculate themselves against claims of consumerism by investing in sustainable products or waste reduction in their operations. This approach comes with its own questions. Tracing Nike's and Walmart's journeys toward greater sustainability illustrates what comes of Mode 2 and Mode 3 action, and how companies can respond when the trade-offs seem insurmountable (that's Mode 4). This chapter will take us through the whole journey from the business case to its limits, to innovation, and finally to strategies for coping with impasses.

Adam Werbach, then-president of the Sierra Club, wrote this about Walmart in his 1997 book, *Act Now, Apologize Later*: They are a "a new breed of toxin . . . [that] could wreak havoc on a town . . . Wal-Mart has proven this—they're big and greedy. They have no compassion for the community or the individual."[1] Ten years later, he landed on the cover of *Fast Company* magazine with the headline, "He Sold His Soul to Wal-Mart."[2] How did one of the world's most vocal environmentalists, board member of the Apollo Clean Energy Alliance, and founder of environmental film and consulting company Act Now end up working with Wal-Mart? And why?

Did Werbach sell his soul? Some people, including Robert Greenwald, the director of the critical documentary *Wal-Mart: The High Cost of Low Price*, thought so. "It's sad. It's really sad . . . They've bought a bunch of people instead of taking care of their employees. And they bought environmental people because they knew that was the weak link."[3] A blogger for the *San Francisco Bay Guardian* wrote, "Adam Werbach makes me puke." Arguing that Walmart's business model was fundamentally opposed to sustainability principles, he stated, "You can't make Wal-Mart anything but an environmental train wreck and an economic disaster, and to even try gives credibility to a truly awful corporation with a horrible business model."[4] A blogger for Grist wrote that Werbach had abandoned his principles:

> Let's be really blunt: there is *no such thing* as a green big box that is full of exploited workers selling you cheap disposable stuff made in sweatshops on the other side of the planet. Whenever environmentalists help Wal-Mart score easy 'corporate responsibility' points [. . .], they set back the efforts of working people in *their* battle with Wal-Mart.[5]

The author of the *Fast Company* article wondered if Werbach was "just being used."

Perhaps one could not help but be skeptical of a company that was under assault for its labor practices, discrimination against women, and impact on communities making an announcement that it would focus on sustainability. It sounded like the ultimate greenwashing exercise. Walmart hired McKinsey & Company to do a study for it, which ended up showing that 2 to 8 percent of Walmart shoppers had stopped shopping there because of all of the negative press the company had received. People inside and outside the company had started referring to the problem as "headline risk."[6] Others thought of it as the "funeral problem": in the headquarters town of Bentonville, Arkansas, everything seemed fine, but when an executive went out of town for a funeral, he was inevitably confronted with the question, "You work for *that* company?"[7] Further, if Walmart has exhausted most of the rural locations that were the origins of its growth and needs to move into cities, then maybe positive PR around sustainability could open doors in San Francisco or New York.

It is worth exploring what Walmart set out to do and what it has accomplished. In 2005, Walmart CEO Lee Scott announced three goals for the company: to be supplied 100 percent by renewable energy, to create zero waste, and to sell products that sustain our resources and the environment. The next year, he got his own cover story. He appeared in the August 7, 2006, issue of *Fortune* with the caption, "Wal-Mart Saves the Planet. Well, not quite. But CEO Lee Scott's green campaign, which started as PR, is becoming a force of nature."[8]

As part of this initiative, Scott consulted with a number of environmental experts, including Werbach, who had left the Sierra Club and was running an environmental consulting firm, Act Now (his firm was later acquired by Saatchi & Saatchi advertising to become Saatchi & Saatchi S, where the *S* stands for sustainability). Werbach's move had come after his own disillusionment with environmental activism, which he felt had not achieved its objectives. In a speech in December 2004, he said, "I am done calling myself an environmentalist." He wanted a "plan to activate the values we share with the majority of Americans" rather than focused on the elites. He wanted to make sustainability personal to everyone.[9] He concluded, "We will get to where we want to go, but we can't get there on the road we've been on."[10]

This speech made him persona non grata with the environmental movement, but it caught the attention of Walmart executives. The new head of sustainability at Walmart, Andy Ruben, asked Werbach for a meeting. Fearing that he might get "bought," Werbach demurred. As is Walmart's way, Ruben persisted. In their first meeting, Werbach insisted, as many environmentalists had, that Walmart's business model ran counter to the very notion of sustainability. Ruben talked about Walmart's environmental ambitions; Werbach responded that this might be a fig leaf for problems with labor conditions. Said Werbach later, "I didn't buy it . . . I thought I was being spun." Then, he thought, just as many others have thought when dealing with Walmart, that the company's size and reach could enable a tremendous amount of impact. His spouse, Lyn, who was the CFO of Act Now, said, "Imagine that struggle of knowing there's an opportunity that has unprecedented reach and not taking it." Long story short: Werbach ended up working with "the enemy."[11]

WALKING THE TALK?

Walmart began to take steps to improve its sustainability. Said CEO Lee Scott, "It wasn't a matter of telling our story better, we had to create a better story."[12]

Who better than Walmart to make a kilowatt of electricity go twice as far, or a gallon of diesel take our trucks twice the distance? Or three times? Who better than Walmart to stretch our energy and material dollars farther than anyone ever has? To help lower our energy bills and gas prices for years to come? . . . The environment is begging for EDLC [everyday low cost] . . . for the Walmart business model. And if we do that, everyone will benefit.[13]

As described in Chapter 2, Scott listened to critics such as Steven Hamburg whose 1994 report criticized Walmart's environmental record. Hamburg later reflected, "It was a lot of green-wash. [Lee Scott] needed to do better . . . I said, 'What really matters is what's on the shelves. Wal-Mart's influence is much greater in the marketplace than in the built environment.'"[14]

Here is where Walmart's power over suppliers comes in handy. When it wanted to reduce use of water for manufacturing, plastic resin and cardboard for packaging, and fuel for shipping laundry detergent by only selling concentrated versions, the retailer could put the pressure on its suppliers, even major ones like P&G, to make the change. A. G. Lafley, CEO of P&G at the time, said, "Lee pushed me. We totally, totally changed the way we manufacture liquid laundry detergents in the US and, now, around the world."[15] Similarly, when environmentalist Hamburg focused Walmart on the light bulb—advocating for switching its product line to more energy-efficient compact fluorescent light (CFL) bulbs—as a win-win, Walmart leaned on GE and other suppliers.[16] GE was hesitant. It did not want to give up the prime shelf space for its then best-selling product, the standard incandescent bulb. GE leaders weren't sure that CFLs would perform well enough to satisfy consumers' expectations. As journalist Charles Fishman pointed out at the time, "GE can either help Wal-Mart sell [CFL] swirls, or some other light bulb company will. In either case, GE's regular-bulb business shrivels . . . The only way to survive creative destruction, in fact, is to get out in front of the tsunami, to catch the wave." And GE did. Said Lorraine Bolsinger, GE's ecomagination VP, "The business case is pretty clear. If we don't grab the market share of CFLs, we lose." Later, as technology changed, the conversation evolved from CFLs to LEDs, with the same logic repeating itself over again.[17]

Getting Walmart into the green-products game means that going green does not have to be a luxury. If only those who can afford to shop at Whole Foods (known to many as Whole Paycheck) can afford to buy environmentally friendly products, then the market (and the impact) will remain limited. As Jib Ellison, founder of the Blu Skye sustainability consultancy (which has worked with Walmart) said, "If all this sustainability stuff is just for the well-to-do, it's not going to make a difference."[18] Even skeptics seem to think that Walmart is serious. According to Rebecca Calahan Klein, president of nonprofit Organic Exchange, which works to get big brands to use organic cotton, Walmart passes her tests for commitment: that it will be completely transparent, that it is not just following a fad, and that it uses its power to alter the business model. "I've worked with businesses for 20 years," she said. "You can tell when someone is not being sincere. They don't put it in their business strategy. They don't put their best people on it." She said Walmart wasn't one of those. It was walking the talk.[19]

Indeed, Walmart has achieved quite a lot in the past decade. Nearly 1,300 suppliers use Walmart's Sustainability Index to report progress on improving production, and 3,000 more have registered to use it in the future. The index is a tool that suppliers can use to track the environmental impact of their products from sourcing through to end use.[20] By 2015, 26 percent of electricity used by Walmart was from renewable sources such as solar and wind, and 34 percent of the water used in stores was recycled. Fleet efficiency—the number of cases delivered per mile driven—has improved more than 87 percent since 2005. The company diverted—to recycling or reuse—82.4 percent of waste in the US and 68 percent internationally. And so on. Its 146-page "2015 Global Responsibility Report" devoted nearly half of its space to enumerating the company's environmental plans and accomplishments.[21] Perhaps, as one journalist asked, if Walmart can turn "conservation into a good old-fashioned American value, will it beat one of its fiercest competitors, the environmental movement, at its own game?"[22] This was certainly Adam Werbach's hope.

On the other hand, by 2015, only 65 percent of the goods sold in Walmart stores are covered by its Sustainability Index. Although its energy use and greenhouse gas emissions are down on a per-square-foot basis, Walmart has grown, so overall energy use and emissions are up. Refrigerant emissions from hydrofluorocarbons were down, but they still comprised 2.5 million metric tons per year. As environmental critics have pointed out, Walmart's business is still about selling products and doing so at the lowest prices possible. It is pressured to increase sales year over year. These business goals would seem to run counter to those of environmental goals. If lawnmowers are so cheap as to be nearly disposable, what is the impact on landfills? Now that clothing is so cheap, 10.5 million tons of it makes it to US landfills each year. Fast fashion means that it is easier for consumers to follow the latest trends. And the availability of inexpensive clothing means that one might as well buy something new rather than mend what is ripped.[23]

IS SUSTAINABILITY ALWAYS WIN-WIN?

When Lee Scott announced the sustainability initiative, he argued that

> For Walmart to be successful and continue to grow, we must operate in a world that is healthy and successful. Of course, we are acutely aware that we have a business to run, and run it we will. At the same time, we believe that these initiatives and many more to come will make us a more competitive and innovative company, and one that is more relevant to our customers. Again, for us there is virtually no distinction between being a responsible citizen and a successful business . . . they are one and the same for Walmart today.[24]

Scott claimed that there was no conflict in the pursuit of profits and the pursuit of sustainability. By this logic, the sustainability initiative had a business case and not just an environmental-benefits case. In fact, according to MIT researchers, this is the new mantra of many companies promoting sustainability initiatives, where sustainability-oriented innovation is "about dispelling the notion of trade-offs between what seem to be competing goals—performance versus impact, profit versus purpose, human wellbeing versus environmental protection."[25]

I wanted to know what happens when Walmart cannot make the business case for a particular environmental initiative. In the context of a webinar on waste management hosted by UL Environment, I asked the senior director of business strategy and sustainability for Walmart Stores, Inc., whether the company moves forward with programs to reduce waste if it can't make the business case. What happens when the financials are not positive? He said,

> We always create a business case around the initiatives. Sometimes it is easier or harder depending on available data. If it doesn't show a positive fi-

nancial outcome, we will ask two questions. If we do a pilot, Do we see a path that would shorten a path to profitability? Then, we will move forward with the intention that, as we scale, the financials will come in line. Or, if we can't get there with scaling, What are changes to process and technology required in order to move forward? We had a number of processes or technologies that didn't originally show a strong business case to begin with, but six months or two years later, they have matured to the point that, when we look at it again, we do see the path to profitability and will move forward with a pilot and then full implementation.[26]

The summary is that Walmart needs a business case. Without that ammunition for action, the company often launches experiments. When there is no consensus, it is ultimately up to the individual business units to decide whether or not to implement the programs. The corporate team at Walmart works with the stores and regions to develop waste-management programs. Ultimately, the corporate team will help the businesses gather the right information. They partner with outside organizations such as UL Environment and the Environmental Defense Fund "to inform our approach with science and best practice." They develop pilots (experiments) in solutions that could prove out the business case in the future. Sometimes there is no agreement on whether the numbers support action: "We put on a business lens, but it also boils down to the question about whether it is the right thing to do or not, and often that is the tiebreaker."

This is where the Mode 2 notion of shared value breaks down. The principle behind this concept popularized by Michael Porter and Mark Kramer—one that has been extraordinarily motivating for many managers in companies around the world—is that it would be possible to "generat[e] economic value in a way that also produces value for society by addressing its challenges."[27] As Porter and Kramer propose, and as Walmart and many other companies have found, there are many occasions to create such win-win outcomes. Companies are often wasteful simply due to habit or lack of knowledge about new technologies or new processes. Uncovering these opportunities has huge upsides for both the companies that find them and for society, which benefits from an improved environment.

There are two challenges. The first, as I showed in earlier chapters, is that pursuing opportunities for shared value is not cost free. Some are fairly easy to implement, such as switching the compact fluorescent bulbs to eye level in stores and moving more-wasteful incandescent ones to lower shelves, selling laptops with the energy-saving mode set as the default, or stocking organic products. But even retrofitting stores with energy-efficient LED lights is a knotty problem. Though LED lights save energy directly by using less electricity to make light and indirectly by emitting less heat and thus saving on cooling costs in refrigerator and freezer cases, Walmart did not adopt these measures immediately. As its vendor from GE admitted, achieving the target internal rate of return was the barrier to implementation:

> Across the board, it had to align [with the internal rate of return], but where the trick of it was, it didn't align everywhere. We had to understand where it made sense to achieve a win-win. LED didn't make sense in most applications at that time [when Walmart began considering LED]. That's why we started in signage and then refrigeration lighting. After Walmart implemented the solution, we took it to the rest of the market. At that time, it didn't make sense in parking lots and on the sales floor, where the bulk of energy use was. Now it does. LED technology has improved, and costs and color properties have improved significantly. Now it's starting to make sense in all applications.[28]

Again, we see that where there is a win-win, Walmart will adopt the changes. Where the economics don't work, it will not (at least not yet). This, of course, sounds like common sense from a business standpoint. What it implies, though, is that sharing value only works to the extent that the business imperatives are met. One of the wins dominates the other. The risk is that we get only environmental initiatives that meet corporate priorities and none that do not.

As I mentioned in Chapter 6, C. K. Prahalad and colleagues have taken this concern head-on, suggesting that social goods such as those embodied in sustainability goals can be sources of innovation that can lead to new sources of competitive advantage. They say optimistically, "Becoming environment-friendly lowers costs because companies end up reducing the inputs they use. In addition, the process generates additional revenues from better products or enables companies to create new businesses."[29] Indeed, this was the logic behind Lee Scott's sustainability initiative: he felt that focusing the company on sustainability could save money, sell products consumers wanted, reinvigorate the culture, and attract and retain the best talent.[30]

Thus, the second challenge is that achieving the win-win requires innovation. This is Mode 3. Most of the potentially win-win solutions are not immediately available or evident. They often require innovation to come up with alternative approaches that meet both the economic and social obligations.

At the most basic level, Prahalad and colleagues argue, companies can see compliance with regulation (or with anticipated future regulation) as an opportunity rather than a constraint. They cite Hewlett-Packard's anticipation of restrictions on the use of lead in electronics. The company innovated in alternative solders using tin, silver, and copper, which enabled the manufacturer to easily comply with a 2006 European hazardous substance directive when it came into effect. This anticipation avoided the dislocation that would have occurred if the company had waited until the last minute to comply with these regulations. More ambitiously, companies have the opportunity, they argue, to increase efficiencies throughout their value chains or develop sustainable offerings that will appeal to more-demanding customers or open up new markets. P&G's Tide Coldwater detergent, which allows laundry to be done with cold water alone, thus saving energy for end users, or Clorox's Green Works (the first nonsynthetic line of cleaning products sold by a major consumer products company) are innovations that do good and could also increase sales.

Still, investing in sustainability-oriented innovation, as with all innovation, can be costly, takes time, and comes with substantial uncertainties about whether solutions can be found. Companies must make investments today for uncertain payoffs in the future. Just because companies pursue sustainability, there is no guarantee that they will be able to achieve the desired outcomes. Expensive innovation efforts might reduce short-term financial performance because they are costly, and they might not produce improved environmental benefits because they are uncertain. Instead of win-win, there is a possibility that a sustainability initiative might end up being lose-lose. This is in part why we see more companies pursuing those initiatives that can be very clearly associated with short-term financial or market benefits.

What about the situations where there isn't a clear win-win? Where innovation is not (yet) possible or is much too expensive? In these cases, there is no shared value. There is not a bigger pie from which everyone can eat. Companies are faced, at least in that moment, with real trade-offs. It is not just a matter of banishing the sustainability trade-off mind-set. The question is, How will these cases be decided? If the bottom line always trumps other factors, if the first win of the win-win equation is the rate limiter, then progress on sustainability will always and only be dictated by corporate agendas.

This is the risk of putting the establishment of environmental standards in the hands of corporations. Some have said of Walmart's Sustainability Index that the company has become "a sort of privatized Environmental Protection Agency, only with a lot more clout."[31] Much as in the case of labor standards in the manufacturing supplier base, self-regulation means that we may be beholden to only getting the environmental win if the bottom-line win is ensured.[32]

PERHAPS IT IS UP TO CONSUMERS?

Many have argued that market mechanisms are the best means to motivate environmental progress. If consumers changed what they wanted, then companies like Walmart would follow. Werbach's work with Walmart was focused in part on making sustainability something that consumers cared about. In a visit to the Rotman School, Werbach talked about the Personal Sustainability Project program that he helped launch at Walmart. The goal was to connect an individual worker's personal goals with their impact on the greater environment. Some wanted to lose weight, so they decided to bike to work some days. Not only is this healthy for the individual, but it puts less pollution into the air and less wear and tear on the roads. Another decided not to eat meat at least one meal per week. Reducing meat eating is generally good for one's health, but it also reduces consumption of proteins that are produced with large amounts of water and food resources. Werbach's insight was that the environmental movement might have focused too much on

> blunt-force scare tactic[s] . . . For too long, environmentalists have been telling people they need to sacrifice. But the great modern challenge is how to be happy. This is the missing link . . . People care about themselves first, so you have to start with what's important in their lives.[33]

Werbach next turned to a new business idea, launching Yerdle.com, which originally was focused on what he calls "personal sustainability." He seemed more and more convinced that improvements to the environment will be driven by consumers as they make individual decisions. Yerdle is another of the businesses being built in the "sharing economy." As it was initially designed, individuals would post pictures of items they did not need anymore and then ship the items free of charge to others who wanted them. In exchange, consumers got Yerdle Reuse Dollars that let them get other items posted on the site. The organization's mission was "to reduce the number of new things we all need to buy by 25%."

In the Black Friday (November 23, 2012) blog post announcing the creation of Yerdle, Werbach and cofounder Andy Ruben argued that the corporate sustainability movement is "still failing at its most fundamental goal: to protect the future of life on the planet." Corporations, they argued, will always be focused on the bottom line, and therefore their efforts will mostly stop at reducing packaging or selling more energy-efficient light bulbs. Inspired by books like Rachel Botsman's *What's Mine Is Yours* and Lisa Gansky's *The Mesh*, they suggested that real change would come only when consumers move from an "ownership" to an "access" model for using things.[34]

One worries, of course, about pushing the responsibility down to individuals. Can we and should we rely on the actions of individuals as consumers to change the tide on environmental degradation? Do we have to accept the existing system as the constraint on action, forcing us to work within it rather than change it? Might this approach be an accession to the neoliberal project to push all social responsibility down to individuals such that market mechanisms are the only force at play? One might argue that people should think of themselves not only as consumers, shaping society through their choice of where to spend their money, but also as citizens, making a difference through collective political and social action. By focusing on individual personal sustainability, are we giving up somehow on making change at a larger scale than one individual at a time? Werbach became frustrated with the progress of the political agenda he pursued through the Sierra Club and abandoned it for an effort to change large corporations through his work with Act Now and later Saatchi & Saatchi S. Frustrated with the inability to move companies beyond the quick wins or solutions that still meet the bottom line, he is now focusing on individual consumption. When it comes to the environment, simply consuming less—while helpful—is unlikely to be enough.

Rotman School researchers Nina Mažar and Chen-Bo Zhong shed some light on this dilemma. They wondered what effect green products might have on consumer behavior. In a series of experiments, they showed that shoppers who bought a basket of products such as Tom's of Maine Natural Deodorant Stick, NOMA compact fluorescent light bulbs, and Seventh Generation paper towels were more likely to cheat and steal in a subsequent task than those who purchased more traditional products such as Speed Stick deodorant stick, Dura-Max incandescent light bulbs, or Bounty paper towels. Why would this be? Wouldn't green consumption be part of a broader sense of social responsibility and morality? Mažar and Zhong argue that such purchases actually give people "moral credentials" that license less-savory behavior. Buying green products increases people's sense of themselves as moral and therefore can be seen to balance out their other less-moral actions.[35] This licensing effect is evident in all sorts of related domains, where gender-egalitarian acts license gender discrimination, reminders of humanitarian traits reduce charitable donations, and the presence of healthy food items on a menu actually increases the likelihood that people will order a side of fries rather than a side salad.[36]

By 2018, Yerdle.com had pivoted. Its model has moved toward focusing on reselling items returned to retailers. It turns out consumers don't really want to reuse products as much as Werbach would hope.[37]

So perhaps we cannot depend on market mechanisms such as consumer demand to place checks and balances on the achievement of environmental wins. People as citizens rather than as consumers can also change the economic equation such that it becomes too costly for companies not to make decisions that favor the environment. That's what protests and social-media campaigns can do. Think of Greenpeace's long efforts to stymie Shell Oil's attempts to drill in the Arctic. By having activists board a ship carrying a drilling rig in the Pacific Ocean on the way to Alaska, use kayaks in a Seattle port as a blockade to impede movement of another drilling rig there, and dangle from the St. Johns Bridge in Portland, Oregon, to block an icebreaker that had gone there for repairs, Greenpeace called global attention to Shell's activities. When Shell later announced that, after $7 billion of investment in Arctic explorations, it was ceasing its efforts, Greenpeace UK's executive director announced that "Big oil has sustained an unmitigated defeat . . . The Save the Arctic movement has exacted a huge reputational price from Shell for its Arctic drilling program."[38] One might argue that a more important impetus might have been falling oil prices, but Shell had sustained drilling even as prices fell. At a minimum, the protests and the resulting reputational costs began to figure into Shell's calculations, making already expensive exploration efforts even more costly.

Many social activists have sought to keep Walmart in check too, whether in the class-action lawsuit claiming discrimination against women, the local protests in towns across the US and around the world when Walmart is planning to bring a store to town, or in the OUR Walmart labor advocacy group that has staged strikes over labor standards. Although most of these efforts have not achieved their aims—the class action was not certified by the US Supreme Court; many Walmart stores still open despite protests; Walmart stores in the US are not unionized—they have had their impact. As some have claimed, they may have even put more energy behind Walmart's environmental activities as a way to balance out some of the negative claims in these other areas. Similarly, the global boycott movement against Nike's sweatshop practices in the 1990s put so much pressure on the company that Nike has become the gold standard in manufacturing (even if the gold standard is not really as golden as activists might hope it would be).

THRIVING WITHIN TRADE-OFFS

Perhaps because consumers cannot be relied upon to create demand for sustainability initiatives, companies have to find ways to achieve sustainability without compromising the other features of products that consumers actually demand. The Nike Air Jordan XX3 is an example.

On January 8, 2008, Nike announced the launch of the Air Jordan XX3. The number 23 represented the number of years that Nike had been making Air Jordans. It was also Michael Jordan's number when he played for the Chicago Bulls. So it is no surprise that Jordan himself said in the press release, "The AIR JORDAN XX3 is deeply meaningful to me, as a celebration of both my life and career. The number 23 is obviously of great significance to me and the release of the XX3 is a pinnacle moment in the Brand's history." Fans agreed. Said one collector,

Any fan would understand the surge of adrenalin that rushes through your body when you find out that there's a launch of the latest shoe in the series. Each and every Jordan sneaker is like a piece of art. I have more than half the collection and I'm attempting to collect the entire series. Needless to say, 23 is the most important piece in the collection because it's his number.[39]

Nike treated this product as it did all of its elite products: with a limited release. On January 25, the company provided 23 pairs of shoes in each of only 23 stores (at a price of $230). Then it offered an All-Star release on February 16 and a nationwide launch on February 23 (at a price of $185).[40] The star-studded launch party included sports stars Ray Allen, Chris Paul, Alonzo Mourning, Carmelo Anthony, Warren Sapp, Dre Bly, Kevin Durant, Brandon Roy, and Paul Pierce, as well as music and media personalities Bun B, Chamillionaire, Chris Tucker, Stuart Scott, and Gabrielle Union.[41] So popular was the shoe—it was the most sought after of Jordan's post-playing-day models—that it was "retro'd" (reintroduced) in 2015 in an all-red Chicago version. The original Air Jordan XX3s show up on eBay today for a thousand dollars or more.

What is perhaps more interesting is that it was also the first basketball shoe that was designed using the Nike Considered approach, which aimed to improve the environmental impact of the company's products. Said star Nike designer Tinker Hatfield,

> Our goal was to make the Air Jordan XX3 the best basketball shoe ever, both in performance and sustainability . . . By infusing the ultimate in technology, setting a new trend in style and designing a shoe with the environment in mind, we hope these ingredients will cause people to say this is one of their favorite Air Jordans ever.[42]

Starting in 1997, as Nike was reeling from the protests and boycotts targeting manufacturing practices and labor standards in its factories, the company began an effort to rethink how its products were made. This extended not just to working conditions but also instigated a conversation about the whole manufacturing approach. After announcing new initiatives to integrate sustainability into all major business decisions and look at environmental impacts in every stage of the product life cycle, Nike began, starting in 1999, to eliminate the use of polyvinyl chloride in shoes, a compound that had previously made up almost 30 percent of the total shoe. Recognizing that cotton production uses more chemicals than any other crop, Nike also began using organic cotton in knit products. It extended the Reuse-a-Shoe program (launched in 1993) to keep used athletic shoes out of landfills by grinding them up to create the Nike Grind product for use in basketball courts, playgrounds, and athletic tracks. In 2000, the company began assessing the chemical composition and environmental impact of the materials and processes used to produce Nike shoes, creating a positive list of materials that met eco-friendly criteria and a negative list of those that should be targeted for elimination. Also in 2000, Nike initiated a corporate-wide sustainability-training program. In 2001, it created a corporate responsibility committee chaired by the CEO. In 2003, it began assessing the environmental impact of inbound logistics.[43] In 2004, Hannah Jones was appointed to the new position of VP of corporate responsibility.

Yet despite or perhaps because of these efforts, Jones discovered a company averse to any corporate responsibility activities. The people designing the products and running the businesses were tired of "moral judgments" being imposed on them. They cared more about performance and profits. Jones's first step was Mode 2 action: she had to "show the business people how we're going to help them deliver returns on investment to our shareholders." She needed to find a way to infuse sustainability into the daily activities of designers. She, along with Mark Parker (then co-president of the Nike brand, now Nike's CEO) and John Hoke (VP of footwear design), formed the Considered Group, whose mandate was to provide tools and inspiration to the product design teams. Importantly, they created the Considered Index, which gave targets and guidelines for use of environmentally preferred materials, reducing the use of solvents, and eliminating waste. Each product design would be rated according to a series of criteria and would earn—borrowing from the Olympics—gold, silver, bronze, or "unrated" scores. Only gold and silver were deemed to have met the Considered targets. This approach activated the competitiveness of the design teams who, coming from a sports mind-set, all wanted top ratings.[44]

The second step was Mode 3 innovation. The first Nike Considered shoe was released in 2005. It was a boot that definitely looked "eco-friendly." The upper was woven from a single hemp shoelace, and it was made out of "Vege-tan" leather in earthy tones. And it was ecological. The production of the shoe reduced manufacturing waste by 61 percent, energy consumption by 35 percent, and use of solvents by 89 percent.[45] Although it won a gold IDEA award for environmental design, some mocked the shoes by calling them "Air Hobbits."[46]

FIGURE 8.1. Nike's "Considered" boot. Source: Nike.

That is, Nike seemed to think that to be environmentally friendly, the product must also look environmentally friendly.

The boot itself was not a huge sales success. The real success was that it allowed Nike to experiment with whole new processes, rethinking the design approach, the materials used, and the assembly process. It was that experience that contributed to the company's ability to use the Considered approach in the Air Jordan XX3. Here's how the Jordan XX3 designers did it. To reduce the use of adhesives, they designed the outsole, midsole, and other parts of the shoe to fit together like pieces of a jigsaw puzzle. They also used more stitching, which involved the invention of a sewing machine that could make what they called 3D stitches around the whole shoe (where previously sewing could be done only on flat portions). They used a water-based bonding process that attached the carbon fiber plate in the shoe without solvent-based cements. The shoe also used several of Nike's environmentally preferred materials such as reused material from the Nike Grind program for the outsole.

The significance of making the Air Jordan XX3 a Nike Considered product is that it attempts to abolish the trade-off between environmental performance and athletic and design performance. In fact, in some ways, the desire for environmental performance drove innovations that contributed to unique design features, such as the 3D stitching that became the signature look of the shoe but was instigated by the goal to reduce the use of adhesives. Said Mark Smith, one of the members of Nike's R&D group, the Innovation Kitchen,

It was the most important thing we could do with this shoe—to take the best playing shoe and make the best playing shoe a shoe that could stand as a new way to build shoes. So much of the way the shoe looks is dependent on it being Considered.[47]

More importantly, it signaled to designers throughout the company that there was no excuse for not using the Considered approach. Designers often assumed that there would necessarily be a trade-off with performance. For Nike, performance is everything. But the Air Jordan XX3 forced designers to ask if there was necessarily a trade-off. According to Lorrie Vogel, manager of the Considered team, "Before, somebody might have said, 'I can't do it. My product has so much stress on it. It's in the Olympics.' The Jordan XX3 stopped them from talking on that end."[48] Of course, the shoe isn't perfectly environmentally friendly. As Nike designer Tinker Hatfield said, "We didn't completely eliminate adhesives, but came close."[49] The trade-offs are still there, but the Jordan XX3 showed that getting over the hurdle was more possible than many had thought. It is worth keeping in mind that getting over the hurdle for the Jordan

FIGURE 8.2. Nike Air Jordan XX3. Source: Flight Club. Reprinted with permission.

XX3 required the invention of a machine that could stitch a shoe while holding it upright and create the spectacular design patterns that were one of the important signatures of the shoe, the creation of alternative glues, the development of new jigsaw-puzzle component design principles, and so on. In short, it was the product of a lot of innovation.

Indeed, Nike's "FY16/17 Sustainable Business Report" called out the "innovation gap," stating,

> Simply hitting . . . targets or scaling proven technologies and best practices will not be enough to halve our environmental impact. Achieving our moonshot will require new technologies yet to be invented and partnerships yet to be forged. Our focus on closing this innovation gap means we're doubling down on invention, design, and collaboration unlike ever before. We're challenging ourselves to imagine a different future, using our position at the forefront of manufacturing engineering and science to reimagine technologies and catalyze new processes.[50]

WHAT DO YOU DO WHEN THERE ISN'T A WIN-WIN?

Most Nike executives are quick to point out that the Considered ethos should be good for the bottom line and good for the environment. This is where Mode 2 and Mode 3 action get you. According to Lorrie Vogel, general manager for Nike Considered, "This is good for the environment, and good from a profitability standpoint. Our stakeholders and our stockholders want to see that."[51] Hannah Jones, head of corporate responsibility at Nike, echoes the point: "No work is more powerful in proving the business case for corporate responsibility and driving innovation into the heart of corporate responsibility than that work being undertaken to create sustainable products and business models—this is our Considered Design ethos."[52]

The challenge for Nike is that the company needs to achieve not just win-win but win-win-win. That is, achieving positive environmental impacts is possible only if it can also hit the profit point *and* deliver athletic and design performance. Whether it is the fifteen-year old kid or the top athlete, customers want what is cool and what will give them a performance edge. Designer Tinker Hatfield put it this way: "Being green isn't enough. We want to be a change agent, but also profitable and [to] make good business moves."[53] A fundamental challenge was, of course, cost, as environmentally preferred materials were usually more expensive than the standard materials. This can lead to some impasses. Most companies stop here, if they even get this far. Nike offers us examples of what I call Mode 4 action: thriving within the trade-offs.

Take for example the gases used in the Nike Air pockets in the soles of the shoes to give spring while maintaining flexibility. These pockets are a signature of so many of Nike's shoes, but from their origins were filled with sulfur hexafluoride, a noxious greenhouse gas with 23,000 times the global warming potential of carbon dioxide due to its heat-trapping capacity. By the 1990s, environmental groups were pushing Nike to eliminate use of the gas, listed in the Kyoto Protocol of 1997, which aimed to reduce greenhouse gases. Nike missed deadlines in 2000 and 2003 to make progress. Company leaders knew that nitrogen could be used as a replacement gas, but it did not durably maintain the air pockets. By 2007, and after several million dollars of R&D investment, Nike found a means for packing nitrogen so that it would not break down. The result was smaller and less visible air pockets. It was only then that Nike announced that it had phased out sulfur hexafluoride.

This could be pitched as a negative or a positive story. On the negative side, for nearly a decade while the research was going on, Nike continued to use a product that it knew was troublesome for the environment.[54] Perhaps that is why the environmental product ratings by the Ethical Consumer in the UK gives Nike a score of only a six out of twenty (with Puma also at six and Adidas and Reebok at 5.5). On the other hand, the only big brands that do much better are Patagonia (13.5), Asics (9.5), and Sergio Tacchini (9.5). The big winners are, as you might imagine, small brands focused only on organic and recycled materials such as Gossypium yoga clothing (19.0), THTC organic clothing (16.5), and Yew sportswear made of recycled polyester (16.5).[55] When launched, the goal for the Nike Considered approach was to have all footwear meet baseline Considered standards by 2011, all apparel by 2015, and all other equipment by 2020. Yet even once Nike hits those goals, it will have achieved only a 17 percent decrease in waste, a 20 percent increase in the use of environmentally preferred materials, and the use of organic cotton in only 5 percent of cotton goods (though there would be a 95 percent reduction in the use of dangerous solvents).[56]

On the positive side, it demonstrates how some companies can deal with seemingly intractable trade-offs. Nike didn't give up on the goal; it just used a temporal solution—making the objectives long term while still pursuing profits in the short term. The company didn't stop investing. It kept at the goals until it had overcome the performance trade-offs. Ultimately its solution required design changes in which the air pockets were less visible in the design. Indeed, Nike even discovered that the new method for sealing the air pocket made it possible to put more air bubbles in the sole. This "thermoforming" allowed the manufacturer to "shape and cradle the air sole to the contour of the foot," which then contributed to the development of the hugely successful Air Max 360.[57]

We could also go back to the famous concentrated laundry detergent example from Chapter 3. Walmart didn't implement this strategy overnight. Instead, it designed a pilot with one supplier (Unilever), using the experiment to work out the kinks in the system. When that pilot was successful, the result created the legitimacy Walmart needed to make similar demands of other suppliers. It also built a road map for everyone else to follow. These examples are both approaches to holding the trade-offs in tension while solutions are worked out. Suppliers would not have accommodated Walmart's request if Walmart hadn't worked out agreements on shelf space, consumer education programs, and training for employees on the new products. Finding this model was the key to success.

Is it enough? When companies are left to regulate themselves and set their own targets, do we get enough progress? Whether individual corporate goals or companies banding together to create industry consortia, as Barbara Kyle, direct of the Electronics TakeBack Coalition, points out, "You end up with manufacturers voting only for criteria that they already meet."[58] This is a place where more regulation could be helpful, though we know that companies are prone to navigating around such rules, as the 2015 revelation that Volkswagen used software to get around emissions testing in millions of its vehicles shows.[59] On the other hand, companies can use regulation as an inspiration for innovation: rather than circumvent regulations (as Volkswagen did), companies can innovate with the regulations.

BACK TO CREATIVE DESTRUCTION

One commentator, inspired by the rapid decline of Volkswagen's brand image, sales, and profits after its emissions deceptions were uncovered in 2015, remarked, "Sustainability is an evolutionary force of creative market destruction and is slowly weeding out the firms and products unfit for a sustainable future."[60] The pressure is on—whether from consumers, activists, employees, investment funds and others—and companies are being challenged to address the increasingly urgent social and environmental challenges that face us today.

So what can a company do to survive and thrive in the face of intractable tensions between the needs and interests of different stakeholders?

First, and yet again, I'm going to start with getting granular on the trade-offs. If you can figure out exactly where the business case for change breaks down (Mode 1), you can work in a more targeted way on answers. The more specific you can be, the more likely a new solution can emerge.

Second, given that you might hit a wall, the most-effective companies will break ties in favor of doing something new. If there isn't agreement about whether there is a business case for action or not (Mode 2), decide on the side of action. Forward movement may provoke innovative solutions (Mode 3). Just as Nike did with its ultimately failed Nike Considered boot (also known colloquially as the Air Hobbit), combining a bias for action with a learning mind-set can eventually turn tough trade-offs into more tractable solutions.

Third, when solutions aren't readily apparent, that's where Mode 4 action comes in. It's worth the effort to identify pilots that break the trade-offs. You don't have to change the whole organization at once. You can use experiments to learn about what future solutions might look like. Even those experiments that fail in the lab or the marketplace may be tremendous sources of learning and stepladders to the next experiment. One way of doing this is to separate out activities aimed at pursuing one goal from those aimed at pursuing others. Successful companies can think about framing some of the conflicting goals as long-term objectives. Sometimes you can pursue the social objective in hopes that profits will come in the long run. Sometimes you can pursue profits now and make the social goal a longer-term objective, as Nike did with substituting less-dangerous chemicals in shoe air pockets. All of these are strategies for living with the tensions created by the trade-offs.

It is precisely the impasses that can provoke the biggest insights. Impasses are uncomfortable, but the discomfort can lead to breakthroughs, experiments, and new ways of thinking. Facing impasses also takes courage. Organizations naturally fight back on change. Managers with incentives based on the bottom line will object to the perceived moral judgments (as Nike managers originally did) imposed by corporate social responsibility. Our models of authoritative leadership push away ambiguity in favor of clear choices. What I have found is that the best companies and the best leaders thrive within these tensions.

• PART IV SIGNPOSTS

- Not all trade-offs are readily amenable to the creation of business cases for action (Mode 2) or innovative solutions (Mode 3). Some trade-offs appear to be truly intractable.

- If you can figure out exactly where the business case for change breaks down (Mode 1), you can work in a more targeted way on answers. The more specific you can be, the more likely it is that a new solution can emerge.

- If you hit a wall, follow the lead of the most effective companies: break ties in favor of doing something new. If there isn't agreement about whether there is a business case for action or not, decide on the side of action. Combining a bias for action with a learning mind-set can eventually turn tough trade-offs into more tractable solutions.

- When solutions aren't readily apparent, that's where Mode 4 action comes in. It's worth the effort to identify pilots that break the trade-offs. You don't have to change the whole organization at once. You can use experiments to learn about what future solutions might look like. Even those experiments that fail in the lab or the marketplace may be tremendous sources of learning and stepladders to the next experiment.

- One way of pursuing Mode 4 action is to separate out activities aimed at pursuing one goal from those aimed at pursuing others. Sometimes you can pursue the social objective in hopes that profits will come in the long run. Sometimes you can pursue profits now and make the social goal a longer-term objective. All of these are strategies for living with the tensions created by the trade-offs.

- It is precisely the trade-off impasses that can provoke the biggest insights. Impasses are uncomfortable, but the discomfort can lead to breakthroughs, experiments, and new ways of thinking. Facing impasses also takes courage. Organizations naturally fight back on change. Managers with incentives based on the bottom line will object to perceived moral judgments imposed by corporate social responsibility. Models of authoritative leadership push away ambiguity in favor of clear choices. The best companies and the best leaders thrive within these tensions.

PART V

SPEARHEADING THE 360° REVOLUTION

CHAPTER 9

THE 360° CEO

Signposts for the Organizational Leader

LET'S RETURN TO WHERE I started this book: Hurricane Katrina. When I asked Kathleen McLaughlin, Walmart's chief sustainability officer, about what started her company's journey toward sustainability, she said it started at that moment:

> That event [Katrina] was so cataclysmic that it literally changed the way our leadership team thought. In the weeks that followed, they sat back and asked themselves, "What if we could be that kind of company every single day? What would that be like?" Lee had a personal epiphany: "We are the largest retail[er] in the world—we are truly driving consumption on a global basis; maybe we should figure out a way to make this all circular." That fall, he gave a speech titled "21st Century Leadership," and in it, he set three broad goals for Walmart: to be supplied by 100 per cent renewable energy, to create zero waste and to sell sustainable products. At the time, I was, like, what? Walmart? It was a great surprise. One thing I've come to appreciate since joining the company is that, when Walmart says it's going to do something, it does it. It's a very execution-oriented company. For ten years now,

this is what people have been working on. *The whole system has changed*, and it's just getting better and better, as our people develop these programs and work closely with hundreds of suppliers, other retailers, government agencies and non-profits.[1]

What does it take to spearhead the 360° revolution? The first thing you are likely thinking is that this book made the problem seem harder than you wanted it to be. As Kathleen McLaughlin says, the whole system may have to change. Telling you that some trade-offs might be, at least for the moment, intractable is perhaps not the most inspiring message (though it may be a bit of a relief to those of you who thought you should be able to find shared value lying around everywhere).

On the flip side, the modes of action I introduce in this book can be the signposts toward progress. Sometimes you can make a business case for taking into account new sets of stakeholders. Sometimes there is no business case to be had. Thus, leaders must mobilize an organization's innovative abilities to create the business case and cope with the unresolved tensions that arise when the needs of stakeholders compete with each other.

The 360° Corporation requires a 360° CEO. CEOs are taking notice of this responsibility. At *Fortune*'s CEO Initiative Summit in the past few years, the recurring theme was CEO engagement in social issues and the need for these executives to participate in a moral revolution. CEOs Tim Cook of Apple, Ed Bastian of Delta, Mikkel Svane of Zendesk, Chip Bergh of Levi Strauss, Blake Irving of GoDaddy, Bernard Tyson of Kaiser Permanente, and Jamie Dimon of JPMorgan Chase all appeared at the events to talk about how they want to change the world. These challenges are clearly top of mind.[2]

Then there's the Monday morning question. You arrive at work, and what should you start doing? Let me propose a few concrete actions that will enable you as a leader to envision, inspire, and manage the necessary organizational change that goes along with becoming a 360° Corporation.

First, an observation. After I initially wrote these recommendations, I realized that they didn't sound much like our traditional notions of the command-and-control leader. I'm not the only one to say that leadership in the twenty-first century is going to require a new set of skills, ones that are more about collaboration than authority, more focused on inquiry than answers, more about mobilizing talented people than instructing them, more about humility than aggrandizement, more about conversation than rapid-fire decision-making. These characteristics become even more important when we consider the new imperative to lead companies not just to achieve shareholder objectives but to address all of the stakeholders that encircle the organization. The leadership challenge for the 360° revolution is one fraught with unknowns, complexity, and sometimes unresolvable tensions. Yet it is also filled with inspiration, creativity, passion, and meaning. The difficulties are what make possible the breakthroughs.

Second, an exhortation. Leading the 360° Corporation is a transformative process. You don't add on social goals to the day-to-day business, sprinkling some "feel good" on top of profit-and-loss statements. It's going to take courage to lead the revolution. Courage to be open to new conversations; courage to listen to criticisms and transform them into opportunities; courage to challenge employees, peers, and bosses to think differently about the business and change their habits; courage to take actions with uncertain futures; courage to learn along the way; courage to do the right thing even as others might press you not to; courage to take the heat after you make tough choices. I could go on with the list. In short, it is going to be potentially uncomfortable and inconvenient, but it is still worth doing.

Here's what you can do.

1. **Ask questions.** Start with inquiry. Solutions are hard to find if no one is asking people to find them. Questions are a critical starting point for any action, and they should be asked at all levels of the organization, from the front line to the C-suite. In my last book, *Creative Destruction*, I wrote about the leader of the organization as a creator of conversations. The recommendation does not change here, except that the need for conversation is even more intense in the face of the sometimes-intractable tensions created by trade-offs among stakeholders. These questions (see Table 9.1) will lead the organization to look 360 degrees around you.

2. **Cocreate with stakeholders.** Engage them in an open dialogue about the issues, concerns, and perspectives. This could be through stakeholder advisory boards, open-source initiatives, town halls, and other two-way (or multidirectional) methods of engagement. By engaging in good faith with stakeholders, companies will be clearer about what value is being

TABLE 9.1. Questions for the 360° CEO

Mode 1	**Ask:** For whom is value being created? For whom is value being destroyed? Who has a seat at the table? Who has been shut out? What power dynamics might make certain stakeholders more or less visible?
Mode 2	**Ask:** Are there win-win solutions that benefit stakeholders, support the profitability of internal business operations, or reduce constraints in the external competitive context? Are we using the business case as an excuse not to take action?
Mode 3	**Ask:** What innovations can we introduce that would alter the costs and benefits or eliminate the trade-offs? What if we started with the innovation imperative and worked backward to a viable economic model?
Mode 4	**Ask:** If we can't break the trade-off today, what experiments in future solutions can we run? Can we work on long-term goals while still paying attention to short-term returns? How can we use the impasses to provoke insight?

created or destroyed, and for whom. Further, these dialogues can lead to co-production of solutions in each of the modes—reframes of business models, new innovative ideas, or partnerships for running experiments for future solutions. We need to see through the eyes of each stakeholder—their points of view provide new lenses to examine the issues and, ultimately, opportunities.

3. **Use the tension** generated by opposition from stakeholders as a source of creative friction that can promote innovative solutions. Rather than fighting opponents, consider what would be possible if creative minds are put to co-producing solutions. Creative insights come from the intersections of different ways of thinking. Walmart's move toward sustainability really took off once the company gave environmentalists such as academic critic Steve Hamburg or former Sierra Club president Adam Werbach a seat at the table. Walmart listened to their concerns and invited them to participate in generating solutions. The retailer did the same with its suppliers, working to make any solutions such as concentrated liquid laundry detergent the proverbial win-win.

4. **Be willing to let go** of your current business model. More than techno-
   logical capabilities and more than market readiness, the thing that holds
   back organizations from making change is the resistance to changing
   the understanding of "how we make money."[3] The existing structure of
   the profit-and-loss statement and the existing ways that the organization makes money can come to be the frame of reference through which
   everything else is filtered. Without breaking these frames, change is impossible. This is true whether we are talking about disruptive technologies or solutions to stakeholder concerns. Changing the business model
   has important implications for how organizations function, how employees are rewarded, and what skills are needed to operate. Still, staying in the existing business model means that most trade-offs will be
   hard to break. You will likely operate only in Mode 2 (if that) and never
   get to Mode 3 or 4. Nike's efforts to improve worker conditions in the
   supply chain required transformations in how the company produced
   products globally, how it designed its products, how many varieties of
   products it could manufacture, what kinds of materials it could use, and
   ultimately how it marketed the products.

5. **Mobilize** your innovative talent to address questions of trade-offs. We
   treat product innovation as the holy grail in many industries, and we
   put our best and brightest to work on these problems. What if we focused the attention of the best and the brightest on resolving stakeholder trade-offs? What solutions might be possible if they did? Using
   trade-offs as a spur for action will likely lead to all sorts of innovative
   new product or service ideas as well. It is a truism that people work
   better and are happier if they are inspired by their work. Increasingly,
   workers—be they on the shop floor or in the executive suite—are requiring their companies to have an inspirational purpose. Study after study
   shows that millennials, in particular, consider a company's social and
   environmental commitments before deciding to take a job and will even
   take a pay cut to work for socially responsible companies.[4] It turns out
   that what works for millennials actually works for most of us.

6. **Avoid** seeing stakeholders as an add-on to the existing way of doing business. If addressing a stakeholder concern is seen as icing on the cake

rather than an integral part of the recipe for making the cake, companies will risk doing little. One might expect some incremental changes, or perhaps some temporarily positive PR, but little will be accomplished to change the underlying trade-offs. Indeed, separating stakeholder conversations from profit conversations can lead to "CSR PR": you do things to look good, but don't back it up. Think about Volkswagen. Its 24-page Code of Conduct touting the company's "responsible, honest actions" and "the most ecologically efficient advanced technologies available throughout the world" helped get Volkswagen on the Dow Jones sustainability index as the world's most sustainable carmaker in 2015, just a week before the US Environmental Protection Agency revealed the company's falsification of emissions data.[5] Needless to say, the company is not on the sustainability index anymore.

7. **Align your incentives**, both formal and informal, with the challenges posed by trade-offs. Recognize that if you talk about wanting to address stakeholder needs, but you ask about only the bottom line in quarterly reviews, then your organization will not respond to efforts to make change. The Nike and Walmart examples both show how important accountability is for change. Nike Considered comes with measurements, targets, and data. Walmart's goal to source $20 billion of products from women-owned businesses inspired a lot of innovation in order to find, train, and support those entrepreneurs. Ambitious rather than incremental targets are often necessary to break people out of existing mind-sets. When Norway mandated 40 percent quotas for women on boards, companies could no longer simply make the excuses that everyone makes about a lacking a pipeline or being unable to find qualified women. Organization leaders just went out and found female board members: they expanded their networks and rethought the criteria about what kinds of skills were required on a board. They are better off for it. Now leaders in Norway look at the quotas the way we look at no-smoking laws in restaurants. We might once have thought they would be a problem, but now we actually like them.[6] Aligning incentives provokes change in ways we couldn't anticipate and didn't know we would appreciate.

8. **Learn as you go.** Because we are at the forefront of knowledge on how to address the trade-offs between stakeholders, there are sure to be unex-

pected roadblocks to action. The key will be to learn from these experiences and find ways to work around the roadblocks or move in new and more productive directions. Point 9 below tells you to just get started. This is important because of the learning that you get by trying. At some point, analysis will not help you resolve the trade-offs you encounter. You won't have all of the answers, so the key is to figure out how to learn as you go. That's a theme that cuts across all of the recommendations, actually. Engaging stakeholders is about learning. Cocreating is about learning. A growth mind-set—the humility of curiosity—will translate into deeper, disruptive insights and faster action.

9. Finally, **get started**. Nothing I've written about is easy. Trade-offs are by definition difficult to resolve. If it were easy, we wouldn't need skilled leaders. Still, the realities of the twenty-first century demand that companies address all of their stakeholders, not just shareholders concerned only with total returns. No one has the perfect solution, but the only way forward is to start.

One of my students told me that the 360° revolution requires a leap of faith. That's probably right, but that leap makes the discovery of creative new solutions possible. Take the leap. Invite others to leap with you.

A NEW PERSPECTIVE FOR STAKEHOLDERS

THIS BOOK HAS BEEN devoted to business leaders facing the push and pull of multiple stakeholders. What if we turned the conversation on its head and asked what we can do as participants in society? We are not just workers; we are also citizens. If we care about pollution, energy use, climate change, workers' rights, consumerism, discrimination, or other problems that our current capitalist system creates, what can we do?

We are at a unique moment in time when citizens are increasingly relying on companies to achieve social objectives. Many are now expecting companies to substitute for weak or slow or damaging government action. More and more, companies are living up to those expectations. CEOs of leading US companies—led by the resignation by Kenneth Frazier, CEO of Merck, on August 14, 2017—effectively disbanded the president's American Manufacturing Council after Donald Trump failed to condemn white supremacists. Stated Frazier in a tweet:

> Our country's strength stems from its diversity and the contributions made by men and women of different faiths, races, sexual orientations and politi-

cal beliefs. America's leaders must honor our fundamental values by clearly rejecting expressions of hatred, bigotry and group supremacy, which run counter to the American ideal that all people are created equal. As CEO of Merck and as a matter of personal conscience, I feel a responsibility to take a stand against intolerance and extremism.[1]

When the US government rolled back environmental regulations in 2017, Walmart spokesman Kevin Gardner responded, "This work is embedded in our business. [It is] good for the business, our shareholders, and customers; if ultimately we are able to positively impact the environment in the process, that's a win too." Walmart's goals of getting half of its power from renewables by 2025 didn't change even as government policy changed. Apple, Amazon, Microsoft, and Alphabet (Google's parent company) wrote in a joint statement: "We believe that strong clean energy and climate policies . . . can make renewable energy suppliers more robust and address the serious threat of climate change while also supporting American competitiveness, innovation, and job growth." Procter & Gamble, Nestlé, Ikea, Levi Strauss, and Best Buy also said they wouldn't change any commitments on climate change that they made during the Obama administration.[2]

In the face of increasing mass shootings and gun violence, Levi's CEO Chip Bergh implemented gun restrictions in all of the manufacturer's facilities and invested company resources in the fight for better gun regulations by partnering with Michael Bloomberg to form Everytown Business Leaders for Gun Safety. Said Bergh in an op-ed,

[A]s business leaders with power in the public and political arenas, we simply cannot stand by silently when it comes to the issues that threaten the very fabric of the communities where we live and work. While taking a stand can be unpopular with some, doing nothing is no longer an option.[3]

Of course, the key is that these companies walk the talk. My hope is that *The 360° Corporation*'s inside look at how corporations rethink, innovate around, or live with trade-offs offers clues for how people as citizens, consumers, workers, and investors can shape the role of the corporation in society.

One important insight is that stakeholders can actually change the calculation about the relative trade-offs. If acting in ways that are contrary to the interests of certain stakeholders becomes more expensive (because of bad press, protest, liability, or lawsuits), then this makes it easier for companies to justify action. One head of sustainability at a major corporation told me, "I would never say this inside the company, but protesters help me make the case." We're seeing this, for example, in Silicon Valley companies such as Uber, Google, and Facebook, which have ended forced arbitration for sexual-harassment claims after scandals and employee protests.[4]

I started thinking about these issues in the earliest days of my consulting career. While I was spending my time working with companies to help them become more innovative and achieve greater total returns to shareholders (recall: I'd drunk the TRS Kool-Aid!), my sister Esther Kaplan was working with ACT UP, the AIDS Coalition to Unleash Power, to protest the lack of corporate and government action on AIDS. I saw her and her many compatriots get arrested for blocking the Midtown Tunnel in New York, swarming the Centers for Disease Control in Atlanta, and chaining themselves to the doors of large pharmaceutical companies. These protests got attention. It turns out, though, that attention wasn't enough.

As explored in David France's extraordinary documentary and subsequent book, *How to Survive a Plague* (and many other films, books, and articles),[5] some of these activists (who later formed the Treatment Action Group, TAG) believed that one possible avenue for change was to get a seat at the table where the decisions about clinical-trial design and drug approvals were being made—both in corporations and in the Federal Drug Administration (FDA). They prepared the FDA Action Handbook and did teach-ins on the science of AIDS for ACT UP's membership around the country. A media committee translated the information for the press, making phone calls and scheduling radio and TV appearances. They made very specific and targeted demands based, importantly, on detailed knowledge about the research and drug-approval processes. They trained themselves up on the science and used protest to force open the door. Eventually, they pushed their way to the table, where they could collaborate on drug-trial design and systems to get treatments in the hands of more people.

But protest was a critical element throughout. Even as faulty drugs such as AZT became available, activists held demonstrations at the New York Stock Exchange to protest the high prices charged by Burroughs Wellcome that made

FIGURE E.1. ACT UP protestors on the street in front of the New York Stock Exchange, September 1989. Source: Clary, Tim, The Associated Press, 1989. Reprinted with permission.

AZT unaffordable to most people with HIV. Peter Staley (a former Wall Streeter) and several other ACT UP members blockaded themselves in a Burroughs Wellcome office in April 1989, and then in September of that year, chained themselves to the stock exchange VIP balcony, sounded airhorns, and dropped a banner reading "SELL WELLCOME," interrupting the opening bell for the first time in history. ACT UP photographers who had infiltrated the exchange sent photos out to the press, and the story went as viral as you could go before the days of social media. The result: Burroughs Wellcome lowered the price of AZT a few days later.

The work of ACT UP and of other AIDS organizers such as TAG is still one of the most important templates for effective action against, and also with, corporate actors. Its battle to fight AIDS was eventually won not just in the streets but also in the boardrooms. When ACT UP and TAG got their representatives to be included as participants in the government and corporate decision-making processes to decide how clinical trials could be designed, new drugs that kept HIV from being a death sentence emerged.

Of course, there is a fine line to walk. When Peter Staley of ACT UP and later TAG worked to get into the pharmaceutical firm decision-making processes for AIDS drugs, he was accused of selling out. When Adam Werbach of the Sierra Club started working with Walmart on sustainability, he was vilified as a sellout too.

There's a risk too in writing a book on how companies can cope with trade-offs created by the differing stakeholder interests that surround them. Am I being bold enough? Am I accepting corporations for what they are? Will these guidelines change things only on the margins? I hope not. My image of the 360° Corporation is one that radically changes the corporate and leadership models that have dominated for the last thirty years or so. My view is that true collaboration, real cocreation, honest conversation, and radical innovation can help us construct new economic models.

As citizens, workers, consumers, and even investors, we can get in on the action.

Workers—through protests and strikes (or threats of strikes)—can pressure companies to change policies and practices. The labor movement has been tremendously weakened over the past few decades. Union membership in the US is declining. Yet campaigns by OUR Walmart and Making Change at Walmart around wages created enough pressure at Walmart in 2016 to increase minimum pay to $10 per hour.[6] Workers are also using social media to get their concerns heard. Think of Susan Fowler's viral blog post about the sexual harassment she experienced at Uber.[7] After she went public with her story, Uber hired former Attorney General Eric Holder to investigate. Not so long afterward, the company's board of directors ousted CEO Travis Kalanick and terminated more than twenty other employees. As we saw in Chapter 4, women at Nike used an internal survey to provoke action on the hostile work environment they faced. Job sites like Glassdoor give workers a chance to review their employers, for better or for worse. Now companies risk showing up on Glassdoor ratings-based lists of "the worst companies to work for."[8]

Perhaps, slowly but surely, we can rely on changes in consumer demand too. Despite the caveats noted in Chapter 7, shoppers can and do change their buying patterns when it comes to social issues. As consumers become more aware, for example, of the potential negative effects of food additives and processed sugars and fats, their actions are causing great consternation on the part of many food manufacturers. Sales of breakfast cereals are down 25 percent since 2000. Per-capita sales of soda are down the same amount. Meanwhile, sales of fresh prepared foods have grown 30 percent in just the last five years. What are manufacturers doing? General Mills is eliminating all artificial colors and flavors from its cereals. Hershey's will eliminate such additives as polyglycerol polyricinoleate, which chocolate makers had been using as a replacement for cocoa butter to reduce their costs of production. Meat producers such as Foster Farms are cutting down on the antibiotics they use. Nestlé is investing $50 million in an R&D facility aimed at developing healthy frozen foods.[9] Consumers are also using their power to influence how companies advertise—as they threaten to boycott companies whose ads appear next to white-supremacist content on YouTube and Google's display-ad system. The social movement organization Sleeping Giants has run a campaign specifically to shame companies whose ads appear on the extremist media site Breitbart.[10]

Investors may also play a part. Investors aren't just in it for the money anymore. Indeed, increasingly they want to make sure that they don't do damage while earning returns. When it comes to climate change, for example, shareholders have made proposals to require energy companies to assess the impact of measures to limit global warming to two degrees Celsius (the 2015 Paris Accord target). The idea is that such an analysis would highlight costs and risks to businesses that are contributing to global warming, thus changing the calculus for slow (or no) action. These proposals got a third to a half of votes cast by shareholders at Exxon Mobil, Chevron, and Occidental Petroleum.[11] The rapid rise of socially responsible mutual funds and other investment vehicles is another sign that investors are voting with their dollars (and yen and euros and so on).

Note that none of these actions is cost-free. If you really love the convenience of Amazon Prime delivery but really hate the working conditions in some of the company's warehouses, then you might have to be willing to put up with slower delivery from another store. If cigarette-company stocks pay the best dividends, but you don't want to support smoking, then maybe your investment portfolio produces lower returns. If the highest-paying jobs are in companies with poor records on discrimination, then maybe you have to earn a little less at a company you like more. Protestors spend time, money, and effort (and risk arrest or violence) to get their voices heard. Stakeholders have trade-offs too. Living your values might be costly in some ways, but you might also get to be part of making real change.

This is why I have hope for the 360° Corporation. It takes the interests and needs of different stakeholders seriously. It doesn't let anyone off the hook, not stakeholders, not companies.

As Peter Staley recalls about AIDS activism,

Some of the more common narratives around ACT UP's success . . . focus on how we became very wonkish, and our own experts in AIDS research to adeptly push players like the US government and pharmaceutical companies towards finding treatments. But the less-discussed story is from those early years, and I think it's a more important one, is that initially, we took to the streets. We started doing national actions in 1988. The first was at the FDA; we shut it down for an entire day with over 1,000 protestors . . . We put our bodies on the line at the FDA, and in so doing, we came out of the closet and shattered the myth of the homosexual of being weak, timid, afraid— unwilling to fight back. Instead, the public saw organized anger and determination . . .[12]

This organized anger and determination is precisely what can help create the 360° Corporation. We should not be afraid of the conflict this creates, but rather embrace it. The tensions create the greatest possibilities for change.

• PART V SIGNPOSTS

- We are at a unique moment in time when citizens are increasingly relying on companies to achieve social objectives. Many are now expecting companies to substitute for weak or slow or damaging government
  action. More and more, companies are living up to those expectations.

- Leadership in the twenty-first century is going to require a new set of
  skills, ones that are more collaborative, more focused on inquiry, more
  about mobilizing talented people, more about humility, more about conversation. These characteristics become even more important when
  we consider the new imperative to lead companies not just to achieve
  shareholder objectives but to address all of the stakeholders that encircle the organization.

- The leadership challenge for the 360° revolution is one fraught with unknowns, complexity, and sometimes unresolvable tensions. Yet it is also
  filled with inspiration, creativity, passion, and meaning. The difficulties
  are what make possible the breakthroughs.

- There are nine principles for "Monday morning" action by corporate
  leaders, starting from asking questions, to cocreating with stakeholders, to using creative friction, to being willing to let go of existing business models, to mobilizing talent, to avoiding seeing social responsibility as an add-on, to aligning incentives, to learning as you go. The most
  important action is just to get started.

- Stakeholders also have a role to play. We are citizens and consumers
  and workers and investors too. Protests, boycotts, social-media pressure, proxy voting, and other activities can shape organizational action. This organized determination, and perhaps even anger, is precisely
  what can help create the 360° Corporation. We should not be afraid of
  the conflict this creates, but rather embrace it. The tensions created by

trade-offs are the fodder for the biggest insights and the greatest possibilities for change.

- The 360° Corporation takes the interests and needs of different stakeholders seriously. It doesn't let anyone off the hook, not stakeholders, not companies. And therein lie the possibilities for a new economy.

NOTES

PROLOGUE: THE CORPORATION IN SOCIETY

1. This view has been a core principle of many business schools and is based on Milton Friedman's article "The Social Responsibility of Business Is to Increase Its Profits," *New York Times Magazine*, September 13, 1970, available at https://www.colorado.edu/studentgroups/libertarians/issues/friedman -soc-resp-business.html, accessed June 28, 2018. Gerald F. Davis, in *Managed by the Markets: How Finance Re-Shaped America* (Oxford: Oxford University Press, 2009) discusses how this consensus around shareholder value evolved in the 1970s.

2. "Certified B Corporation," B Labs, https://www.bcorporation.net/what -are-b-corps, accessed June 2, 2018.

3. Andrew Kassoy, Bart Houlahan, and Jay Coen Gilbert, the founders of B Lab, "Your Business Should Be a Force for Good: An Open Letter to Business Leaders," B the Change, February 6, 2017, https://bthechange.com/your -business-should-be-a-force-for-good-an-open-letter-to-business-leaders -b6909beab17f, accessed June 2, 2018.

4. Larry Fink, "Larry Fink's Annual Letter to CEOs: A Sense of Purpose," BlackRock 2018, https://www.blackrock.com/corporate/investor-relations/larry -fink-ceo-letter, accessed June 2, 2018.

5. This is not the first time in business history that questions about corporate social responsibility have emerged. The last time the issue was discussed seriously was in the aftermath of the social unrest and activism of the 1960s

and 1970s, when there were contentious debates about the nature of the firm. It was in this context that Milton Friedman wrote his 1970 piece, "The Social Responsibility of Business Is to Increase Its Profits," to be discussed in more detail in Chapter 1. While Friedman's model ended up mainly triumphing in the 1980s and 1990s, there was a substantial discussion in the management literature about a model for corporate responsibility. Archie Carroll was a major figure in this conversation; see his article, "The Pyramid of Corporate Social Responsibility: Towards the Moral Management of Organizational Stakeholders" (*Business Horizons*, July–August 1991, 39–48). That work pitched social responsibility as being at the top of a pyramid (a sort of Maslow's hierarchy of needs), where economic responsibilities to be profitable were the bedrock; with legal responsibilities to obey the law, and ethical responsibilities to do what is right and fair as the middle layer; and finally, at the peak, what Carroll called philanthropic responsibilities to contribute to the community. Most of this conversation was subsumed by increased government regulations—in the US, this includes the Environmental Protection Agency (EPA), Consumer Product Safety Commission (CPSC), Equal Employment Opportunity Commission (EEOC), and Occupational Safety and Health Administration (OSHA)—that forced companies to take these stakeholders into consideration for legal reasons. Now, in the second decade of the twenty-first century, the conversation is coming in a different form, one that doesn't rely on government regulation for action and one that doesn't put stakeholder needs as a second-order consideration after profits. (Thanks to Bretton Fosbrook for pointing me to these ideas.)

CHAPTER 1: CREATIVE DESTRUCTION REDUX

1. Devin Leonard, "'The Only Lifeline Was the Wal-Mart,'" *Fortune*, October 3, 2005, http://archive.fortune.com/magazines/fortune/fortune_archiv/2005/10/03/8356743/index.htm, accessed January 9, 2019.

2. Michael Barbaro and Justin Gillis, "Wal-Mart at the Forefront of Hurricane Relief," *Washington Post*, September 6, 2005, http://www.washingtonpost.com/wp-dyn/content/article/2005/09/05/AR2005090501598.html, accessed January 9, 2019.

3. Barbaro and Gillis, "Wal-Mart at the Forefront of Hurricane Relief."

4. As quoted in Philip Mattera, "Disaster as Relief: How Wal-Mart Used Hurricane Katrina to Repair Its Image," Corporate Research Project, *Corporate Research E-Letter*, no. 55, September–October 2005, https://www.corp-research.org/e-letter/disaster-relief, accessed January 9, 2019.

5. Mattera, "Disaster as Relief."

6. Kathleen McLaughlin, quoted in Sarah Kaplan, "Walmart's Journey to Sustainability," *Rotman Management Magazine*, Winter 2017, http://www.rotman.utoronto.ca/Connect/Rotman-MAG/Back-Issues/2017/Back-Issues---2017/Winter2017-SmartPower/Winter2017-SarahKaplan-WalmartsJourneytoSustainability, accessed June 21, 2018.

7. Governance and Accountability Institute, "Flash Report: Eighty One Percent of the S&P 500 Index Companies Published Corporate Sustainability Reports in 2015," March 15, 2016, http://www.ga-institute.com/nc/issue-master -system/news-details/article/flash-report-eighty-one-percent-81-of-the-sp-500 -index-companies-published-corporate-sustainabi.html, accessed August 31, 2017.

8. Global Reporting Initiative reports database, https://www.globalreport ing.org/services/Analysis/Reports_List/Pages/default.aspx, accessed August 31, 2017.

9. See, for example, Michael C. Jensen, "Value Maximization, Stakeholder Theory, and the Corporate Objective Function," *Journal of Applied Corporate Finance* 14, no. 3 (2005), 8–21. Jensen argues that it is "logically impossible to maximize more than one dimension," 10.

10. Milton Friedman, "The Social Responsibility of Business Is to Increase Its Profits," *New York Times Magazine*, September 13, 1970, available at https:// www.colorado.edu/studentgroups/libertarians/issues/friedman-soc-resp-busi ness.html, accessed June 28, 2018.

11. Michael E. Porter and Mark R. Kramer, "Strategy and Society," *Harvard Business Review* 84, no. 12 (December 2006): 78–92; Porter and Kramer, "Creating Shared Value," *Harvard Business Review* 89, no. 1–2 (2011): 62–77.

12. Porter and Kramer, "Strategy and Society," 84.

13. Walmart, "Wal-Mart Completes Goal to Sell Only Concentrated Liquid Laundry Detergent," press release, May 29, 2008, http://corporate.walmart .com/_news_/news-archive/2008/05/29/wal-mart-completes-goal-to-sell-only -concentrated-liquid-laundry-detergent, accessed August 31, 2017.

14. Kevin Mahn, "The Changing Face of Socially Responsible Investing," *Forbes*, April 26, 2016, http://www.forbes.com/sites/advisor/2016/04/26/the -changing-face-of-socially-responsible-investing/#3e6f3acf66d0, accessed August 31, 2017.

15. John Acher, "Norway Dumps Wal-Mart from $240 Billion Investment Fund," Reuters, June 6, 2006.

16. Jonathan Cooper, "California Pension System Reconsiders Tobacco Divestment," Associated Press, April 14, 2016, http://bigstory.ap.org/article /daae3889b0bb4bc7a85415e35fe82e22/california-pension-system-reconsiders -tobacco-divestment, accessed August 31, 2017.

17. From the Interfaith Center on Corporate Responsibility website, http:// www.iccr.org/about-iccr, accessed August 31, 2017.

18. *Total returns to shareholders* or *total shareholder return* is a measure of the performance of a company for the holders of its stock. It includes the price appreciation (or depreciation) of the stock as well as the dividends paid over time. The measure assumes that dividends will be reinvested in buying new shares of stock. The measure is reported as a compound annual growth rate. This measure is a way of making more equal comparisons across "growth stocks," those

companies that invest their cash into growth and therefore would expect greater stock price appreciation, and those "value stocks" that use their cash to pay dividends to shareholders. This measure focuses only on financial value created for shareholders and not on any other stakeholder in the company.

19. Richard N. Foster and Sarah Kaplan, *Creative Destruction: Why Companies That Are Built to Last Underperform the Market—And How to Successfully Transform Them* (New York: Currency/Doubleday, 2001).

20. "Creating Shared Value," Nestlé, http://www.nestle.com/csv/what-is-csv, accessed August 31, 2017.

21. "2016 Global Responsibility Report," Wal-Mart Inc., http://cdn.corporate.walmart.com/04/23/176a88fc474c92306f04555815ce/2016-global-responsibility-report.pdf, accessed August 31, 2017. The emphasis is mine.

22. As well summarized in Aseem Kaul and Jiao Luo, "An Economic Case for CSR: The Comparative Efficiency of For-Profit Firms in the Market for Social Goods" (working paper, March 2016), https://papers.ssrn.com/sol3/papers.cfm?abstract_id=2600780, accessed August 31, 2017.

23. Michael E. Porter, *Competitive Strategy: Techniques for Analyzing Industries and Competitors* (New York: Free Press, 1980); *Competitive Advantage: Creating and Sustaining Superior Performance* (New York: Free Press, 1985).

24. M. M. Blair and L. A. Stout, "A Team Production Theory of Corporate Law," *Virginia Law Review* 85, no. 2 (1999): 101–182; P. Klein, J. Mahoney, A. McGahan, and C. Pitelis, "A Property Rights Approach for a Stakeholder Theory of the Firm," *Strategic Organization* 10, no. 3 (2012): 304–315.

25. See examples on LGBTQ benefits, recycling, and biotech: F. Briscoe and S. Safford, "The Nixon-in-China Effect: Activism, Imitation, and the Institutionalization of Contentious Practices," *Administrative Science Quarterly* 53, no. 3 (2008): 460–491; M. Lounsbury, M. J. Ventresca, and P. M. Hirsch, "Social Movements, Field Frames, and Industry Emergence: A Cultural-Political Perspective on US Recycling," *Socio-Economic Review* 1, no. 1 (2003): 71–104; K. Weber, L. G. Thomas, and H. Rao, "From Streets to Suites: How the Anti-Biotech Movement Affected German Pharmaceutical Firms," *American Sociological Review* 74, no. 1 (2009): 106–127.

26. Ingrid Eckerman, *The Bhopal Saga: Causes and Consequences of the World's Largest Industrial Disaster* (Hyderabad, India: Universities Press, 2005).

27. Ram Nidumolu, C. K. Prahalad, and M. R. Rangaswami, "Why Sustainability Is Now the Key Driver of Innovation," *Harvard Business Review* 87, no. 9 (September 2009): 57–64.

28. See, as examples, T. Hahn, L. Preuss, J. Pinkse, and F. Figge, "Cognitive Frames in Corporate Sustainability: Managerial Sensemaking with Paradoxical and Business Case Frames," *Academy of Management Review* 39, no. 4 (2014): 463–487; and Hahn, Pinkse, Preuss, and Figge, "Tensions in Corporate Sustainability: Towards an Integrative Framework," *Journal of Business Ethics* 127, no. 2 (2015): 297–316.

29. N. Slawinski and P. Bansal, "Short on Time: Intertemporal Tensions in Business Sustainability," *Organization Science* 26, no. 2 (2015): 531–549.

30. Jensen, in "Value Maximization, Stakeholder Theory, and the Corporate Objective Function," argues that it is "logically impossible to maximize more than one dimension," 10.

31. P. E. Tetlock, R. S. Peterson, and J. S. Lerner, "Revising the Value Pluralism Model: Incorporating Social Content and Context Postulates," in *The Psychology of Values,* Ontario Symposium, vol. 8, ed. C. Seligman, J. M. Olson, and M. P. Zanna (Mahwah, NJ: L. Erlbaum Associates, 1996), 25–51; R. K. Mitchell, G. R. Weaver, B. R. Agle, A. D. Bailey, and J. Carlson, "Stakeholder Agency and Social Welfare: Pluralism and Decision Making in the Multi-Objective Corporation," *Academy of Management Review* 41, no. 2 (2016): 252–275.

32. These ideas are laid out by John Dewey–inspired pragmatist scholars of experimental governance and experimentalism, such as Charles F. Sabel and Jonathan Zeitlin, "Experimentalist Governance," in *Oxford Handbook of Governance* , ed. David Levi-Faur (Oxford: Oxford University Press, 2012), 2–4; Christopher K. Ansell and Martin Bartenberger, "Varieties of Experimentalism," *Ecological Economics* 130 (2016): 64–73; and D. A. Schön, *The Reflective Practitioner: How Professionals Think in Action* (New York: Basic Books, 1983).

33. R. G. Eccles, I. Ioannou, and G. Serafeim, "The Impact of Corporate Sustainability on Organizational Processes and Performance," *Management Science* 60, no. 11 (2014): 2835–2857.

34. After the review process was complete, I was able to contact the reviewer and received permission to publish this quote from his review.

CHAPTER 2: YOU'VE GOT TO WALK BEFORE YOU CAN RUN

1. Stephen P. Bradley, Pankaj Ghemawat, and Sharon Foley, "Wal-Mart Stores," Harvard Business School Publishing, case no. 794024, January 20, 1994.

2. Quoted in Sam Walton with John Huey, *Made in America: My Story* (New York: Doubleday, 1992), 237.

3. Ann Zimmerman, "Pro-Union Butchers at Wal-Mart Win a Battle, but Lose the War," *Wall Street Journal*, April 11, 2000, http://www.wsj.com/articles/SB955407680495911513, accessed August 31, 2017.

4. As cited and linked to in Steven Greenhouse, "How Walmart Persuades Its Workers Not to Unionize," *Atlantic*, June 8, 2015, https://www.theatlantic.com/business/archive/2015/06/how-walmart-convinces-its-employees-not-to-unionize/395051/, accessed January 12, 2019.

5. Susan Berfield, "How Walmart Keeps an Eye on Its Massive Workforce," *Bloomberg Businessweek*, November 24, 2015, http://www.bloomberg.com/features/2015-walmart-union-surveillance/, accessed August 31, 2017.

6. Steve Greenhouse, "Illegally in US, and Never a Day Off at Wal-Mart," *New York Times*, November 5, 2003, https://www.nytimes.com/2003/11/05/us/illegally-in-us-and-never-a-day-off-at-wal-mart.html, accessed January 12, 2019;

Greenhouse, "Wal-Mart to Pay US $11 Million in Lawsuit on Illegal Workers," *New York Times*, March 19, 2005, https://www.nytimes.com/2005/03/19/business/walmart-to-pay-us-11-million-in-lawsuit-on-illegal-workers.html, accessed January 12, 2019

7. As excerpted in Robert Greenwald's 2005 documentary, *Wal-Mart: The High Cost of Low Price.*

8. Anne D'Innocenzio, "Wal-Mart Raises Pay for Managers," *US News and World Report*, June 2, 2015.

9. Liza Featherstone, "Wage Against the Machine," Slate, June 27, 2008, http://www.slate.com/articles/business/moneybox/2008/06/wage_against_the_machine.html, accessed August 31, 2017.

10. Featherstone, "Wage Against the Machine."

11. Shannon Pettypiece, "Wal-Mart Cuts Some Workers' Hours After Pay Raise Boosts Costs," *Bloomberg Businessweek*, August 31, 2015, http://www.bloomberg.com/news/articles/2015-08-31/wal-mart-cuts-some-workers-hours-after-pay-raise-boosts-costs, accessed August 31, 2017.

12. Tim Worstall, "Of Course Walmart Cut Hours After Raising Pay—What Did You Expect?" *Forbes*, September 1, 2015, http://www.forbes.com/sites/timworstall/2015/09/01/of-course-walmart-cut-hours-after-raising-pay-what-did-anyone-expect/#53f31a1f0223, accessed August 31, 2017.

13. Geraldine E. Willigan, "High-Performance Marketing: An Interview with Nike's Phil Knight," *Harvard Business Review* 70, no. 4 (July–August 1992): 90–101, https://hbr.org/1992/07/high-performance-marketing-an-interview-with-nikes-phil-knight, accessed August 31, 2017.

14. See Nike's website, http://about.nike.com/, accessed August 31, 2017.

15. Bob Herbert, "In America: Nike's Pyramid Scheme," *New York Times*, June 10, 1996, http://www.nytimes.com/1996/06/10/opinion/in-america-nike-s-pyramid-scheme.html, accessed August 31, 2017.

16. David C. Rikert and C. Roland Christensen, "Nike (A)," Harvard Business School, case no. 385024, May 15, 1990; Matthew Kish, "The Cost Breakdown of a $100 Pair of Sneakers," *Portland Business Journal*, December 16, 2014, http://www.bizjournals.com/portland/blog/threads_and_laces/2014/12/the-cost-breakdown-of-a-100-pair-of-sneakers.html?s=image_gallery, accessed August 31, 2017.

17. Phil Knight, "New Labor Initiatives," speech at National Press Club, May 12, 1998, http://business.nmsu.edu/~dboje/NIKphilspeech.html, accessed August 31, 2017. For the original video, see CSPAN's 59-minute recording of the event: "Nike in the Global Economy," C-SPAN, May 12, 1998, https://www.c-span.org/video/?105477-1/nike-global-economy, accessed January 12, 2019.

18. For example, Sarah Kaplan, "Truce Breaking and Remaking: The CEO's Role in Changing Organizational Routines," in *Cognition and Strategy*, Advances in Strategic Management, vol. 32, ed. Giovanni Gavetti and William

Ocasio (Bingley, UK: Emerald Group, 2015), 1–45; J. P. Eggers and Sarah Kaplan, "Cognition and Capabilities: A Multi-Level Perspective," *Academy of Management Annals*, 7 (2013): 295–340; Sarah Kaplan, "Cognition, Capabilities, and Incentives: Assessing Firm Response to the Fiber-Optic Revolution," *Academy of Management Journal* 51, no. 4 (2008): 672–695; Sarah Kaplan and Rebecca Henderson, "Inertia and Incentives: Bridging Organizational Economics and Organizational Theory," *Organization Science* 16, no. 5 (2005): 509–521; Sarah Kaplan, Fiona Murray, and Rebecca M. Henderson, "Discontinuities and Senior Management: Assessing the Role of Recognition in Pharmaceutical Firm Response to Biotechnology," *Industrial and Corporate Change* 12, no. 4 (2003): 203–233.

19. For example, R. E. Freeman, *Strategic Management: A Stakeholder Approach* (Boston: Pitman, 1984).

20. See Tim Koller, Marc Goedhart, and David Wessels, *Valuation: Measuring and Managing the Value of Companies* (Hoboken, NJ: Wiley, 2005), now in its sixth edition. A nice summary can be found in Koller, "What Is Value-Based Management?" *McKinsey Quarterly*, August 1994, http://www.mckinsey.com/business-functions/strategy-and-corporate-finance/our-insights/what-is-value-based-management, accessed August 31, 2017.

21. "FY 16/17 Sustainable Business Report," Nike, Inc., https://sbi-stg-s3-media-bucket.s3.amazonaws.com/wp-content/uploads/2018/05/18175102/NIKE-FY1617-Sustainable-Business-Report_FINAL.pdf, accessed January 12, 2019.

22. Matthew Hall, Yuval Millo, and Emily Barman, "Who and What Really Counts? Stakeholder Prioritization and Accounting for Social Value," *Journal of Management Studies* 52, no. 7 (2015): 907–934.

23. "2018 Global Responsibility Report," Wal-Mart Inc., https://corporate.walmart.com/2018grr/, accessed January 12, 2019; "FY 16/17 Sustainable Business Report," Nike, Inc., https://sbi-stg-s3-media-bucket.s3.amazonaws.com/wp-content/uploads/2018/05/18175102/NIKE-FY1617-Sustainable-Business-Report_FINAL.pdf, accessed January 12, 2019.

24. Charles Fishman, "How Many Lightbulbs Does It Take to Change the World? One. And You're Looking at It," *Fast Company*, September 1, 2006, https://www.fastcompany.com/57676/how-many-lightbulbs-does-it-take-change-world-one-and-youre-looking-it, accessed January 12, 2019; and Stephanie Rosenbloom and Michael Barbara, "Environmental Sustainability, Now at Wal-Mart," *New York Times*, February 5, 2009, https://www.nytimes.com/2009/01/25/business/worldbusiness/25iht-25walmart.19647095.html, accessed January 12, 2019.

25. Matthew Heimer, "'Do Some Uncomfortable and Inconvenient Things': A Civil Rights Champion's Call to Action for CEOs," *Fortune*, June 27, 2018, http://fortune.com/2018/06/26/bryan-stevenson-ceo-initiative/, accessed June 28, 2018.

CHAPTER 3: IS THERE A WIN-WIN? THE SEARCH FOR SHARED VALUE

1. "2018 Global Responsibility Report," Wal-Mart Inc., https://corporate
.walmart.com/2018grr/, accessed May 30, 2018.

2. "FY 16/17 Sustainable Business Report," Nike, Inc., https://sbi-stg-s3
-media-bucket.s3.amazonaws.com/wp-content/uploads/2018/05/18175102
/NIKE-FY1617-Sustainable-Business-Report_FINAL.pdf, accessed January 12,
2019.

3. Wal-Mart, "Wal-Mart to Sell Only Concentrated Products in Liquid
Laundry Detergent Category by May 2008," press release, September 26, 2007,
https://corporate.walmart.com/_news_/news-archive/2007/09/26/wal-mart-to
-sell-only-concentrated-products-in-liquid-laundry-detergent-category-by
-may-2008, accessed May 30, 2018; Wal-Mart, "Wal-Mart Completes Goal
to Sell Only Concentrated Laundry Detergent," press release, May 29, 2008,
https://corporate.walmart.com/_news_/news-archive/2008/05/29/wal-mart
-completes-goal-to-sell-only-concentrated-liquid-laundry-detergent, accessed
May 30, 2018.

4. Good summaries can be found in Rebecca Henderson, "Making the Busi-
ness Case for Environmental Sustainability" (working paper 15–068, Harvard
Business School, February 19, 2015); and "The Business Case for Corporate
Social Responsibility," Conference Board, June 2011, https://www.conference
-board.org/publications/publicationdetail.cfm?publicationid=1954, accessed
May 30, 2018.

5. "FY 16/17 Sustainable Business Report," Nike, Inc.

6. I develop this argument in more detail in Sarah Kaplan, "Beyond the
Business Case for Social Responsibility," *Academy of Management Discoveries* (in
press), https://journals.aom.org/doi/10.5465/amd.2018.0220.

7. This argument is based on the system-justification theory as represented
in the following articles: Sebastian Hafenbrädl and Daniel Waeger, "Ideology
and the Micro-Foundations of CSR: Why Executives Believe in the Business
Case for CSR and How This Affects Their CSR Engagements," *Academy of Management Journal* 60, no. 4 (2017): 1582–1606; D. Proudfoot and A. C. Kay, "System Justification in Organizational Contexts: How a Motivated Preference for
the Status Quo Can Affect Organizational Attitudes and Behaviors," *Research in
Organizational Behavior* 34 (2014): 173–187; J. T. Jost and M. R. Banaji, "The Role
of Stereotyping in System-Justification and the Production of False Conscious-
ness," *British Journal of Social Psychology* 33 (1994): 1–27; J. T. Jost, M. R. Banaji,
and B. Nosek, "A Decade of System Justification Theory: Accumulated Evidence of Conscious and Unconscious Bolstering of the Status Quo," *Political
Psychology* 25 (2004): 881–919.

8. Indeed, legal scholar Jamillah Bowman Williams shows that civil rights–
based arguments are more likely to provoke inclusive behaviors while business-
case justifications can lead to negative beliefs about inclusion. See Williams,
"Breaking Down Bias: Legal Mandates vs. Corporate Interests," *Washington*

Law Review 92, no. 3 (2017): 1473–1513. Similarly, Miguel M. Unzueta and Eric D. Knowles suggest that embedding justifications in sociocultural explanations of inequalities (such as understandings of privilege) may be more effective than profit-maximizing justifications. See Unzueta and Knowles, "The 'Business Case' for Diversity May Not by Itself Make the Strongest Case for Diversity," in *Diversity Ideologies in Organizations*, ed. Kecia M. Thomas, Victoria C. Plaut, and Ny Mia Tran (New York and London: Routledge), 257–267.

9. H. J. Birnbaum, E. P. Apfelbaum, and A. Waytz, "When the Business Case Backfires: Competitive Advantage Standards Jeopardize Lasting Support for Diversity" (working paper, MIT Sloan, 2018).

10. Andrew Crane, Guido Palazzo, Laura J. Spence, and Dirk Matten, "Contesting the Value of 'Creating Shared Value,'" *California Management Review* 56, no. 2 (2014): 130–153.

11. "A Response to Andrew Crane et al.'s Article by Michael E. Porter and Mark R. Kramer," *California Management Review* 56, no. 2 (Winter 2014): 130–153.

12. David Kiron, Gregory Unruh, Nina Kruschwitz, Martin Reeves, Holger Rubel, and Alexander Meyer Zum Felde, "Corporate Sustainability at a Crossroads," *MIT Sloan Management Review*, May 2017, reprint number 58480.

CHAPTER 4: GETTING STUCK IN THE BUSINESS CASE

1. Tim Smedley, "The Evidence Is Growing—There Really Is a Business Case for Diversity," *Financial Times*, May 14, 2014, https://www.ft.com/content /4f4b3c8e-d521-11e3-9187-00144feabdc0, accessed March 13, 2018. Vivian Hunt, Lareina Yee, Sara Prince, and Sundiatu Dixon-Fyle, "Delivering Through Diversity," McKinsey & Company, January 2018, https://www.mckinsey.com /business-functions/organization/our-insights/delivering-through-diversity, accessed March 13, 2018.

2. Michel Landel, "Gender Balance and the Link to Performance," *McKinsey Quarterly*, February 2015, https://www.mckinsey.com/featured-insights/leader ship/gender-balance-and-the-link-to-performance, accessed March 13, 2018.

3. Oliver Cann, "Gender Equality Is Sliding Backwards Finds Our Global Report," World Economic Forum, https://www.weforum.org/agenda/2016/10 /gender-gap-report-2016-equality-sliding-backwards/, accessed October 26, 2016.

4. Declaration of Claudia Renati in Support of Plaintiffs' Motion for Class Certification, US District Court, Northern District of California, case no. C-01-2252 MJJ, http://walmartclass.com/staticdata/walmartclass/declarations/Renati _Claudia.htm, accessed November 12, 2015.

5. Declaration of Ramona Scott in Support of Plaintiffs' Motion for Class Certification, US District Court, Northern District of California, case no. C-01-2252 MJJ, http://walmartclass.com/staticdata/walmartclass/declarations/Scott _Ramona.htm, accessed November 12, 2015.

6. Wal-Mart Stores, Inc. v. Dukes, 564 U.S. 338, 131 S. Ct. 2541 (2011). The US Supreme Court decided the case on June 20, 2011.

7. Ira Kalb, "Wal-Mart vs. 1.5 Million Women: Can the Company's Reputation Be Saved?" *CBS Moneywatch*, March 31, 2011, https://www.cbsnews.com/news/wal-mart-vs-15-million-women-can-the-companys-reputation-be-saved/, accessed March 14, 2018. Information about Robert Greenwald's 2005 documentary, *Walmart: The High Cost of Low Price* can be found at https://www.bravenewfilms.org/walmartmovie.

8. "Statistical Overview of Women in the Workplace," Catalyst, March 3, 2014, http://www.catalyst.org/knowledge/statistical-overview-women-workplace, accessed November 13, 2015; "Women CEOs of the S&P 500," Catalyst, October 9, 2015, http://www.catalyst.org/knowledge/women-ceos-sp-500, accessed November 13, 2015.

9. Claire Cain Miller, Kevin Quealy, and Margot Sanger-Katz, "The Top Jobs Where Women Are Outnumbered by Men Named John," *New York Times*, April 24, 2018, https://www.nytimes.com/interactive/2018/04/24/upshot/women-and-men-named-john.html, accessed November 12, 2018.

10. Francine D. Blau and Lawrence M. Kahn, "The Gender Pay Gap: Have Women Gone as Far as They Can?" *Academy of Management Perspectives* 21, no. 1 (February 2007): 7–23; Catherine Hill, "The Simple Truth About the Gender Pay Gap," American Association of University Women, 2015, http://www.aauw.org/files/2015/09/The-Simple-Truth-Fall-2015.pdf, accessed November 14, 2015.

11. Justin Wolfers, "Fewer Women Run Big Companies Than Men Named John," *New York Times*, March 2, 2015, https://www.nytimes.com/2015/03/03/upshot/fewer-women-run-big-companies-than-men-named-john.html, accessed November 13, 2015; "Poverty and the Social Safety Net," Institute for Women's Policy Research, https://iwpr.org/issue/poverty-welfare-income-security/poverty/, accessed March 13, 2018; Ontario Securities Commission, http://www.osc.gov.on.ca/en/55517.htm, accessed March 13, 2018.

12. This only began changing in the United States in the 1970s under the pressure of women's movement activists. Stephanie Gilmore, *Groundswell: Grassroots Feminist Activism in Postwar America* (New York: Routledge, 2013).

13. "Charges Alleging Sex-Based Harassment (Charges Filed with EEOC) FY 2010-FY 2018," US Equal Employment Opportunity Commission, https://www.eeoc.gov/eeoc/statistics/enforcement/sexual_harassment_new.cfm, accessed March 13, 2018.

14. Peter Glick and Susan Fiske, "The Ambivalent Sexism Inventory: Differentiating Hostile and Benevolent Sexism," *Journal of Personality and Social Psychology* 70, no. 3 (1996): 491–512; P. Glick, S. T. Fiske, A. Mladinic, J. L. Saiz, D. Abrams, B. Masser, B. Adetoun, J. E. Osagie, A. Akande, A. Alao, A. Brunner, T. M. Willemsen, K. Chipeta, B. Dardenne, A. Dijksterhuis, D. Wigboldus, T. Eckes, I. Six-Materna, F. Expósito, M. Moya, M. Foddy, H.-J. Kim, M. Lameiras, M. J. Sotelo, A. Mucchi-Faina, M. Romani, N. Sakallı, B. Udegbe, M. Yama-

moto, M. Ui, M. C. Ferreira, and W. López, "Beyond Prejudice as Simple Antipathy: Hostile and Benevolent Sexism Across Cultures," *Journal of Personality and Social Psychology* 79, no. 5 (2000): 763–775.

15. In an interview by Philip Galanes, "Seeking a Level Playing Field," *New York Times*, October 24, 2014, https://www.nytimes.com/2014/10/26/fashion/kirsten-gillibrand-and-julianna-margulies-share-more-than-fame.html, accessed March 13, 2018.

16. This comparison was constructed by Jennie Dusheck in a blog post, "Family Man Who Invented Relativity and Made Great Chili Dies," April 1, 2013, http://www.lastwordonnothing.com/2013/04/01/guest-post-physicist-dies-made-great-chili/, accessed November 13, 2015.

17. Melanie Tannenbaum, "The Problem When Sexism Just Sounds So Darn Friendly . . . ," PsySociety, *Scientific American*, April 2, 2013, http://blogs.scientificamerican.com/psysociety/benevolent-sexism/, accessed November 13, 2015.

18. The controversy continued, however, as the obituary still managed to claim that she took eight years off work to raise her children, when in fact she had worked consistently part-time as a consultant. Amy Davidson, "Yvonne Brill and the Beef-Stroganoff Illusion," *New Yorker*, April 1, 2013, http://www.newyorker.com/news/amy-davidson/yvonne-brill-and-the-beef-stroganoff-illusion, accessed November 13, 2015.

19. "Education," Project Implicit, https://implicit.harvard.edu/implicit/education.html, accessed November 14, 2015.

20. There is a huge amount of research on this topic. I have summarized an entire field of study in one paragraph. Selected references include Danielle Gaucher, Justin Friesen, and Aaron C. Kay, "Evidence That Gendered Wording in Job Advertisements Exists and Sustains Gender Inequality," *Journal of Personality and Social Psychology* 101, no. 1 (2011): 109–128; R. E. Steinpreis, K. A. Anders, and D. Ritzke, "The Impact of Gender on the Review of the Curricula Vitae of Job Applicants and Tenure Candidates: A National Empirical Study," *Sex Roles* 41, nos. 7–8 (1999): 509–528; M. Bertrand and S. Mullainathan, "Are Emily and Greg More Employable than Lakisha and Jamal? A Field Experiment on Labor Market Discrimination," *American Economic Review* 94, no. 4 (2004): 991–1013; F. Trix and C. Psenka, "Exploring the Color of Glass: Letters of Recommendation for Female and Male Medical Faculty," *Discourse and Society* 14, no. 2 (2003): 191–220; E. J. Castilla, "Gender, Race, and Meritocracy in Organizational Careers," *American Journal of Sociology* 113, no. 6 (2008): 1479–1526; A. Joshi, J. Son, and H. Roh, "When Can Women Close the Gap? A Meta-Analytic Test of Sex Differences in Performance and Rewards," *Academy of Management Journal* 58, no. 5 (December 2014): 1516–1545; C. J. Turco, "Cultural Foundations of Tokenism: Evidence from the Leveraged Buyout Industry," *American Sociological Review* 75, no. 5 (2010): 894–913; I. Fernandez-Mateo and Z. King, "Anticipatory Sorting and Gender Segregation in Temporary Employment," *Management*

Science 57 (2011): 989–1008; R. M. Fernandez and M. L. Mors, "Competing for Jobs: Labor Queues and Gender Sorting in the Hiring Process," *Social Science Research* 37, no. 4 (2008): 1061–1080; A. H. Eagly and S. J. Karau, "Role Congruity Theory of Prejudice Toward Female Leaders," *Psychological Review* 109, no. 3 (2002): 573–598; S. T. Fiske, A. J. C. Cuddy, and P. Glick, "Universal Dimensions of Social Cognition: Warmth and Competence," *Trends in Cognitive Sciences* 11, no. 2 (2007): 77–83; M. E. Heilman, A. S. Wallen, D. Fuchs, and M. M. Tamkins, "Penalties for Success: Reactions to Women Who Succeed at Male Gender-Typed Tasks," *Journal of Applied Psychology* 89, no. 3 (2004): 416–427. I have also written more on this: Sarah Kaplan, "Meritocracy: From Myth to Reality," *Rotman Magazine,* Spring 2015, 48–53, http://www.rotman.utoronto.ca/Connect /Rotman-MAG/Back-Issues/2015/Back-Issues---2015/Spring-2015---Smarten -Up/Spring-2015-Free-Feature-Article---Meritocracy-From-Myth-to-Reality -by-Sarah-Kaplan, accessed June 3, 2018.

21. Louise Matsakis, Jason Koebler, and Sarah Emerson, "Here Are the Citations for the Anti-Diversity Manifesto Circulating at Google," Motherboard, August 17, 2017, https://motherboard.vice.com/en_us/article/evzjww/here-are -the-citations-for-the-anti-diversity-manifesto-circulating-at-google, accessed June 3, 2018.

22. Nellie Bowles, "Equality in Tech? Some Men Say It's Gone Too Far," *New York Times*, September 23, 2017, https://www.nytimes.com/2017/09/23/technol ogy/silicon-valley-men-backlash-gender-scandals.html, accessed June 3, 2018.

23. Quote from Ernst & Young, *Groundbreakers: Using the Strength of Women to Rebuild the World Economy*, 2010, http://www.womenable.com/content/user files/E&Y-Groundbreakers.pdf, accessed January 12, 2019. See also Georges Desvaux, Sandrine Devillard, Alix de Zelicourts, Cecile Kossoff, Eric Labaye, and Sandra Sancier-Sultan, "Women Matter: Ten Years of Insights on Gender Diversity," *McKinsey & Company*, October 2017, https://www.mckinsey.com /featured-insights/gender-equality/women-matter-ten-years-of-insights-on -gender-diversity, accessed January 12, 2019; and Amanda Hindlian, Sandra Lawson, Sonya Banerjee, Deborah Mirabal, Hui Shan and Emma Campbell-Mohn, "Closing the Gender Gaps: Advancing Women in Corporate America," *Goldman Sachs Global Markets Institute*, October 2018, https://www.goldman sachs.com/insights/pages/gmi-gender-gaps.html, accessed January 12, 2019.

24. S. E. Jackson, K. E. May, and K. Whitney, "Understanding the Dynamics of Diversity in Decision-Making Teams," in *Team Effectiveness and Decision-Making in Organizations*, ed. Richard A. Guzzo, Eduardo Salas, and associates (San Francisco: Jossey-Bass, 1995), 204–261; K. A. Farrell and P. L. Hersch, "Additions to Corporate Boards: The Effect of Gender," *Journal of Corporate Finance* 11, no. 1 (2005): 85–106; N. Bassett-Jones, "The Paradox of Diversity Management," *Creativity and Innovation Management* 14, no. 2 (2005): 169–175.

25. Carl Bialik, "Who Makes the Call at the Mall, Men or Women?" *Wall*

Street Journal, April 23, 2011, https://www.wsj.com/articles/SB10001424052748 703521304576278964279316994, accessed November 29, 2015.

26. "The 2014 State of Women-Owned Businesses Report," commissioned by American Express Open, http://www.womenable.com/content/user files/2014_State_of_Women-owned_Businesses_public.pdf, accessed November 29, 2015.

27. Betsy Brill, "Women in Philanthropy," *Forbes*, August 18, 2009, http://www.forbes.com/2009/08/18/brill-women-philanthropy-intelligent-investing-wealth.html, accessed November 13, 2015; Ryan Gorman, "Women Now Control More than Half of US Personal Wealth, Which 'Will Only Increase in Years to Come.'" *Business Insider*, April 7, 2015, https://www.businessinsider.com/women-now-control-more-than-half-of-us-personal-wealth-2015-4, accessed November 29, 2015.

28. Ana Revenga and Sudhir Shetty, "Empowering Women Is Smart Economics," *Finance and Development* 49, no. 1 (2012): 40–43, http://www.imf.org/external/pubs/ft/fandd/2012/03/revenga.htm, accessed November 19, 2015.

29. "Women," Calvert Foundation, http://www.calvertfoundation.org/component/content/article/19, accessed November 29,2015.

30. John Kell, "Nike Makes a Big Push into the Fast-Growing Women's Segment," *Fortune*, October 22, 2014, http://fortune.com/2014/10/22/nike-women-business/, accessed November 19, 2015.

31. Rob Strasser, quoted in, J. B. Strasser, *Swoosh: The Unauthorized Story of Nike and the Men Who Played There* (New York: HarperCollins, 1993), 397–398.

32. Quoted in Geraldine E. Willigan, "High-Performance Marketing: An Interview with Nike's Phil Knight," *Harvard Business Review* 70, no. 4 (July-August 1992): 90–101.

33. Strasser, *Swoosh*, 397–398.

34. Barbara Lippert, "The Sole of a Woman," *Adweek*, October 7, 1991.

35. "Can Nike Just Do It?" *Businessweek*, April 17, 1994.

36. Janet Champ, advertising executive at Wieden Kennedy who worked on the Nike account, as quoted in Jean M. Grow, "The Gender of Branding: Early Nike Women's Advertising, a Feminist Antenarrative," *Women's Studies in Communication* 31, no. 3 (2008): 312–343.

37. Quoted in Willigan, "High-Performance Marketing," 99–100.

38. "If You Let Me Play," Nike TV ad, https://www.youtube.com/watch?v=EENUPgWd7-A, accessed November 29, 2015.

39. Janet Champ, from Wieden Kennedy, as quoted in Grow, "The Gender of Branding," 335.

40. Devin Rhodes, 2011, comment on YouTube video of "Nike Ad: If You Let Me Play (1995)," https://www.youtube.com/watch?v=AQ_XSHpIbZE, accessed November 29, 2015.

41. Cynthia Enloe, *The Curious Feminist: Searching for Women in a New Age*

of Empire (Berkeley: University of California Press, 2004), especially Chapter 3, "The Globetrotting Sneaker," and Chapter 4, "Daughters and Generals in the Politics of the Globalized Sneaker."

42. From the Adbusters website, https://www.adbusters.org/spoof-ads, accessed January 12, 2019.

43. Enloe, *The Curious Feminist*, especially Chapters 3 and 4.

44. From the Girl Effect website, http://www.girleffect.org/about-us/?gclid =CL7Zi6fBuMkCFUKQHwodsxAM5w, accessed November 30, 2015.

45. From the Girl Effect YouTube channel, https://www.youtube.com/watch ?v=WIvmE4_KMNw, accessed November 29, 2015.

46. Jad Chaaban and Wendy Cunningham, "Measuring the Economic Gain of Investing in Girls: The Girl Effect Dividend" (World Bank Policy Research Working Paper No. 5753), August 2011, http://papers.ssrn.com/s013/papers.cfm ?abstract_id=1907071, accessed November 29, 2015.

47. Maria Hengeveld, "How Nike's Neoliberal Feminism Came to Rule the Global South," Feminist Wire, September 14, 2015, http://www.thefeminist wire.com/2015/09/nike-neoliberal-feminism/, accessed November 29, 2015. See also Michelle Murphy, "The Girl: Mergers of Feminism and Finance in Neoliberal Times," *Scholar and Feminist Online* 11, nos.1–2 (2012–2013), http://sf online.barnard.edu/gender-justice-and-neoliberal-transformations/the-girl -mergers-of-feminism-and-finance-in-neoliberal-times/, accessed November 29, 2015.

48. "Walmart Launches Global Women's Economic Empowerment Initiative" Wal-Mart Inc., https://www.prnewswire.com/news-releases/walmart -launches-global-womens-economic-empowerment-initiative-129808593 .html, accessed November 30, 2015.

49. Penny Abeywardena, "How Walmart Is Reimagining Its Investments to Empower Girls and Women," Clinton Foundation, April 29, 2014, https://www .clintonfoundation.org/blog/2014/04/29/how-walmart-reimagining-its-invest ments-empower-girls-and-women, accessed November 30, 2015.

50. Abeywardena, "How Walmart Is Reimagining Its Investments to Empower Girls and Women."

51. Valentina Zarya, "Meet the Activists Leading the Fight for Paid Family Leave," *Fortune*, May 1, 2018, http://fortune.com/longform/us-family-leave -parental-leave-activists/, accessed August 29, 2018.

52. United Food and Commercial Workers Union Local 400, "Walmart's Business Practices Cause Systematic Economic Harm to Women in the US and Worldwide," press release, September 15, 2011, http://www.ufcw400.org/2011 /09/15/walmarts-business-practices-cause-systematic-economic-harm-to -women-in-the-u-s-and-worldwide/, accessed March 14, 2018.

53. Jamillah Bowman Williams, "Breaking Down Bias: Legal Mandates vs. Corporate Interests," *Washington Law Review* 92, no. 3 (2017): 1473–1513.

54. O. Georgeac and A. Rattan, "Organizational Diversity Cases: Instrumental Justifications for Organizations' Commitment to Diversity Undermine Anticipated Sense of Belonging Among LGBTQ+ Individuals and Women" (working paper, London Business School, 2018).

55. "Walmart Global Sustainability Report 2009" and "Walmart Global Responsibility Report 2014" (all Walmart responsibility and sustainability reports can be accessed at https://corporate.walmart.com/global-responsibility/global-responsibility-report-archive, accessed January 12, 2019); "Board of Directors," Wal-Mart Inc., http://corporate.walmart.com/our-story/leadership, accessed November 30, 2015; Matthew Boyle and Jordyn Holman, "Women at Walmart Becoming Scarcer Despite C-Suite Promotions," *Bloomberg Businessweek*, February 12, 2018, https://www.bloomberg.com/news/articles/2018-02-12/women-at-walmart-becoming-more-scarce-despite-c-suite-promotions, accessed March 13, 2018; "Road to Inclusion: Culture Diversity and Inclusion 2017 Report," Wal-Mart Inc., https://cdn.corporate.walmart.com/11/0d/f9289df649049a38c14bdeaf2b99/2017-cdi-report-web.pdf, accessed March 13, 2018.

56. Quoted in Amy Westervelt, "Walmart Invests Billions to Buy from Women-Owned Businesses—but Is It Enough?" *Guardian*, March 29, 2017, https://www.theguardian.com/sustainable-business/2017/mar/29/women-gender-gap-walmart-business, accessed March 14, 2018.

57. Maria Hengeveld, "Nike Says It Empowers Women Around the World," Investigative Fund, August 26, 2016, https://www.theinvestigativefund.org/investigation/2016/08/26/nike-says-empowers-women-around-world/, accessed May 25, 2018.

58. Julie Creswell, Kevin Draper, and Rachel Abrams, "At Nike, Revolt Led by Women Leads to Exodus of Male Executives," *New York Times*, April 28, 2018, https://www.nytimes.com/2018/04/28/business/nike-women.html, accessed June 3, 2018; Julie Creswell and Kevin Draper, "Five More Nike Executives Are Out Amid Inquiry into Harassment Allegations," *New York Times*, May 8, 2018, https://www.nytimes.com/2018/05/08/business/nike-harassment.html, accessed June 3, 2018.

59. Sara Germano, "Nike to Adjust Pay for Thousands of Staffers After Internal Review," *Wall Street Journal*, July 23, 2018, https://www.wsj.com/articles/nike-to-adjust-pay-for-thousands-of-staffers-after-internal-review-1532369993, accessed August 22, 2018.

60. Bloomberg, "Nike 'Devalued and Demeaned' Female Employees, Lawsuit Alleges," *Fortune*, August 11, 2018, http://fortune.com/2018/08/11/nike-discrimination-lawsuit/, accessed August 22, 2018.

61. Fara Warner, "Nike's Women's Movement," *Fast Company*, July 31, 2002, https://www.fastcompany.com/45135/nikes-womens-movement, accessed June 3, 2018.

62. Nike, "Nike Women's-Only Store with Fitness Studio Opens in New-

port Beach," press release, November 20, 2014. http://news.nike.com/news/new-nike-experience-store-in-newport-beach-california-combines-best-of-women-s-products-with-fitness-studio, accessed November 29, 2015.

63. Vanessa Friedman, "The 2016 Pirelli Calendar May Signal a Cultural Shift," *New York Times*, November 30, 2015, https://www.nytimes.com/2015/12/03/fashion/the-2016-pirelli-calendar-may-signal-a-cultural-shift.html, accessed June 3, 2018.

64. Quoted in Friedman, "The 2016 Pirelli Calendar May Signal a Cultural Shift."

65. L. Babcock and S. Laschever, *Women Don't Ask: Negotiation and the Gender Divide* (Princeton, NJ: Princeton University Press, 2003).

66. Sarah Kaplan and Natassia Walley, "The Rhetoric of Female Risk Aversion, *Stanford Social Innovation Review* 14, no. 2 (2016): 48–54.

67. For more information on the risks of getting the mechanisms of discrimination wrong, see Isabel Fernandez-Mateo and Sarah Kaplan, "Gender and Organization Science," *Organization Science* 29, no. 6 (2018): 1229–1236.

CHAPTER 5: CSR IS NOT AN ADD-ON

1. Charles Fishman, "The Wal-Mart You Don't Know," *Fast Company*, December 1, 2003, http://www.fastcompany.com/47593/wal-mart-you-dont-know, accessed August 31, 2017.

2. Milton Friedman, "The Social Responsibility of Business Is to Increase Its Profits," *New York Times Magazine*, September 13, 1970, https://www.colorado.edu/studentgroups/libertarians/issues/friedman-soc-resp-business.html, accessed June 28, 2018.

3. "Bangladesh Arrests Three over Deadly Factory Fire," BBC News, November 28, 2012, http://www.bbc.com/news/world-asia-20522593, accessed August 31, 2017.

4. Sarah Stillman, "Death Traps: The Bangladesh Garment-Factory Disaster," *New Yorker*, May 1, 2013, http://www.newyorker.com/news/news-desk/death-traps-the-bangladesh-garment-factory-disaster, accessed August 31, 2017.

5. Agence France Presse, "A Huge Clothing Factory Fire in Bangladesh Is Leading to Pressure on P Diddy," Business Insider, November 27, 2012, https://www.businessinsider.com/a-clothing-factory-fire-which-killed-over-a-hundred-people-was-producing-diddys-new-fashion-line-2012-11, accessed November 12, 2018.

6. As quoted by Laila Al-Arian, "Statements from Gap and Walmart for the Made in Bangladesh Episode," Fault Lines (blog), Al Jazeera America, August 20, 2013, http://america.aljazeera.com/watch/shows/fault-lines/FaultLinesBlog/2013/8/20/what-gap-and-walmarthavetosayforthemselves.html, accessed August 31, 2017.

7. Quoted in Steven Greenhouse, "Documents Reveal New Details About

Walmart's Connection to Tazreen Factory Fire," *New York Times*, December 10, 2012, http://www.nytimes.com/2012/12/11/world/asia/tazreen-factory-used-by-2nd-walmart-supplier-at-time-of-fire.html, accessed August 31, 2017; and Greenhouse, "Documents Indicated Walmart Blocked Safety Push in Bangladesh," *New York Times*, December 5, 2012, http://www.nytimes.com/2012/12/06/world/asia/3-walmart-suppliers-made-goods-in-bangladeshi-factory-where-112-died-in-fire.html, accessed August 31, 2017.

8. "Walmart 2014 Global Responsibility Report," Wal-Mart Inc., http://cdn.corporate.walmart.com/db/e1/b551a9db42fd99ea24141f76065f/2014-global-responsibility-report.pdf, accessed August 31, 2017. Its "2015 Global Responsibility Report" no longer included factory audit figures. There appears to be no explanation for why the numbers do not add up to 100 percent, https://cdn.corporate.walmart.com/f2/b0/5b8e63024998a74b5514e078a4fe/2015-global-responsibility-report.pdf, accessed August 31, 2017.

9. James Pogue, "Disasters Made in Bangladesh," Vice, February 19, 2013, http://www.vice.com/read/disasters-made-in-bangladesh-000321-v20n2, accessed August 31, 2017.

10. Clare O'Connor, "These Retailers Involved in Bangladesh Factory Disaster Have Yet to Compensate Victims," *Forbes*, April 26, 2014, http://www.forbes.com/sites/clareoconnor/2014/04/26/these-retailers-involved-in-bangladesh-factory-disaster-have-yet-to-compensate-victims/, accessed August 31, 2017.

11. Steven Greenhouse, "As Firms Line Up on Factories, Wal-Mart Plans Solo Effort," *New York Times*, May 14, 2013, http://www.nytimes.com/2013/05/15/business/six-retailers-join-bangladesh-factory-pact.html, accessed August 31, 2017.

12. Sujeet Sennik, "I Designed That Cheap Garment. I Lit That Factory Fire in Bangladesh," *Globe and Mail*, January 18, 2013, http://www.theglobeandmail.com/globe-debate/i-designed-that-cheap-garment-i-lit-that-factory-fire-in-bangladesh/article7498897/, accessed August 31, 2017.

13. Josh Eidelson, "Documents Undermine Walmart Account on Deadly Bangladesh Fire," *Nation*, December 6, 2012, http://www.thenation.com/article/documents-undermine-walmart-account-deadly-bangladesh-fire/, accessed August 31, 2017.

14. Tripti Lahiri and Syed Zain Al-Mahmood, "Bangladesh: How Rules Went Astray," *Wall Street Journal*, December 6, 2012, http://www.wsj.com/articles/SB10001424127887323401904578159512118148362, accessed August 31, 2017.

15. As quoted by Pogue, "Disasters Made in Bangladesh."

16. Quoted in Renee Dudley and Arun Devnath, "Wal-Mart Nixed Paying Bangladesh Suppliers to Fight Fire," Bloomberg, December 5, 2012, https://www.bloomberg.com/news/articles/2012-12-05/wal-mart-nixed-paying-bangladesh-suppliers-to-fight-fire, accessed August 31, 2017.

17. Ben W. Heineman Jr., "The Cost of Saving Lives in Bangladesh," *Atlantic*, May 10, 2013, http://www.theatlantic.com/international/archive/2013/05/the-cost-of-saving-lives-in-bangladesh/275749/, accessed August 31, 2017.

18. Jim Yardley, "Export Powerhouse Feels Pangs of Labor Strife," *New York Times*, August 23, 2012, http://www.nytimes.com/2012/08/24/world/asia/as-bangladesh-becomes-export-powerhouse-labor-strife-erupts.html, accessed August 31, 2017.

19. From the Accord on Fire and Building Safety in Bangladesh website, https://bangladeshaccord.org/, accessed January 12, 2019.

20. For more information, see the Accord website, http://bangladeshaccord.org/remediation/, accessed August 31, 2017.

21. As made known by the Clean Clothes Campaign, an organization founded to support garment workers around the world, https://cleanclothes.org/news/2013/07/10/safety-scheme-gap-and-walmart, accessed January 12, 2019.

22. Kathleen McLaughlin, as quoted in Sarah Kaplan, "Walmart's Journey to Sustainability," *Rotman Management Magazine*, Winter 2017, http://www.rotman.utoronto.ca/Connect/Rotman-MAG/Back-Issues/2017/Back-Issues---2017/Winter2017-SmartPower/Winter2017-SarahKaplan-WalmartsJourneytoSustainability, accessed June 21, 2018. See also CSA staff, "Women in Factories Training Funded by Walmart," *Chain Store Age*, November 10, 2014, https://www.chainstoreage.com/news/women-factories-training-funded-walmart/, accessed June 21, 2018.

23. Kathleen McLaughlin, as quoted in Kaplan, "Walmart's Journey to Sustainability."

CHAPTER 6: STAKEHOLDERS AS A SOURCE OF INNOVATION

1. Jeffrey Ballinger, "The New Free-Trade Heel," *Harper's*, August 1992, http://harpers.org/archive/1992/08/the-new-free-trade-heel/, accessed August 31, 2017.

2. Steven Greenhouse, "Nike Shoe Plant in Vietnam Is Called Unsafe for Workers," *New York Times*, November 8, 1997, http://www.nytimes.com/1997/11/08/business/nike-shoe-plant-in-vietnam-is-called-unsafe-for-workers.html, accessed August 31, 2017.

3. Nike's 1997 Code of Conduct is available at http://hrlibrary.umn.edu/links/nikecode.html, accessed January 12, 2019. It covered forced labor, child labor, compensation, benefits, overtime, health and safety, the environment, and inspection. Its Code of Conduct as of January 2019 is available at https://sustainability.nike.com/code-of-conduct, accessed January 12, 2019.

4. Dana Canedy, "Nike's Asian Factories Pass Young's Muster," *New York Times*, June 25, 1997, https://www.nytimes.com/1997/06/25/business/nike-s-asian-factories-pass-young-s-muster.html, accessed August 31, 2017.

5. All quotes of the speech are from Philip Knight, "New Labor Initiatives," speech at National Press Club, May 12, 1998, http://business.nmsu.edu/~dboje

/NIKphilspeech.html, accessed August 31, 2017. See CSPAN's 59-minute video-recording of the event: "Nike in the Global Economy," C-SPAN, May 12, 1998, https://www.c-span.org/video/?105477-1/nike-global-economy, accessed January 12, 2019.

6. Tim Connor, "Still Waiting for Nike to Do It: Nike's Labor Practices in the Three Years Since CEO Phil Knight's Speech to the National Press Club," Global Exchange, May 2001, https://works.bepress.com/tim-connor/3/download/, accessed January 12, 2019.

7. Aaron Bernstein, "Nike's New Game Plan for Sweatshops," *Bloomberg Businessweek*, September 20, 2004, https://www.bloomberg.com/news/articles/2004-09-19/online-extra-nikes-new-game-plan-for-sweatshops, accessed July 29, 2015.

8. Shelly Banjo, "Inside Nike's Struggle to Balance Cost and Worker Safety in Bangladesh," *Wall Street Journal*, April 21, 2014, http://www.wsj.com/articles/SB10001424052702303873604579493502231397942, accessed August 31, 2017.

9. Banjo, "Inside Nike's Struggle."

10. Quoted in Banjo, "Inside Nike's Struggle."

11. Ram Nidumolu, C. K. Prahalad, and M. R. Rangaswami, "Why Sustainability Is Now the Key Driver of Innovation," *Harvard Business Review*, September 2009, 57–64.

12. All Nike sustainability and social responsibility reports can be found at https://sustainability.nike.com/reports, accessed January 12, 2019.

13. Quoted in Banjo, "Inside Nike's Struggle."

14. Richard M. Locke, *The Promise and Limits of Private Power: Promoting Labor Standards in the Global Economy* (Cambridge: Cambridge University Press, 2013). Much of the argument here is drawn from Chapters 3, 4, and 5.

15. Information from "FY07/09 Corporate Responsibility Report" and "FY12/13 Sustainable Business Performance Summary," Nike, Inc., both available at https://sustainability.nike.com/reports, accessed January 12, 2019.

16. Anita M. McGahan, Rahim Rezaie, and Donald C. Cole, "Embedded Innovation in Health," in *Innovating for the Global South: Towards an Inclusive Innovation Agenda*, ed. Dilip Soman, Janice Gross Stein, and Joseph Wong (Toronto: University of Toronto Press, 2014), 94–114.

17. See the discussion of his speech to CEOs in Chapter 2; Matthew Heimer, "'Do Some Uncomfortable and Inconvenient Things': A Civil Rights Champion's Call to Action for CEOs," *Fortune*, June 27, 2018, http://fortune.com/2018/06/26/bryan-stevenson-ceo-initiative/, accessed June 28, 2018.

18. The information and quotes for the Levi's story come from Erika Fry, "Can Levi's Make Life Better for Garment Workers?" *Fortune*, September 8, 2017.

19. As discussed in Chapter 5. Sujeet Sennik, "I Designed That Cheap Garment. I Lit That Factory Fire in Bangladesh," *Globe and Mail*, January 18, 2013,

http://www.theglobeandmail.com/globe-debate/i-designed-that-cheap-garment -i-lit-that-factory-fire-in-bangladesh/article7498897/, accessed August 31, 2017.

20. Quoted in Banjo, "Inside Nike's Struggle."

21. From one survivor of the Triangle Shirtwaist Factory fire:

I saw the fire in the tables, where they were all full with lingerie material, you know, and that had come up in a flame. When I saw that, I ran out. I went to the door that was closed. I didn't know that was closed. I went there, knocked on the door. Closed. I just stood there 'til they opened it. Forty people going down the steps, we all tumbling one right after another. And I saw people throwing themselves from the window. And as soon as we went down, we couldn't get out, because the bodies were coming down. It was terrible.

From a survivor of the Tazreen Fashions fire:

When we heard "Fire!" we all rushed and were trying to get out of the factory. The factory worker broke a window, and one of the workers pulled me through the window. Immediately after the fire broke, we tried to run out, but the door was locked.

As quoted in Francesca Rheannon, "From Triangle to Tazreen: A Century of Lessons," *CSRwire Talkback*, December 13, 2012, http://www.csrwire.com /blog/posts/641-from-triangle-to-tazreen-a-century-of-lessons, accessed August 31, 2017.

22. Sources: James Pogue, "Disasters Made in Bangladesh," Vice, February 19, 2013, http://www.vice.com/read/disasters-made-in-bangladesh-000321 -v20n2, accessed August 31, 2017; Jim Yardley, "Export Powerhouse Feels Pangs of Labor Strife," *New York Times*, August 23, 2012, http://www.nytimes .com/2012/08/24/world/asia/as-bangladesh-becomes-export-powerhouse -labor-strife-erupts.html, accessed August 18, 2015; Amy Yee, "Labor Unions Gaining Ground in Bangladesh Garment Industry," Voice of America, May 1, 2015, http://www.voanews.com/content/labor-unions-bangladesh-garment-industry /2744414.html, accessed August 31, 2017; Stephanie Clifford and Steven Greenhouse, "Fast and Flawed Inspections of Factories Abroad," *New York Times*, September 1, 2013, http://www.nytimes.com/2013/09/02/business/global/super ficial-visits-and-trickery-undermine-foreign-factory-inspections.html, accessed August 31, 2017.

23. Gendy Alimurung, "Sweatshops Are Fashion's Dirty Little Secret. But They Don't Exist in L.A.—Do They?" *LA Weekly*, July 26, 2012, http://www .laweekly.com/news/sweatshops-are-fashions-dirty-little-secret-but-they-dont -exist-in-la-do-they-2175796, accessed August 31, 2017; Michelle Chen, "Yes, Your T-Shirt Was 'Made in LA'—and the Worker Got 4 Cents for It," *Nation*, September 11, 2015, http://www.thenation.com/article/the-jobs-that-were-going -to-leave-theyve-already-left/, accessed August 31, 2017.

24. Said Walmart spokesperson Kevin Gardner, "Walmart has been advocating for improved fire safety with the Bangladeshi government, with industry groups and with suppliers. We have been actively developing and implementing proactive programs to raise fire safety awareness and increase fire prevention. We firmly believe factory owners must meet our Standards for Suppliers and we recognize the cost of meeting those standards will be part of the cost of the goods we buy." As quoted in Josh Eidelson, "Documents Undermine Walmart Account on Deadly Bangladesh Fire," *Nation*, December 6, 2012, http://www.thenation.com/article/documents-undermine-walmart-account-deadly-bangladesh-fire/, accessed August 31, 2017.

CHAPTER 7: DEALING WITH PARADOXES

1. "Police Use Pepper Spray on Crowd Waiting for New Air Jordans," WAFF 48, December 20, 2012, http://www.waff.com/story/20390749/pepper-spray-used-on-unruly-crowd-at-madison-square-mall, accessed March 15, 2018; "Air Jordan Ticket Grab 'Complete Chaos' at Willowbrook Mall," ABC7Chicago, December 14, 2014, http://abc7chicago.com/news/air-jordan-ticket-grab-complete-chaos--at-mall/436375/, accessed March 15,2018.

2. The video and description of the ad campaign can be found in Tobias Peterson, "It's Gotta Be the Shoes, Money," Popmatters, November 30, 2006, https://www.popmatters.com/its-gotta-be-the-shoes-money-2495745463.html, accessed January 12, 2019. In 2018, Nike relaunched the "It's gotta be the shoes" campaign with this ad, https://www.msn.com/en-us/video/l/nike-shoe-therapy-%E2%80%93-it%E2%80%99s-gotta-be-the-shoes-extended-session/vp-BBOswXN, accessed January 12, 2019.

3. The expression "Be Like Mike" originated in a 1991 Gatorade ad campaign. Gavin Evans, "'Be Like Mike': The Story Behind Michael Jordan's Iconic Gatorade Commercial Song," Complex, May 6, 2016, https://www.complex.com/sports/2016/05/be-like-mike-michael-jordan-gatorade-commercial-song, accessed January 12, 2019.

4. As quoted in "Nike (A)," Harvard Business School Publishing, case no. 9–385–025, May 1990. In 2014, Nike was the twenty-second most valuable brand in the world, at $20 billion in value (Apple, Google, Coca-Cola, and IBM are numbers one through four) according to Interbrand, http://www.bestglobalbrands.com/2014/ranking/, accessed August 27, 2015.

5. As quoted in Justin Tejada, "Your Sneakers or Your Life: Behind the Story That Shook Up the Industry," Sole Collector, May 14, 2015, http://solecollector.com/news/sports-illustrated-sneakers-or-your-life/, accessed March 15, 2018.

6. Rick Telander, "Senseless," *Sports Illustrated*, May 14, 1990, https://www.si.com/vault/1990/05/14/121992/senseless-in-americas-cities-kids-are-killing-kids-over-sneakers-and-other-sports-apparel-favored-by-drug-dealers-whos-to-blame, accessed August 31, 2017.

7. A question raised in Robert Goldman and Stephen Papson, *Nike Culture:*

The Sign of the Swoosh (London: Sage, 1998). See also, Michael Eric Dyson, "Be Like Mike? Michael Jordan and the Pedagogy of Desire," *Cultural Studies* 7, no. 1 (1993): 64-72.

8. Tejada, "Your Sneakers or Your Life." The editorial "Will the NRA Ever Wake Up?" appeared in the April 2, 1990, issue of *Advertising Age*.

9. Geraldine E. Willigan, "High-Performance Marketing: An Interview with Nike's Phil Knight," *Harvard Business Review*, July-August 1992, https://hbr.org/1992/07/high-performance-marketing-an-interview-with-nikes-phil-knight, accessed August 31, 2017.

10. Sam Walton's philosophy as quoted in Brian O'Keefe, "Meet the CEO of the Biggest Company On Earth," *Fortune*, September 9, 2010, http://archive.fortune.com/2010/09/07/news/companies/mike_duke_walmart_full.fortune/index.htm, accessed August 31, 2017.

11. All quotes from Anonymous, student assignment, Corporation 360°, October 2014.

12. Charles Fishman, *The Wal-Mart Effect: How the World's Most Powerful Company Really Works, and How It's Transforming the American Economy* (New York: Penguin, 2006).

13. "Self Storage Fact Sheet," Easy Storage Solutions, https://www.storageunitsoftware.com/blog/self-storage-fact-sheet, accessed March 15, 2018.

14. Juliet Schor, *The Overspent American: Upscaling, Downshifting, and the New Consumer* (New York: Basic Books, 1998).

15. These ideas about preferences are reviewed in S. Frederick, G. Loewenstein, and T. O'Donoghue, "Time Discounting and Time Preference: A Critical Review," *Journal of Economic Literature* 40, no. 2 (2002): 351–401. A good overview of the psychology in behavioral economics can be found in Nobel Prize-winning psychologist Daniel Kahneman's book, *Thinking, Fast and Slow* (New York: Farrar, Straus, and Giroux, 2011).

16. Thorstein B. Veblen, *The Theory of the Leisure Class: An Economic Study in the Evolution of Institutions* (New York: Macmillan, 1899) as discussed in Juliet Schor, *The Overspent American*.

17. Robert Hendrickson, *The Facts on File Encyclopedia of Word and Phrase Origins*, 4th ed. (New York: Facts on File, 2008).

18. Joseph Heath and Andrew Potter, *The Rebel Sell: Why the Culture Can't be Jammed* (Toronto: HarperCollins Canada, 2004).

19. Rick Telander, "Senseless."

20. Naomi Klein, *No Logo: Taking Aim at the Brand Bullies*, (Toronto: Knopf Canada, 2000), 3.

21. According to the Advertising Education Foundation, "A Brief Overview of the History of Branding," https://s20896.pcdn.co/wp-content/uploads/2016/12/landa_history_rev2.pdf, accessed January 12, 2019. I wasn't able to verify Klein's claim in *No Logo: Taking Aim at Brand Bullies*, but evidence from Angela Orend and Patricia Gagné suggests that Nike was one of the more popular

of the corporate-based tattoos; see Orend and Gagné, "Corporate Logo Tattoos and the Commodification of the Body," *Journal of Contemporary Ethnography* 38, no. 4, (2009): 493–517.

22. Tirtha Dhar and Kathy Baylis, "Fast-Food Consumption and the Ban on Advertising Targeting Children: The Quebec Experience," *Journal of Marketing Research* 48, no. 5 (2011): 799–813.

23. Schor, *The Overspent American*.

24. "The Case for Brands," *Economist*, September 6, 2001, http://www.economist.com/node/771049, accessed March 15, 2018; and "Pro Logo vs. No Logo" debate, WNYC, New York, September 25, 2002, http://www.wnyc.org/story/84896-pro-logo-vs-no-logo/, accessed March 15, 2018.

25. M. J. Lee, "Walmart, Amazon, Sears, eBay to Stop Selling Confederate Flag Merchandise," CNN, June 24, 2015, http://www.cnn.com/2015/06/22/politics/confederate-flag-walmart-south-carolina/, accessed March 15, 2018; Phil Wahba, "Walmart to Stop Selling Assault Rifles," *Fortune*, August 26, 2015, www.fortune.com/2015/08/26/walmart-assault-rifles/, accessed March 15, 2018; Chris Wilson, "Why Walmart's New Gun Rules Won't Actually Reduce Homicides," *Time*, March 7, 2018, http://time.com/5187583/walmart-sells-guns-age-homicides/, accessed June 25, 2018.

26. Roy S. Johnson, "The Jordan Effect: The World's Greatest Basketball Player Is Also One of Its Great Brands. What Is His Impact on the Economy?" *Fortune*, June 22, 1998.

27. Ira Berkow, "Jordan's Bunker View on Sneaker Factories," *New York Times*, July 12, 1996.

28. The story is compiled from the following articles: Stephanie Strom, "A Sweetheart Becomes Suspect: Looking Behind Those Kathie Lee Labels," *New York Times*, June 27, 1996, https://www.nytimes.com/1996/06/27/business/a-sweetheart-becomes-suspect-looking-behind-those-kathie-lee-labels.html, accessed August 31, 2017; Emily Farache, "Kathie Lee's Latest Sweatshop Scandal," E!online, September 22, 1999, https://www.eonline.com/news/38744/kathie-lee-s-latest-sweatshop-scandal, accessed August 31, 2017. On the other hand, Kathie Lee continues to participate in the system. As John Oliver of the Comedy Central television show *This Week Tonight* pointed out, even after the Rana Plaza disaster where products from the Children's Place were found in the rubble, she was featured on the *Today Show* exclaiming excitedly about the low price of some Children's Place clothes for the holidays. See Parker Molloy, "John Oliver Digs into the Low-Cost, Child Labor Hypocrisy in the Fashion Industry," Upworthy, April 27, 2015, http://www.upworthy.com/john-oliver-digs-into-the-low-cost-child-labor-hypocrisy-in-the-fashion-industry?c=ufb2, accessed August 31, 2017.

29. Bob Harig, "Tiger Woods Signs New Nike deal," ESPN, July 17, 2013, http://espn.go.com/golf/story/_/id/9485529/tiger-woods-signs-new-endorsement-contract-nike-agent-confirms, accessed March 15, 2018; Associated Press,

"Nike Re-signs Michael Vick as Endorser," ESPN, July 4, 2011, http://sports
.espn.go.com/nfl/news/story?id=6730833, accessed March 15, 2018; Martha
Bellisle, "Ben Roethlisberger Settles Lawsuit Alleging 2008 Rape," *Reno Ga-
zette-Journal*, USA Today, January 20, 2012, http://usatoday30.usatoday.com
/sports/football/nfl/steelers/story/2012-01-20/ben-roethlisberger-settles-law
suit/52702798/1, accessed March 15, 2018; "Police Statement Details Roethlisberger's Alleged Assault," CNN, April 16, 2010, http://www.cnn.com/2010
/CRIME/04/16/roethlisberger.incident/, accessed March 15, 2018.

30. Alissa Walker, "Nike's Tiger Woods Ad: Too Soon?" *Fast Company*,
April 7, 2010, https://www.fastcompany.com/1610066/nikes-tiger-woods-ad-too
-soon, accessed March 15, 2018.

31. Alice Gomstyn, "From Ben Roethlisberger to Tiger Woods: Why Nike
Didn't Flee," ABC News, April 15, 2010, https://abcnews.go.com/Business/ben
-roethlisberger-tiger-woods-nike-flee/story?id=10375523, accessed August 15,
2015.

32. Timothy Egan, "Nike's Women Problem," *New York Times*, April 21,
2010, https://opinionator.blogs.nytimes.com/2010/04/21/nikes-women-problem/,
accessed August 15, 2015.

33. Erika Eichelberger, "10 Things Elizabeth Warren's Consumer Protection Agency Has Done for You," *Mother Jones*, March 14, 2014, https://www
.motherjones.com/politics/2014/03/elizabeth-warren-consumer-financial-pro
tection-bureau-2/, accessed August 15, 2015.

34. From the Adbusters website, https://www.adbusters.org/spoof-ads, accessed August 15, 2015.

35. "Names &," *Washington Post*, May 13, 1999, https://www.washington
post.com/archive/lifestyle/1999/05/13/names-38/07e9829a-e023-45dc-b170
-ffce9b6b846c/?utm_term=.09e2e819d772, accessed August 15, 2015.

36. See, as examples, T. Hahn, L. Preuss, J. Pinkse, and F. Figge, "Cognitive
Frames in Corporate Sustainability: Managerial Sensemaking with Paradoxical and Business Case Frames," *Academy of Management Review* 39, no. 4 (2014):
463–487; and Hahn, Pinkse, Preuss, and Figge, "Tensions in Corporate Sustainability: Towards an Integrative Framework," *Journal of Business Ethics* 127, no. 2
(2015): 297–316; N. Slawinski and P. Bansal, "Short on Time: Intertemporal Tensions in Business Sustainability," *Organization Science* 26, no. 2 (2015): 531–549.

CHAPTER 8: EXPERIMENTATION

1. Adam Werbach, 1997, *Act Now, Apologize Later* (New York: Harper-
Collins/Cliff Street Books), 248, 256.

2. Retitled for the online edition, Adelle Sacks, "Working with the Enemy,"
Fast Company, September 1997, https://www.fastcompany.com/60374/working
-enemy, accessed January 12, 2019.

3. As quoted in Amanda Witherell, "Is Wal-Mart Going Green or Just
Greenwashing?" *San Francisco Bay Guardian*, August 16, 2006.

4. Tim Redmond, "Adam Werbach Makes Me Puke," *San Francisco Bay Guardian*, April 7, 2008, http://sfbgarchive.48hills.org/sfbgarchive/2008/04/07 /adam-werbach-makes-me-puke/, accessed January 12, 2019.

5. John Sellers, "In Working with Wal-Mart, Activist Adam Werbach Is Abandoning His Principles," Grist, July 20, 2006, http://grist.org/article/sellers/, accessed March 15, 2018.

6. Stephanie Rosenbloom and Michael Barbaro, "Green-Light Specials, Now at Wal-Mart," *New York Times*, January 24, 2009, https://www.nytimes .com/2009/01/25/business/25walmart.html, accessed March 15, 2018.

7. As described by Adam Werbach in his public talk at the Rotman School, November 11, 2009.

8. Retitled for the online article, Marc Gunther, "The Green Machine," *Fortune*, July 31, 2006, http://archive.fortune.com/magazines/fortune/fortune_ar chive/2006/08/07/8382593/index.htm, accessed January 12, 2019.

9. As quoted in Sacks, "Working with the Enemy."

10. As quoted in Chris Turner, "If You Can't Beat 'Em . . ." *Globe and Mail*, March 15, 2008, https://www.theglobeandmail.com/technology/science/if-you -cant-beat-em/article669270/, accessed March 15, 2018.

11. As quoted in Sacks, "Working with the Enemy."

12. Rosenbloom and Barbaro, "Green-Light Specials, Now at Wal-Mart."

13. Lee Scott, "Twenty First Century Leadership," speech to associates, October 23, 2005, http://corporate.walmart.com/_news_/executive-viewpoints /twenty-first-century-leadership, accessed March 15, 2018.

14. Quoted in Charles Fishman, "How Many Lightbulbs Does It Take to Change the World? One. And You're Looking at it." *Fast Company*, September 2006, https://www.fastcompany.com/57676/how-many-lightbulbs-does-it -take-change-world-one-and-youre-looking-it, accessed March 15, 2018.

15. Quoted in Rosenbloom and Barbaro, "Green-Light Specials, Now at Wal-Mart."

16. Quoted in Charles Fishman, "How Many Lightbulbs Does It Take to Change the World?"

17. Diana Budds, "GE Lighting Plans to Stop CFL Bulb Production by Year End," *Fast Company*, February 1, 2016, https://www.fastcompany.com/3056104 /ge-lighting-plans-to-stop-cfl-bulb-production-by-years-end?cid=search, accessed January 12, 2019.

18. Rosenbloom and Barbaro, "Green-Light Specials, Now at Wal-Mart."

19. Quoted in Witherell, "Is Wal-Mart Going Green or Just Greenwashing?"

20. Walmart's Sustainability Index Program, https://www.walmartsustain abilityhub.com/sustainability-index, accessed January 12, 2019.

21. All of Walmart's Global Responsibility and Sustainability Reports can be found at https://corporate.walmart.com/global-responsibility/global-respon sibility-report-archive, accessed January 12, 2019.

22. Witherell, "Is Wal-Mart Going Green or Just Greenwashing?"

23. Elizabeth Cline, "Where Does Discarded Clothing Go?" *Atlantic*, July 18, 2014, https://www.theatlantic.com/business/archive/2014/07/where-does-discarded-clothing-go/374613/, accessed March 15, 2018.

24. Scott, "Twenty First Century Leadership."

25. Jason Jay, Sergio Gonzalez, and Mathew Swibel, "Sustainability-Oriented Innovation: A Bridge to Breakthroughs," Big Idea: Leading Sustainable Organizations, *MITSloan Management Review*, November 10, 2015, http://sloanreview.mit.edu/article/sustainability-oriented-innovation-a-bridge-to-breakthroughs, accessed March 15, 2018.

26. "More Than Just Trash Talk: Turning Waste into Opportunities," UL Environment webinar, June 24, 2015, archived at https://ul.wistia.com/medias/m2nbom4tlw, accessed March 15, 2018.

27. Michael E. Porter and Mark R. Kramer, "Creating Shared Value," *Harvard Business Review* 89, nos. 1–2 (2011): 62–77.

28. As quoted in Peter Kelly-Detwiler, "How Walmart and G.E. Are Leading Transformation in the Energy Market," *Forbes*, September 30, 2013, http://www.forbes.com/sites/peterdetwiler/2013/09/30/walmart-ge-and-lighting-a-case-study-in-market-transformation/, accessed March 15, 2018.

29. Ram Nidumolu, C. K. Prahalad, and M. R. Rangaswami, "Why Sustainability Is Now the Key Driver of Innovation," *Harvard Business Review* 87, no. 9 (September 2009): 57–64.

30. Rosenbloom and Barbaro, "Green-Light Specials, Now at Wal-Mart."

31. Jack Neff, "Why Wal-Mart Has more Green Clout Than Anyone," *Advertising Age*, October 15, 2007.

32. "You end up with manufacturers voting only for criteria that they already meet," as quoted in Stacy Mitchell, "Walmart's Greenwash: How the Company's Much-Publicized Sustainability Campaign Falls Short, While Its Relentless Growth Devastates the Environment," Institute for Local Self-Reliance, March 2012, http://ilsr.org/wp-content/uploads/2012/03/walmart-greenwash-report.pdf, accessed March 15, 2018.

33. Sacks, "Working with the Enemy."

34. Adam Werbach and Andy Ruben, "Black Friday Today, Personal Sustainability Tomorrow," Triple Pundit, November 23, 2012, http://www.triplepundit.com/2012/11/personal-sustainability-black-friday/, accessed March 15, 2018.

35. Nina Mažar and Chen-Bo Zhong, "Do Green Products Make Us Better People?" *Psychological Science* 21 (2010): 494–498.

36. B. Monin and D. T. Miller, "Moral Credentials and the Expression of Prejudice," *Journal of Personality and Social Psychology* 81 (2001): 33–43; S. Sachdeva, R. Iliev, and D. L. Medin, "Sinning Saints and Saintly Sinners: The Paradox of Moral Self-Regulation," *Psychological Science* 20 (2009): 523–528; Keith Wilcox, Beth Vallen, Lauren Block, and Gavan J. Fitzsimons, "Vicarious Goal

Fulfillment: When the Mere Presence of a Healthy Option Leads to an Ironi-cally Indulgent Decision," *Journal of Consumer Research* 36, no. 3 (October 2009): 380–393.

37. "How It Works," Yerdle.com, https://www.yerdlerecommerce.com/in dex.html#how-it-works, accessed March 15, 2018.

38. Quoted in BBC News, "Shell Stops Arctic Activity After 'Disappointing' Tests," September 28, 2015, https://www.bbc.com/news/business-34377434, ac-cessed March 15, 2018. See also Reuters, "Arctic Oil Rig Departs Seattle-Area Port Despite Protest," June 30, 2015, https://www.reuters.com/article/us-usa -shell-arctic/arctic-oil-rig-departs-seattle-area-port-despite-protest-idUSKC N0PA10X20150630, accessed March 15, 2018; and "Greenpeace Protesters Claim Symbolic Victory as Shell Oil Ship Leaves Portland," *Oregonian*, July 30, 2015, https://www.oregonlive.com/portland/index.ssf/2015/07/greenpeace_pro testers_claim_sy.html, accessed March 15, 2018.

39. Adeline Yeo, "23 Is the Number," theurbanwire.com, February 26, 2008, http://theurbanwire.com/2008/02/23-is-the-number/, accessed March 15, 2018.

40. Nike, "Jordan Brand Launches Air Jordan XX3," press release, Janu-ary 8, 2008, http://news.nike.com/news/jordan-brand-launches-air-jordan-xx3, accessed March 15, 2018; Reena Jana, "Quality over Green: Nike's New Air Jor-dan," *Businessweek*, January 25, 2008, https://www.bloomberg.com/news/arti cles/2008-01-25/quality-over-green-nikes-new-air-jordanbusinessweek-busi ness-news-stock-market-and-financial-advice, accessed March 15, 2018.

41. Brandon Richard, "Flashback//Air Jordan XX3 Launch Event in 2008," Sole Collector, February 12, 2013, http://solecollector.com/news/flashback-air -jordan-xx3-23-launch-event-in-2008, accessed March 15, 2018.

42. Nike, "Jordan Brand Launches Air Jordan XX3."

43. "Nike 'Considered'—An Environmental Sustainability Initiative" (case study 710-016-1, ICMR Center for Management Research, 2010), http://www .icmrindia.org/casestudies/catalogue/Business%20Ethics/BECG111.htm, ac-cessed March 15, 2018.

44. Information in this paragraph comes from Rebecca Henderson, Rich-ard M. Locke, Christopher Lyddy, and Cate Reavis, "Nike Considered: Getting Traction on Sustainability" (case 08-077, MITSloan Management, January 21, 2009).

45. "IDSA Awards, Gold 2005: Nike Considered Boot," *Businessweek*, http:// www.bloomberg.com/ss/05/06/idea2005/source/29.htm, accessed November 6, 2015; "Nike Considered Boot," IDSA, http://www.idsa.org/awards/idea/com puter-equipment/nike-considered-boot, accessed June 3, 2018.

46. Jana, "Quality over Green: Nike's New Air Jordan."

47. As quoted in Michael Andersen, "How Nike's Considered Line Changed the Company for Good," Sole Collector, April 22, 2015, http://solecollector.com /news/the-history-of-nike-considered/, accessed March 15, 2018.

48. Eugenia Levenson, "Citizen Nike," *Fortune*, November 17, 2008, http://archive.fortune.com/2008/11/17/news/companies/levenson_nike.fortune/index.htm, accessed March 15, 2018.

49. Jana, "Quality over Green: Nike's New Air Jordan."

50. "Nike 16/17 Sustainable Business Report," 13, https://sustainability.nike.com/reports, accessed November 12, 2018.

51. "A Natural Step Case Study: Nike," by the Natural Step consulting firm, which worked with Nike to develop the Considered approach, https://thenaturalstep.org/project/nike/, accessed March 15, 2018.

52. Tilde Herrera, "Nike: From Considered Design to Closing the Loop," Green Biz, October 19, 2009, http://www.greenbiz.com/blog/2009/10/19/considered-design-closing-loop, accessed March 15, 2018.

53. Jana, "Quality over Green: Nike's New Air Jordan."

54. "Nike 'Considered'—An Environmental Sustainability Initiative."

55. Ethical Consumer describes itself as "the UK's leading alternative consumer organization." The group rates companies on their performance related to the environment, animals, people, politics, and product sustainability. See Heather Webb, "Sportswear," Ethical Consumer, September 10, 2016, http://www.ethicalconsumer.org/buyersguides/clothing/sportswear.aspx, accessed March 15, 2018.

56. "A Natural Step Case Study: Nike."

57. Stanley Holmes, "Nike Goes for the Green," *Businessweek*, September 25, 2006, https://www.bloomberg.com/news/articles/2006-09-24/nike-goes-for-the-green, accessed November 4, 2018.

58. Mitchell, "Walmart's Greenwash."

59. Coral Davenport and Jack Ewing, "VW Is Said to Cheat on Diesel Emissions; US to Order Big Recall," *New York Times*, September 18, 2015, https://www.nytimes.com/2015/09/19/business/volkswagen-is-ordered-to-recall-nearly-500000-vehicles-over-emissions-software.html, accessed March 15, 2018.

60. Gregory Unruh, "The Changing Business Climate Is Causing Product Die-Offs," *Sloan Management Review*, October 9, 2015, http://sloanreview.mit.edu/article/the-changing-business-climate-is-causing-product-die-offs/, accessed March 15, 2018.

CHAPTER 9: THE 360° CEO

1. Kathleen McLaughlin in an interview by Sarah Kaplan at an event at the Rotman School, as printed in Sarah Kaplan, "Walmart's Journey to Sustainability," *Rotman Management Magazine*, Winter 2017, http://www.rotman.utoronto.ca/Connect/Rotman-MAG/Back-Issues/2017/Back-Issues---2017/Winter2017-SmartPower/Winter2017-SarahKaplan-WalmartsJourneytoSustainability, accessed June 21, 2018. The emphasis is mine.

2. See http://fortune.com/tag/ceo-initiative/ for *Fortune*'s coverage of the yearly events, accessed June 28, 2018.

3. Sarah Kaplan and Rebecca Henderson, "Inertia and Incentives: Bridging Organizational Economics and Organizational Theory," *Organization Science* 16, no. 5 (2005): 509–521; Kaplan, "Truce Breaking and Remaking: The CEO's Role in Changing Organizational Routines," *Cognition and Strategy (Advances in Strategic Management)* 32 (2015): 1–45.

4. Cone Communications, "Millennial Employee Engagement Study," press release, November 2, 2016, https://static1.squarespace.com/static/56b4a7472b8d de3df5b7013f/t/5819e8b303596e3016ca0d9c/1478092981243/2016+Cone +Communications+Millennial+Employee+Engagement+Study_Press+Re lease+and+Fact+Sheet.pdf; PWC, "Millennials at Work: Reshaping the Workplace," 2011, https://www.pwc.de/de/prozessoptimierung/assets/millennials-at -work-2011.pdf; Peggie Pelosi, "Millennials Want Workplaces with Social Purpose. How Does Your Company Measure Up?" Talent Economy, February 20, 2018, http://www.talenteconomy.io/2018/02/20/millennials-want-workplaces -social-purpose-company-measure/, accessed June 16, 2018.

5. Richard Hardyment, "CSR After the Volkswagen Scandal," Triple Pundit, October 28, 2015, https://www.triplepundit.com/2015/10/csr-volkswagen -scandal/, accessed June 3, 2018.

6. Aaron Dhir, *Challenging Boardroom Homogeneity: Corporate Law, Governance, and Diversity* (Cambridge: Cambridge University Press, 2015); Margarethe Wiersema and Marie Louise Mors, "What Board Directors Really Think of Gender Quotas," *Harvard Business Review*, https://hbr.org/2016/11/what-board -directors-really-think-of-gender-quotas, accessed February 20, 2018.

EPILOGUE: A NEW PERSPECTIVE FOR STAKEHOLDERS

1. Sarah Whitten, "Trump Attacks Merck CEO for Stepping Down from Manufacturing Council in Protest," CNBC, August, 14, 2017, https://www .cnbc.com/2017/08/14/merck-ceo-resigns-from-trumps-american-manufactur ing-council.html, accessed June 27, 2018.

2. Jeva Lange, "Major American Companies Say Thanks but No Thanks to Trump's Environmental Regulation Rollbacks," Week, March 30, 2017, http:// theweek.com/speedreads/689276/major-american-companies-say-thanks-but -no-thanks-trumps-environmental-regulation-rollbacks, accessed June 27, 2018.

3. Chip Bergh, "Levi Strauss CEO: Why Business Leaders Need to Take a Stand on Gun Violence," *Fortune*, September 4, 2018, http://fortune.com/2018 /09/04/levi-strauss-gun-violence-parkland/, accessed September 9, 2018.

4. For example, Kate Conger and Daisuke Wakabayashi, "Google Overhauls Sexual Misconduct Policy After Employee Walkout," *New York Times*, November 8, 2018, https://www.nytimes.com/2018/11/08/technology/google-arbi tration-sexual-harassment.html, accessed November 10, 2018.

5. This section was informed by David France, *How to Survive a Plague: The Inside Story of How Citizens and Science Tamed AIDS* (New York: Knopf, 2016); information on both the book and the documentary on which it was based can be found at https://surviveaplague.com/, accessed June 27, 2018. Douglas Crimp, "Before Occupy: How AIDS Activists Seized Control of the FDA in 1988," *Atlantic*, December 6, 2011, https://www.theatlantic.com/health/archive/2011/12/before-occupy-how-aids-activists-seized-control-of-the-fda-in-1988/249302/, accessed June 27, 2018; "ACT UP Demonstration at the New York Stock Exchange," NYC LGBT Historic Sites Project, https://www.nyclgbtsites.org/site/act-up-demonstration-at-the-new-york-stock-exchange/, accessed June 27, 2018; Tom Carson, "When the Fringe Shapes the Center," *American Prospect*, September 28, 2012, http://prospect.org/article/when-fringe-shapes-center, accessed June 27, 2018.

6. Dave Jamieson, "Labor Groups Are Taking on Walmart and McDonald's. But Who Will Fund Their Fight?" HuffPost, June 2, 2016, https://www.huffingtonpost.com/entry/our-walmart-funding_us_574f4b70e4b0eb20fa0cac8b, accessed June 27, 2018.

7. Susan Fowler, "Reflecting on One Very, Very Strange Year at Uber," susanjfowler.com, February 19, 2017, https://www.susanjfowler.com/blog/2017/2/19/reflecting-on-one-very-strange-year-at-uber, accessed June 27, 2018; Johana Bhuiyan, "With Just Her Words, Susan Fowler Brought Uber to Its Knees," Recode, December 6, 2017, https://www.recode.net/2017/12/6/16680602/susan-fowler-uber-engineer-recode-100-diversity-sexual-harassment, accessed June 27, 2018.

8. Grant Suneson and Samuel Stebbins, "What Are the Worst Companies to Work for? New Report Analyzes Employee Reviews," *USA Today*, June 15, 2018, https://www.usatoday.com/story/money/business/2018/06/15/worst-companies-to-work-for-employee-reviews/35812171/, accessed June 27, 2018.

9. Hans Taparia and Pamela Koch, "A Seismic Shift in How People Eat," *New York Times*, November 6, 2015, https://www.nytimes.com/2015/11/08/opinion/a-seismic-shift-in-how-people-eat.html, accessed June 27, 2018.

10. Osita Nwanevu, "'Sleeping Giants' Is Borrowing Gamergate's Tactics to Attack *Breitbart*," Slate, December 14, 2016, http://www.slate.com/articles/news_and_politics/politics/2016/12/sleeping_giants_campaign_against_breitbart.html, accessed June 27, 2018.

11. Gretchen Morgenson, "Want Change? Shareholders Have a Tool for That," *New York Times*, March 24, 2017, https://www.nytimes.com/2017/03/24/business/proxy-climate-change-executive-pay.html, accessed June 27, 2018.

12. Peter Staley, "What I've Learned from Thirty Years of AIDS Activism," Vice, March 30, 2017, https://www.vice.com/en_us/article/mgdxy3/what-ive-learned-from-thirty-years-of-aids-activism, accessed June 27, 2018.

INDEX

Page references in *italics* refer to figures.

for, 37–39, 85–86; and safety disasters, 86–90, 87; and supply chain complexity, 94–96

The Overspent American (Schor), 125

P

paradoxes, dealing with: branding as paradox, 128–31; consumer choice as paradox, 124–28; intractable tension of, 27, 117–18, 131–32; Nike example, 118–21; Walmart example, 121–24

Parker, Mark: on Considered approach, 147; on factory conditions, 103; on sexual harassment, 77; on sustainability, 49, 52–53

Pax World Fund, 17

Pirelli, 78–79

Porter, Michael, 16, 22, 56–57, 139

Prahalad, C. K., 102, 104–5, 140–41

Procter & Gamble (P&G), 32, 136, 141, 168

The Promise and Limits of Private Power (Locke), 103

"The Pyramid of Corporate Social Responsibility" (Carroll), 178n5

Q

questions, asking, 161, 162

R

Rahman, Sakr, 110

Rana Plaza building collapse, 89, 93, 97, 101, 111, 199n28

Rattan, Aneeta, 75

Reebok, 68–71, 151

regulation: auditing for compliance, 88–89, 92–94; cultural views of, 109–10; and responsibility to diverse stakeholders, 12; and sustainability reports, 11

Reich, Robert, 129

Renati, Claudia, 61–62

rethinking trade-offs. *See* Mode 2 (rethink trade-offs)

return on invested capital (ROIC) tree, 40–41

risk reduction, as business-case justification, 51

Roethlisberger, Ben, 129–31

Rosita Knitwear factory, 111–12

Rotman School of Management, University of Toronto: Corporation 360° course, 3, 20–21; MBA strategy course of, 32

Ruben, Andy, 135, 143

Ryanair, 22

S

Saatchi & Saatchi S (Act Now), 133, 135, 143

Sadisah (Nike factory worker), 97

safety issues. *See* supply chain

Sam's Club, 35–36, 61–62

San Francisco Bay Guardian, on Werbach, 134

Save the Arctic movement, 144–45

Schor, Juliet, 125, 127, 131

Scott, Lee, 8, 42, 133, 135–41

Scott, Ramona, 62

self-storage industry, consumerism and, 124

Sellers, Joseph, 62–64

Sennik, Sujeet, 90–91, 109

sexism: "benevolent sexism", 64–66; and hostile work environment, 64, 65, 69–70, 172

shared value, 47–57; for balancing stakeholder trade-offs, 16–20; business case as undermining objectives of social responsibility, 54–57; business-case logic as problem for, 56, 59–61; making business case for social responsibility, 51–54; Mode 2, defined, 13, 15, 23–25; successful examples of, 47–51; sustain-